"A MASTERFUL EXPOSITION of the life and teachings of Chinese Chan master Dongshan, the ninth century founder of the Caodong school, later transmitted by Dōgen to Japan as the Sōtō sect. Leighton carefully examines in ways that are true to the traditional sources yet have a distinctively contemporary flavor a variety of material attributed to Dongshan. Leighton is masterful in weaving together specific approaches evoked through stories about and sayings by Dongshan to create a powerful and inspiring religious vision that is useful for students and researchers as well as practitioners of Zen. Through his thoughtful reflections, Leighton brings to light the panoramic approach to kōans characteristic of this lineage, including the works of Dōgen. This book also serves as a significant contribution to Dōgen studies, brilliantly explicating his views throughout."

—STEVEN HEINE, author of *Did Dōgen Go to China? What He Wrote and When He Wrote It*

"IN HIS WONDERFUL NEW BOOK, *Just This Is It*, Buddhist scholar and teacher Taigen Dan Leighton launches a fresh inquiry into the Zen teachings of Dongshan, drawing new relevance from these ancient tales. His inclusive and wide-ranging commentary applies these ancient Tang dynasty teachings of sentience and suchness to the problems of materialism and climate change that we face on our planet, today. Time-traveling from Dongshan to Dōgen to Bob Dylan, by way of Rimbaud and others, Leighton's approach brings this old Zen ancestor to life with immediacy and intimacy, strengthening our vital connections through lineage and across time."

—RUTH OZEKI, author of *A Tale for the Time Being*

三十八世洞山良价禪師

TAIGEN DAN LEIGHTON

Just This Is It

Dongshan and the Practice of Suchness

Shambhala BOULDER | 2015

Shambhala Publications, Inc.
2129 13th Street
Boulder, Colorado 80302
www.shambhala.com

FRONTISPIECE: Traditional Chinese Woodcut of Dongshan Liangjie.

Dongshan Looking into the Stream (*Horayama Do-sui View*, partial; in Japanese: 洞山渡水図 部分) image reproduced by permission of TNM (Tokyo National Museum, 東京国立博物館) Image Archives.

9 8 7 6 5 4

Printed in the United States of America

Shambhala Publications makes every effort to print on acid-free, recycled paper.

Shambhala Publications is distributed worldwide by Penguin Random House, Inc., and its subsidiaries.

Designed by Michael Russem

LIBRARY OF CONGRESS CATALOGING-IN-PUBLICATION DATA

Leighton, Taigen Daniel, author.
Just this is it: Dongshan and the practice of suchness / Taigen Dan Leighton.
pages cm
ISBN 978-1-61180-228-3 (paperback)
1. Liangjie, 807–869—Teachings. 2. Caodong (Sect) I. Title.
BQ9449.L527L45 2015
294.3'420427—dc23
2014019630

This work is Gratefully Dedicated to my Teacher,
Tenshin Reb Anderson Roshi,
who adeptly introduced me to the depths
of Dongshan's subtle teachings.
I am not him, but he actually is me.

Contents

Major Figures Mentioned from the Caodong/Sōtō Lineage

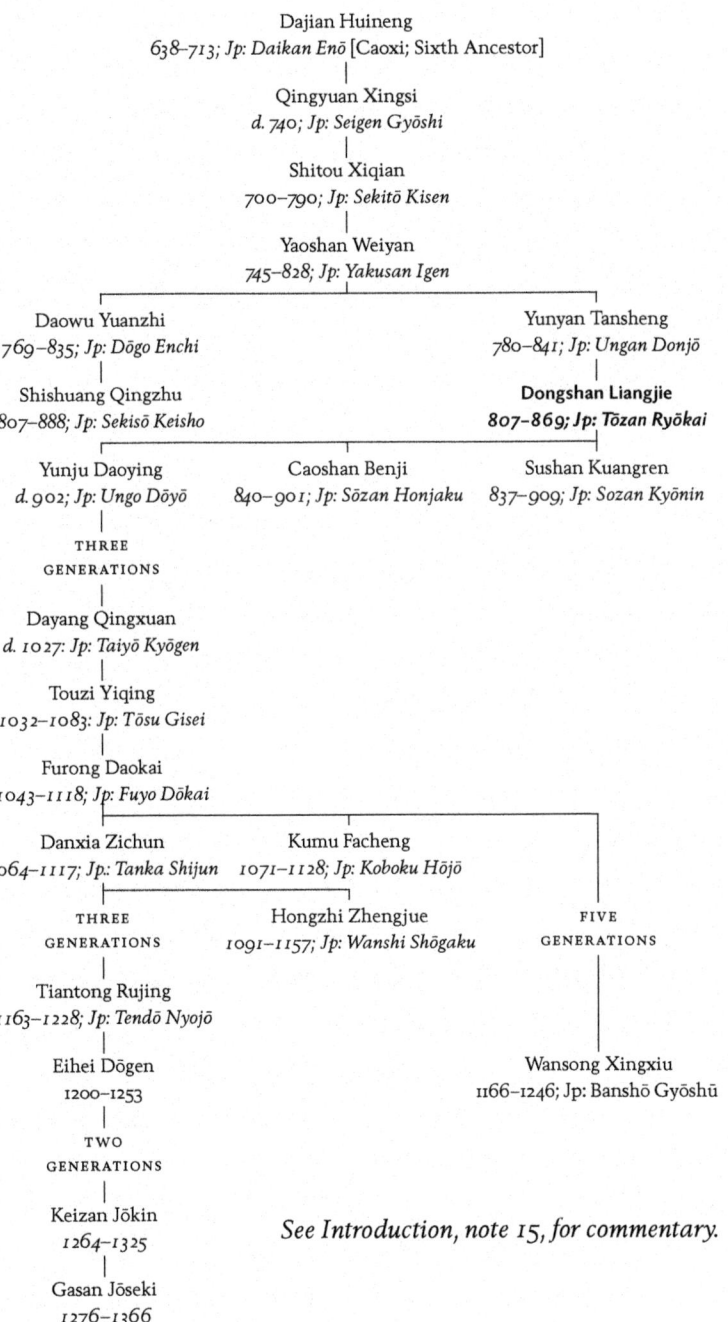

Dajian Huineng
638–713; Jp: Daikan Enō [Caoxi; Sixth Ancestor]
|
Qingyuan Xingsi
d. 740; Jp: Seigen Gyōshi
|
Shitou Xiqian
700–790; Jp: Sekitō Kisen
|
Yaoshan Weiyan
745–828; Jp: Yakusan Igen
|

Daowu Yuanzhi
769–835; Jp: Dōgo Enchi
|
Shishuang Qingzhu
807–888; Jp: Sekisō Keisho
|

Yunyan Tansheng
780–841; Jp: Ungan Donjō
|
Dongshan Liangjie
807–869; Jp: Tōzan Ryōkai

Yunju Daoying
d. 902; Jp: Ungo Dōyō
|
THREE
GENERATIONS
|
Dayang Qingxuan
d. 1027: Jp: Taiyō Kyōgen
|
Touzi Yiqing
1032–1083: Jp: Tōsu Gisei
|
Furong Daokai
1043–1118; Jp: Fuyo Dōkai
|

Caoshan Benji
840–901; Jp: Sōzan Honjaku

Sushan Kuangren
837–909; Jp: Sozan Kyōnin

Danxia Zichun
1064–1117; Jp: Tanka Shijun
|
THREE
GENERATIONS
|
Tiantong Rujing
1163–1228; Jp: Tendō Nyojō
|
Eihei Dōgen
1200–1253
|
TWO
GENERATIONS
|
Keizan Jōkin
1264–1325
|
Gasan Jōseki
1276–1366

Kumu Facheng
1071–1128; Jp: Koboku Hōjō
|
Hongzhi Zhengjue
1091–1157; Jp: Wanshi Shōgaku

FIVE
GENERATIONS
|
Wansong Xingxiu
1166–1246; Jp: Banshō Gyōshū

See Introduction, note 15, for commentary.

Acknowledgments

I first express appreciation to all the students at Mountain Source Sangha in the San Francisco Bay Area from 1995 to 2006, as well as the students at Ancient Dragon Zen Gate in Chicago from 2007 through the present. In both sanghas I spoke on many occasions about Dongshan's stories and his teaching, and their various responses certainly have benefited this book. Thanks to Jennifer Obst of Ancient Dragon Zen Gate for transcribing a number of talks of mine related to Dongshan, which helped with the writing of this book.

I am deeply grateful to the anonymous donor whose generous grant allowed me to initiate and make significant progress on this project. A number of readers or others who heard portions of this material helped clarify and improve this work in various ways with their suggestions and encouragement. These included especially Tonen O'Connor, Gib Robinson, Douglas Floyd, Roy Wyman, Rosalind Leighton, Nyozan Eric Shutt, Keizan Titus O'Brien, Alan Senauke, Tenkei Coppens, Naomi Leighton, Harry Miller, Norman Fischer, Brook Ziporyn, and my bright late student Harry Jackson. Kenshu Shimada of DePaul University and Paul Mayer of the Field Museum provided helpful information about echinoderms and their history. I am very grateful to Steven Heine, Paul Copp, and Andy Ferguson for a variety of valuable scholarly and historical assistance. Of course, any errors regarding source information, and all misguided or misleading interpretations or commentaries concerning Dongshan's teachings, are solely my own responsibility.

Thanks to my agent, Victoria Shoemaker, for helpful encouragement and a range of practical assistance. I am grateful to Dave O'Neal of Shambhala Publications, along with Hazel Bercholz, Ben Gleason, and many others at Shambhala for the actual production of this book. Many thanks to Bob Dylan for permission to use the lines from "All I Really Want to Do," and also for five decades of profound and ongoing inspiration. Thanks to my friends Preston and Michiyo Houser for their kind assistance and support with permissions issues. Thanks to Ven. Heng Sure and the Buddhist Text Translation Society / Dharma Realm Buddhist University for providing the traditional Chinese woodcut image of Dongshan. Henry Frum kindly provided permission to use his photographs from Dongshan's temple. The painting of Dongshan crossing the stream by Mayuan is used with the permission of the Tokyo National Museum and TNM Image Archives. I am grateful to editors Steven Heine and Dale Wright, and to Oxford University Press, for publishing an abbreviated version of portions of the material in this book as the article "Dongshan and the Teaching of Suchness" in their book *Zen Masters*, published by Oxford University Press in 2010.

I want to express my deep appreciation for the work of Thomas Cleary, whose incisive translations of the Dongshan-related stories in the *Book of Serenity* have considerably benefited this book. In addition to the *Book of Serenity*, Dr. Cleary's monumental translations of the *Flower Ornament Scripture* and the *Blue Cliff Record* (in collaboration with his brother J. C. Cleary), along with his translations of Dōgen, have all been important to my own work. My deep thanks go to William Powell for his translation of Dongshan's *Recorded Sayings*, the base text for my commentaries. Much thanks to Charlie Pokorny for his helpful, extensive notes on the Dongshan and related materials available in English. I am deeply indebted to all of my Buddhist teachers, too numerous to name. Especially I am thankful to my friends Shohaku Okumura and Kaz Tanahashi. The privilege of working with each of them cotranslating and thereby closely studying the writings of Eihei Dōgen was helpful background for the study of Dongshan.

I am grateful to my wife, Naomi, for her patience and all her gracious support throughout the long work required on this book.

Finally, I am unspeakably grateful to Tenshin Reb Anderson, senior dharma teacher and former abbot at San Francisco Zen Center and my ordination and dharma transmission teacher. Through many classes and in individual discussion, starting thirty-five years ago, Reb provided an extensive and insightful introduction to the work of Dongshan, including the stories discussed herein, the "Jewel Mirror Samādhi," and the five degrees teachings. Reb's long, patient guidance has been foundational to my practice and understanding of the Way. But again, any faulty interpretations herein are solely my own responsibility.

Just This Is It

Dongshan's Context in Zen

Themes from the Golden Age

Tang dynasty China, from the seventh to the tenth century, has traditionally been considered the Golden Age of Chan, to use the Chinese name, transmitted to Japan with its Japanese pronunciation, Zen. A great many Chan figures particularly from the ninth century have been celebrated ever since in Zen lore, their stories studied intently by many centuries of Zen practitioners. This book will address many spiritual issues key to this tradition through the stories and writings about the Tang master Dongshan. Major topics include the nature of reality itself, and how the realization of this may be most carefully conveyed. Also of importance is the spiritual role of nature, including nonhuman and even nonsentient beings, a matter very relevant to modern environmental concerns. How to explore these issues in practice and how to teach about them are other key areas addressed in these stories. Many spiritual traditions, within Buddhism and others, present a system of stages of progress on a path of realization. The Dongshan stories present a deeper view and a critique of the manner in which we imagine and engage such paths. Implicit in these stories is an approach to spiritual practice that is at once challenging and comforting, offering an immediacy that can further unfold in diligent practice.

Dongshan Liangjie (807–69; Jpn.: Tōzan Ryōkai), one of the most prominent teachers of Tang dynasty Chan, is considered the founder of the Caodong lineage, one of the Chan "five houses," as they were described in later Chan.[1] After it was transmitted to

Japan by Eihei Dōgen (1200–53), this lineage was known as Sōtō Zen, and it is now a significant factor in the transporting of Buddhism to the West. But Dōgen's teachings, now widely studied in the West, cannot be truly appreciated without realizing his inspiration from Dongshan. As founder of one of the five houses, Dongshan had a major impact in the classic Chan/Zen literature attributed to the legendary Tang dynasty masters. The colorful stories about Dongshan and the verses attributed to him have been avidly studied by practitioners through various approaches since at least the Song dynasty in the twelfth and thirteenth centuries, when Chan saw a literary flowering that celebrated and commented on the legendary Tang figures. Dongshan's teachings present a subtle and stimulating view of spiritual truth, and of modes of conveying and realizing its reality. His teachings became important as a dialectical underpinning for much of later Zen philosophical speculations.

Colorful stories and images from Dongshan include that of his early awakening upon seeing his reflection in a stream soon after departing from his master. Dongshan's sayings inspired by that experience are subtle and evocative lessons on the deeper reality of our cherished self. Earlier important stories involve that of his quest to hear the truth declared by inanimate objects, which led him to find his teacher. Stories from later on, when Dongshan became a noted master himself, show him challenging his students by asking them to go beyond their comfort zones to face extreme weather or see through the promise of familiar roadmaps to a supposed success. He spoke of the path of the bird, flying freely beyond any obvious road signs. The "Jewel Mirror Samādhi" verse attributed to Dongshan includes many seemingly enigmatic but actually fertile phrases or images, such as a silver bowl filled with snow, the danger of either turning away or grasping, cowering rats, a battle-scarred tiger, and a stone woman arising to dance when a wooden man breaks out in song.

Sources and Questions about History

Modern scholars generally accept that the various recorded sayings and lamp transmission documents attributed to Tang masters are often not historically reliable, as many of these texts were not recorded until well after the teacher lived.[2] The historical questions are not insignificant. How Chan figures in that period saw basic issues including transmission and lineage identities is uncertain, and our traditional views may well have been molded later. The source material about the Tang personages appears in three genres: their recorded sayings; transmission of the lamp texts; and later collections of koans, or paradigmatic stories sometimes used as meditative objects. The many recorded sayings (Ch.: *yulu*; Jpn.: *goroku*) purport to be compilations of talks, dialogues, and activities of particular masters. The lamp transmission texts (Ch.: *chuandenglu*; Jpn.: *dentōroku*) instead usually present brief excerpts from various masters, presented along with others in their same contemporary generation following in sequence from the accepted Chan founders.[3] There are exceptions to the gap between the masters and the production of their recorded sayings texts, such as the prominent masters Huangbo Xiyun (d. 850; Jpn.: Ōbaku Kiun) and Yunmen Wenyan (864–949; Jpn.: Unmon Bun'en), whose records were supposedly compiled by direct students of the masters.[4] But the questionable history is especially true in the case of Dongshan, whose earliest extant *Recorded Sayings* was not compiled until eight centuries after his death.[5] Some of the stories we have about major figures from the Tang dynasty might have been invented in the Song period, and many were certainly embellished or significantly modified then. However, many of the stories about Dongshan can be found in earlier versions in the lamp transmission or classical koan texts, and we may note that oral traditions carried on through generations of monastic study might sometimes be reliable, so the historical veracity of these records and stories may be highly suspect, but not necessarily disproved except where contradictions with reliable historical records are found.

In this book, rather than analyzing questions of historical accuracy of the information attributed to Dongshan, I will consider not the literal historical personage of Dongshan, but rather his position as an exemplary, iconic figure in Chan lore, based on the material that has been conveyed about him in his *Recorded Sayings* and in major koan collections. Readers of this work are welcome to enjoy the challenging and playful stories about Dongshan in the chapters to follow without focusing on the information about historical sources presented here. However, historical investigation of Chan figures can be highly valuable to both scholars and practitioners in deepening our understanding of the context of the teachings. Although scholars may legitimately question, for example, whether the plays of William Shakespeare were actually written by him or by somebody else using the same name, we nevertheless examine and enjoy the works attributed to him. Similarly, this study will consider the stories attributed to the figure of Dongshan, as received (or partially conceived) in Song Chan and consequently studied as a whole in Japanese Zen. The stories and verses attributed to Dongshan, whether or not reliable to the actual historical person Dongshan, are vitally important to Zen philosophy, lore, and practice teachings and have been studied by and informed a millennium of Zen students. But, just to be perfectly clear, none of the stories about Dongshan to be recounted in this book can be verified as historically reliable, and, similarly, none of the many other related stories of his contemporaries can be factually verified. Still, I find them worthy of extended discussion. I will hereafter in this work generally speak of Dongshan as if the historical person were responsible for all the teachings attributed to him, although I will add some pertinent historical questions where they apply. For the reader's convenience, I will also refer to him as "Dongshan" even in the early stories before he settled to teach at Mt. Dong, or Dongshan, and received that name. I hope that in the future, historical scholars of Tang and Song Chan might clarify some of the relevant historical issues.

The *Recorded Sayings* attributed to Dongshan include many stories of encounter dialogues between Dongshan and his teachers, and then with his students. Many of these challenging stories from Dongshan and his contemporaries became objects of awakening study for students, compiled during the Song dynasty in the classic koan collections (some of which were published before the various recorded sayings anthologies). Along with the recorded sayings and lamp transmission texts, these koan collections are the third major source for stories about Dongshan. A great many different koan collections were created in the Song, and many others were created later in Japan, and some even in modern times. But the three most important collections, still studied today, are the *Blue Cliff Record*, the *Book of Serenity*, and the *Gateless Barrier*.[6] The *Blue Cliff Record* was initiated with a hundred cases selected and ordered with his own verse comments by Xuedou Chongjian (980–1052; Jpn.: Setchō Jūken) from the Yunmen lineage. The *Blue Cliff Record* collection was created later by the important Linji lineage master Yuanwu Keqin (1063–1135; Jpn.: Engo Kokugon), who wrote introductions to the cases and commentaries with added sayings to both the cases and Xuedou's verses. This collection was the model for the later *Book of Serenity*, which was a product of the Caodong lineage founded by Dongshan. The *Book of Serenity* was based on a hundred stories selected in sequence with his own verse comments by the important twelfth-century Caodong master Hongzhi Zhengjue (1091–1157; Jpn.: Wanshi Shōgaku). The *Book of Serenity* includes commentaries by a later Caodong teacher, Wansong Xingxiu (1166–1246; Jpn.: Banshō Gyōshū), that are formatted like the *Blue Cliff Record*, and includes a handful of cases featuring Dongshan and numbers of others referring to him.[7] The third major collection, the *Gateless Barrier*, had less extensive commentary than the other two and was created by Wumen Huikai (1183–1260; Jpn.: Mumon Ekai). The *Blue Cliff Record* and the *Gateless Barrier* generally followed the style of the Linji/Rinzai lineage, named after Dongshan's contemporary Linji Yixuan (d. 867; Jpn.: Rinzai Gigen). The *Book of Serenity* presents the approach of the

Caodong/Sōtō tradition founded by Dongshan, although certainly it is not the only koan collection from that tradition.

In addition to encounter dialogues, Dongshan's *Recorded Sayings* includes various teaching verses attributed to Dongshan. Dongshan is perhaps best known for the teaching poem the "Jewel Mirror Samādhi" (Ch.: Baojing Sanmei; Jpn.: Hōkyō Zammai), which is also considered the first enunciation of the five degrees teaching that is the dialectical philosophy underlying much of Caodong, and indeed Chan discourse as a whole. However, the Baojing Sanmei text does not appear in any source before around 1119 and is not mentioned in any earlier sources. Juefan Huihong (1071–1128; Jpn.: Kakuban Keikō), who first published the text, claimed it had been transmitted secretly since Dongshan. Nevertheless, the text has circulated widely and been studied as a work of Dongshan's since the early twelfth century.[8]

Most available discussions of Dongshan focus on the five degrees teaching.[9] Often called the five ranks, this teaching has also been translated as five positions or modes. One modern Chinese commentator states astutely, "This doctrine and others like it are not of central importance in the teachings of Tung-shan's school [Tung-shan is the older Wade-Giles transliteration for Dongshan]. They are merely expedient means or pedagogical schemata for the guidance of the less intelligent students. It is regrettable that historians of Ch'an have a tendency to treat these incidents as essentials and to ignore the true essentials altogether."[10] Ironically, this commentary is presented just preceding an extensive discussion of the five degrees and Dongshan's related teachings. Indeed, although the five degrees stand as an important theoretical product of Dongshan, there is much more to the practical unfolding of the stories attributed to him. Later figures in his lineage, especially Dōgen, have sharply criticized excessive emphasis on the five degrees, even while reverently celebrating Dongshan's teaching. For example, Dōgen says, "Peasants or stray cats who never understood the inner chamber of Dongshan, and have not passed the threshold of buddha-dharma, mistakenly say that Dongshan guided students with his theory of Five Ranks of differentiation and oneness. This is an inadequate view. You should not pay attention to it." But Dōgen then proclaims that "the ancient ancestor [Dongshan] has the treasury of the true dharma eye."[11]

The Dongshan Lineage

The "Jewel Mirror Samādhi" is still chanted as an important part of the liturgy in modern Sōtō Zen. The figure of Dongshan has been venerated and kept alive historically through the Caodong/Sōtō lineage, in China and Japan. The name Caodong is often suggested to be based on Dongshan's name combined with that of one of his main disciples, Caoshan Benji (840–901; Jpn.: Sōzan Honjaku). While Caoshan was instrumental in developing five degrees theory, he was not the successor whose line was predominant in the Caodong development, and he appears only once in all of Dongshan's *Recorded Sayings*.[12] More to the point, the order of the name Caodong implies the "Cao" preceding "Dong," so it is more likely that the "Cao" in Caodong actually refers to Caoxi, the teaching site and thus a name used for the famed Chan Sixth Ancestor Dajian Huineng (638–713; Jpn.: Daikan Enō), and so also the source of Caoshan's name. Therefore, the name Caodong probably refers to Huineng and Dongshan.[13]

Thus, the name Caodong may well be taken to refer to all six teachers in the lineage between and including the Sixth Ancestor Caoxi Huineng and Dongshan. All of the Chan five houses descend from Huineng. But the official Caodong lineage after Huineng passed to Qingyuan (d. 740; Jpn.: Seigen Gyōshi), then to Shitou Xiqian (700–790; Jpn.: Sekitō Kisen), Yaoshan Weiyan (745–828; Jpn.: Yakusan Igen), and from Yaoshan to Dongshan's own teacher, Yunyan Tansheng (781–841; Jpn.: Ungan Donjō), about whom much more will be said in the stories of Dongshan's training that follow. Such a list might be seen as a series of Bible-like begettings, of interest in East Asian Zen only for Confucian-influenced ancestor veneration. However, stories that survive concerning each of these foundational figures can be seen as informative of the emerging Caodong teaching style and its approach to practice.

Of the early Caodong figures, Shitou is especially important as author of two long teaching poems, "Harmony of Difference and Sameness" (Ch.: Cantongqi; Jpn.: Sandōkai) and "Song of the Grass Hut" (Ch.: Caoanke; Jpn.: Soanka).[14] The latter poem presents a commentary on the space of practice, while the former has been highly influential in the Caodong/Sōtō lineage as presenting a fundamental dialectical polarity of the universal, or sameness, and the particular, or differentiations. This verse can readily be seen as a direct precursor of Dongshan's "Jewel Mirror Samādhi."

It is noteworthy, as many of the stories make clear, that there was often more than one single teacher who was formative to each successor, although the official lineages designate single teachers and successors in each generation. See the chart in the front of the book for names and official lineage relationships of Caodong/Sōtō teachers mentioned in this book.[15]

Suchness and Its Teaching

The "Jewel Mirror Samādhi" begins, "The teaching of suchness is intimately transmitted by buddhas and ancestors." The passages from this poem will be discussed later in this work, as will the five degrees implied therein, but the first line of the "Jewel Mirror Samādhi" provides two of the central issues that run throughout the writing and stories attributed to Dongshan. The first theme is the nature of suchness, and the Zen process of engaging this reality through the practice of meditative attention and in practice more generally. Many of the central stories about Dongshan relate to recognizing, exploring, or expressing reality, or the suchness of things. Known in Sanskrit as *tathatā*, this suchness is described in Indian Buddhism as ultimate truth, reality, the source, or the unattainable.[16] Experientially, this suchness might imply the direct apprehension of the immediate present reality, harking back to early Buddhist mindfulness practices of bare attention. So, in varying contexts suchness may refer to our clear perception of reality, or else to the nature of that reality itself.

Suchness might be seen as a more positive way of describing the reality indicated also in Mahāyāna Buddhism by the term for emptiness, *śūnyatā* in Sanskrit. *Emptiness* as a technical term in Buddhism is not about some abstract "nothingness," but indicates the emptiness or insubstantiality of all persons and entities, understood as empty of inherent substantive existence. Things are empty because of their interdependence, as each particular event is the elaborate product of the dependent causation of many conditions. Nothing exists as a separate entity unto itself. But historically the teaching of emptiness, developed in the branch of Indian Mahāyāna Buddhism called Mādhyamika, came to be seen by some as too negative in its rhetorical style. The later Mahāyāna philosophical branch called Yogācāra instead discussed this reality more positively as suchness. Both approaches of emptiness and suchness are amply present in Tang period Chan discourse and rhetoric. But the Buddhist teaching of suchness becomes an important touchstone in the material related to Dongshan. And in Dongshan's usage, the sense of this teaching is put into common conversation, or rather expressed spontaneously not as theoretical teaching, but in the immediacy of Chan inquiry and discourse.

I should note and emphasize here as an important disclaimer, that although I am using the term *suchness*, in reality there is no such thing as suchness. Speaking about a Japanese term, *immo*, which will be discussed further in chapter 9, the scholar Thomas Kasulis makes an astute, important point. He adds, "This term is often improperly construed substantially and metaphysically as 'Suchness.' [But it] is not a thing; it is a *way* things are experienced."[17] I agree about this term, and generally about such things. Suchness is not some thing to be acquired, any more than emptiness is. Suchness is not a thing at all, and neither is emptiness.

I would add that from a Buddhist perspective, ultimately and in reality *all* things are not things, are not substantially and inherently existent objects. In actuality, there are no nouns, but all words and supposed entities are verbs or adverbs. This is perhaps somewhat easier to express grammatically in Japanese than in English. In English, coherency requires the use of nouns. So regardless of suchness not being such a thing, in the interest of intelligibility I will use the term *suchness* throughout this work, including in its title. In the East Asian Mahāyāna philosophical tradition, going back to the Lotus Sutra, a whole discussion of varieties of suchness did become important, as will be further discussed in chapter 9.

This grammatical disclaimer is most important in not attaching to suchness as an object to grasp, but rather seeing such reality as a mode of practice of meditative awareness and activity. Ultimately, there is no such thing as suchness and, similarly, no such thing as emptiness. Emptiness is not a thing to seek, but rather the way a thing is, just as Kasulis says being such "is a way things are experienced." Emptiness itself is empty, and attachment to emptiness is considered the most dangerous attachment. Dongshan and Caodong lineage teachers emphasize the ungraspability of suchness as they engage it.

The Teaching of Such

The second issue highlighted in the first sentence of the "Jewel Mirror Samādhi" is the teaching itself, how this reality is "intimately transmitted." Many of the stories about Dongshan concern his subtle style of teaching, the Zen pedagogy for conveying the truth of suchness, or the teaching as such. The approaches to teaching that Dongshan experienced with his teacher Yunyan, and that are later reflected in Dongshan's own engagement with his students, are especially subtle and slippery. This reflects both the ephemeral nature of the reality to be conveyed and the importance of the student's own personal experiential realization of this reality. This is not available via some easily digestible presentation readily dispensed by the teacher.

These two main issues of suchness and approaches to its teaching will be addressed in three contexts through the course of this book. First I will closely explore the intricate narratives about Dongshan's own training, his relationship to his teachers, and the circumstances of his own awakening and receiving of Dharma transmission or teaching authorization. These stories focus explicitly on the issues of the nature of reality and the complexity of the relationship of Chan student and master. The second section of the book will discuss a number of the encounter dialogues about Dongshan and his own disciples that were commemorated in his *Recorded Sayings* and in koan collections. These dialogues deal with questions such as how to escape hot and cold, where to find a place without grass for ten thousand miles, and which embodiment of Buddha goes beyond classifications. We will explore how these often pithy narratives or dialogues elucidate the issues of suchness and of Chan teaching. Finally, in the third section I will comment on how these two issues of suchness and approaches to its teaching are reflected in evocative passages from the "Jewel Mirror Samādhi." I will also explore the incisive and influential five degrees teachings about the process of the interactions between our conventional reality and ultimate truth, and how these issues of suchness and its transmission are relevant to these five degrees presented by Dongshan.

A Tradition of Commentary

After presenting each of the stories or verses attributed to Dongshan, I will be offering my own comments and interpretations. These are certainly not intended to be the final word on these teachings. Rather, I hope to provoke further interest and reflection on these stories and writings. The stories attributed to Dongshan have been studied for close to a millennium or more because of their range and profundity. At present there is no active field of Dongshan studies, either among academic scholars or among practitioners, but I hope that this volume might help inspire such a focus, long overdue in Zen studies. I offer these teachings not as mere historical artifacts, but because they can be illuminating to current and ongoing modes of practice, understanding, and the present experience of the workings of spiritual reality. I do not wish to merely create some hagiographical sanctifying account of a great founding figure, but rather to promote inquiry into the philosophical, practical teachings embedded in the stories about Dongshan. My comments will include practical application to Zen meditation and other aspects of spiritual life. As an authorized successor in the spiritual lineage of Dongshan and Dōgen, I have a responsibility to offer my own commentary on these stories and teachings. As discussed further in chapter 2, Dongshan said that he only half agreed with his own teacher, that "If I completely agreed, then I would be unfaithful to my teacher."[18] So to be true to Dongshan, I offer my own perspectives on his teachings.

The modes with which these traditional teaching stories have been engaged by Chan and Zen people, including how the stories were eventually incorporated into formal koan collections, is a complex and controversial issue in Zen history and studies. The panoramic Sōtō approach to koan practice stands as an alternative to the more commonly recognized Rinzai koan tradition, with both ancient approaches still used in practice. At least since the elaborations of these stories by Dōgen, the thirteenth-century transmitter of Dongshan's tradition to Japan, the style of koan practice in the ensuing Sōtō lineage has involved playful amplification of the stories, including a variety of potential associations that may evoke illuminating perspectives on the spiritual issues involved.[19] Accordingly, my commentaries will sometimes suggest provocative modern or Western comparisons so as to be faithful as well to our own time and context.

In addition to my observations, I will offer commentaries by various noted teachers in the lineage of Dongshan. These will include especially the twelfth-century Chinese master Hongzhi, best known for his silent or serene illumination meditation teachings. But Hongzhi also initiated koan collections, including the previously mentioned *Book of Serenity*, which contains a handful of cases featuring Dongshan and numbers of others referring to him. Some of Hongzhi's comments, and those of the *Book of Serenity* commentator Wansong, will be included herein. In addition to Hongzhi's and Dōgen's koan collections, important early Caodong koan collections were initiated by Touzi Yiqing (1032–83; Jpn.: Tōsu Gisei) and by Hongzhi's teacher Danxia Zichun (1064–1117; Jpn.: Tanka Shijun).

Later in the thirteenth century the Dongshan lineage was transported to Japan by Eihei Dōgen, who commented on Dongshan frequently. Indeed, a notable story about Dōgen's first meeting with his own Caodong lineage teacher in China, Tiantong Rujing (1163–1228; Jpn.: Tendō Nyojō), relates that Rujing quickly accepted the foreigner Dōgen as a close student because the night before Dōgen arrived, Rujing had a dream in which Dongshan Liangjie appeared and foretold the Japanese monk's coming.[20] Given Dōgen's founding of Sōtō Zen as a continuation and development of Dongshan's lineage, and the major impact now in the West of Dōgen's writings, I will include many of his comments on Dongshan. Scholars as well as practitioners now are intensively studying Dōgen's teachings. While Dōgen's writings encompass and comment on the whole of the Chinese Chan tradition, and indeed the whole of the major Indian and Chinese Buddhist literature, Dōgen cannot be fully understood without consideration of how his teaching approach reflects Dongshan and the other Caodong lineage founders, whom Dōgen frequently cites. The stories about Dongshan remain as family jewels within the Sōtō tradition.

Finally, I will add a few commentaries on Dongshan by Shunryū Suzuki and other twentieth-century masters who brought the Dongshan and Dōgen lineage to America. These modern commentaries will help illuminate the contemporary relevance of the Dongshan teachings and stories.

Dongshan Looking into the Stream (detail) by Mayuan (12th cent.; Jpn.: Bayen).

Dongshan's stupa. The small original stupa was erected in 870; some renovations were made in 1983. Photo by Henry Frummer, 2004.

Dongshan's temple; current buildings from the 1980s.
Photo by Henry Frummer, 2004.

Dharma hall in back, reportedly from the early eighteenth century.
Photo by Henry Frummer, 2004.

PART ONE   The Search for Suchness

CHAPTER ONE

Nonsentient Beings Expounding Dharma

Dongshan's Childhood Eyes and Ears

The first story in Dongshan's *Recorded Sayings* describes him receiving a basic Buddhist lesson as a child. Reading the Heart Sutra with his tutor, he came to "There is . . . no eyes, no ears, no nose, no tongue, no body, no mind." He immediately felt his face and said, "I have eyes, ears, a nose, a tongue, and so on. Why does the sutra say they don't exist?" The instructor appreciated the depth of the question and said the youth needed to find a more able teacher. The future Dongshan then went to a Chan temple and received novice precepts, later taking full monk ordination at age twenty-one.[1]

The Heart Sutra contains a recapitulation of all the fundamental teachings of Buddhism. But it describes them by means of negation, from the context of emptiness teaching. All beings and all teachings, as well, are essentially empty of inherent separate reality because of their radical interconnectedness and mutual intercausality. In a famous statement of this approach, the Heart Sutra says, "Form does not differ from emptiness, emptiness does not differ from form. Form itself is emptiness, emptiness itself form." Emptiness is not some thing that actually exists somewhere outside form, but emptiness is the way form is. All forms are empty, lacking any inherent existence. This is true for all other categories besides form and its various aspects, including sense perceptions, faculties, and organs such as eyes and ears.

But the very young Dongshan's response recognized that from the reality of conventional and phenomenal truth, he certainly did have eyes and ears. Thus, this early, first story of the boy who would become Dongshan anticipates key issues concerning the nature of perception itself and of the complex relationship between the particulars, or phenomenal reality, and the ultimate, universal reality to which the Heart Sutra points. Just these issues of perception and the interaction between the phenomenal and the ultimate are central to the pivotal story of Dongshan's awakening, discussed in the next chapter, and also to his lifelong teaching of suchness.

Dongshan's Dharma Inquiry

The story of Dongshan's first meeting with his teacher Yunyan involves his questioning as to whether nonsentient beings could expound the Dharma. The story, as presented in Dongshan's *Recorded Sayings*, is extensive and rather elaborate, and somewhat eccentric in how it emphasizes the issues of the nature of Dharma, or reality, and the strategies for conveying it. The story can be summarized as follows: Dongshan first inquired about this question with the great teacher Guishan Lingyou (771–853; Jpn.: Isan Reiyü), who came to be considered a founder of one of the other five houses of Chan. Dongshan repeated to Guishan a story he had heard about a lengthy exchange with a student by National Teacher Nanyang Huizhong (d. 776; Jpn.: Nan'yō Echū), who maintained that nonsentient beings did indeed expound the Dharma, constantly, radiantly, and unceasingly.[2] In the story, Huizhong states that all the sages can hear this nonsentient Dharma. But then, perhaps ironically, he avers that fortunately he himself could not hear the nonsentient beings expounding, because otherwise human students could not hear his teaching. The national teacher then provides a scriptural source for the expounding by nonsentient beings from the Avataṃsaka Sūtra (Flower Ornament; Ch.: Huayan; Jpn.: Kegon), citing the passage "The earth expounds Dharma, living beings expound it, throughout the three times, everything expounds it."[3]

After narrating this story, Dongshan asked Guishan to comment, and Guishan raised his fly-whisk. When Dongshan failed to understand and asked for further explanation, Guishan proclaimed, "It can never be explained to you by means of one born of mother and father." Dongshan would later refer to such nonexplanation with deep appreciation, even though he seems to be grasping for clear elucidation at this point. Guishan finally suggested that Dongshan visit the teacher Yunyan for further illumination on this question. Yunyan had practiced with Guishan under the famed teacher Baizhang Huaihai (794–814; Jpn.: Hyakujō Ekai) and now lived in some linked caves in a cliff face.[4] What would happen between Dongshan and Yunyan, whom Dongshan would recognize as his teacher, both resolved Dongshan's question and shaped his whole teaching career.

The Chinese Buddha Nature Background

This issue of nonsentient beings' relation to the Dharma had arisen over the previous couple of centuries in Chinese Buddhist thought in relationship to the teaching of Buddha nature, which describes the potentiality for awakening in beings. This potentiality of Buddha nature had also come to be presented as an aspect of the very nature of reality itself, a radical innovation. A century before Dongshan, Tiantai school scholar Zhanran (711–82; Jpn.: Tannen) articulated the teaching potential of grasses and trees, traditionally seen as inanimate and thus inactive objects.[5] Zhanran devoted an entire treatise to explicating the Buddha nature of nonsentient things. Previously, the scholar Jizang (549–623; Jpn.: Kichizō) from the Chinese Sanlun school (derived from the Indian Mādhyamika tradition that emphasized emptiness teaching) had argued that the distinction between sentient and nonsentient was false, or empty, and not viable.[6] Jizang said that if one denies Buddha nature to anything at all, "then not only are grasses and trees devoid of buddha-nature, but living beings are also devoid of buddha-nature."[7]

The Tiantai school of Zhanran was the first native Chinese school, and it had developed an inclusive synthesis of all Buddhist teachings, including systems for classifying all the scriptures and schools that had arrived from India. In the Tiantai classification, the Lotus Sutra was the highest teaching. But Zhanran's view of nonsentient beings' dharmic capacity reflected in part his interest in Huayan school cosmology, with its vision of the world as a luminous ground of interconnectedness and of the mutual nonobstruction of particulars. The Huayan school is based on the *Avataṃsaka Sūtra*, which features lofty visionary descriptions of the awareness and activity of awakening beings, or bodhisattvas. The Huayan patriarchs, such as Fazang (643–712; Jpn.: Hōzō), developed a sophisticated philosophical system that includes discussions of the dialectic interrelationship of the world's particulars with the universal, ultimate reality.[8] This Huayan dialectical philosophy is the direct precursor for the Caodong examination and writings about the interrelationship of particular and universal, which began in the eighth century with Shitou's teaching poem, "Harmony of Difference and Sameness." Dongshan would continue to develop this study in his "Song of the Jewel Mirror Samādhi" and his teaching of the five degrees, which became the philosophical underpinning for Caodong/Sōtō teachings.

Zhanran's Huayan influence echoes the National Teacher Huizhong's citation of the Huayan *Avataṃsaka Sūtra* in the story cited by Dongshan. Zhanran had discussed the Huayan school patriarch Fazang's dynamic view of "suchness according with conditions" to support his own teaching of the Buddha nature of nonsentient beings and was the first to connect "the co-arising of suchness and the essential completeness of Buddha nature."[9] For Zhanran, "the very colors and smells of the world around us constitute the Assembly of the Lotus [Sutra]; they are the immediate and undefiled expression of buddhahood."[10] A central inference of the discussion of nonsentient beings expounding the Dharma presented in Dongshan's stories is the limitation, and ultimate inaccuracy, of usual conventional human notions of sentient and nonsentient, and of human awareness generally. But the wonder and splendor of the suchness of the phenomenal world we inhabit is also celebrated, with important consequences for how to see and practice in this world.

The suchness teaching involved in this story about Dongshan meeting his teacher is not a matter of mere human psychological or perceptual realities, but is grounded in ontological, existential reality as a primal expression of Buddha nature. We might also hear, in this question about the dharmic capacity of nonsentient beings, modern concerns about our human relationship to the environment, and even ecological consciousness. What is the role of the phenomenal world and the world of nature in human spirituality? How might one discern the value of supposedly nonsentient elements of the natural order to a vision of spiritual wholeness and awakening? If supposedly nonsentient beings can expound the Dharma, then the world of nature and phenomena itself merits deep respect as an expression and active agent of ultimate transcendence.

A noteworthy implication of the historical background context to this story is the degree to which Chan discourse responds and comments on scholarly Buddhist teaching. This is so despite the widely proclaimed Chan slogan of "going beyond words and letters," attributed to the legendary sixth-century Chan founder Bodhidharma, though long after his lifetime. This Chan/Zen slogan has at times been taken literally, so that Zen students sometimes have even been discouraged from reading the sutras, teaching stories, and commentaries on them. Certainly, Chan functioned in China as a postgraduate movement to bring Buddhist theory into everyday experience and application, beyond the abstract discourse of learned Buddhist scholars and monks. However, it is very clear that the masters in the Chan traditions almost without exception have been very well versed in Buddhist literature, and commonly refer to the sutras, even in their colloquial talks and dialogues.

Buddhist scholar Robert Sharf claims that the Chinese native philosophical concern with human "nature" contributed to this discussion in Chinese Buddhism. "I do not know of any Indian references to mundane objects such as roof tiles or stones becoming buddhas and preaching the dharma. In other words, the extension of buddha-nature to the *insentient* appears to have been a distinctively Chinese innovation."[11] The *tathāgatha garbha* (or Buddha-womb or matrix) teachings from developing Indian Mahāyāna sources formed the roots of Chinese Buddha nature theory, although even a cursory discussion of that extensive literature goes beyond the scope of this work.[12] The related aspect of the innovative Chinese view of plants as imbued with buddha nature is supported as well in Lambert Schmithausen's detailed study of possible early Indian Buddhist antecedents.[13] Interestingly, current scientific observation and experimentation with intelligent behavior in plants has led to fascinating speculation about plant communication and even "plant neurobiology," challenging anthropocentric prejudices about the nature of intelligence and consciousness.[14]

Buddha nature teaching and its application to supposedly nonsentient beings became important fairly early in Chinese Buddhism, even though nonsentient beings were not included in the Indian tathāgatha garbha sources. According to documents recovered in the early twentieth century from the Dunhuang caves along the Silk Road in what is now Western China, as early a Chan figure as the fourth patriarch, Dayi Daoxin (580–651; Jpn.: Dai-i Dōshin) proclaimed that walls, fences, tiles, and stones preach the Dharma and so must possess buddha nature.[15] But the buddha nature of nonsentient beings was much disputed in early Chan, with many prominent teachers denying the awakening capacity of nonsentient beings, and others seeing the phenomenal world as an expression of the ultimate, with the buddha field or land not separate from the Buddha.[16] Nanyang Huizhong, the national teacher cited by Dongshan, was considered the greatest Chan exponent of the Buddha nature of nonsentient beings. When asked whether "mind" and "nature" were different, he replied, "To the deluded mind they are different; to the enlightened they are not different."[17] Eventually, this view generally prevailed in Chan, and endures.

This Chinese view of Buddha nature including nonsentient beings was extremely important to the thought of Dongshan's Japanese successor Dōgen. Dōgen held in the highest esteem Nanyang Huizhong, the great Chan exponent of the Buddha nature of nonsentient beings.[18] Dōgen wrote an entire *Shōbōgenzō* essay, "Mujō Seppō" ("Insentient Beings Speak the Dharma"), in which he discusses the story about Huizhong cited by Dongshan.[19] Near the beginning of this essay, Dōgen says, "Speaking dharma is neither sentient nor insentient," and he goes on to comment extensively on how nonsentient beings do and do not expound the Dharma. Furthermore, one of Dōgen's earliest and most foundational writings about the meaning of his zazen practice, "Bendōwa" ("Talk on Wholehearted Study of the Way"), celebrates the mutual incomprehensible guidance and support of zazen practitioners with "earth, grasses and trees, fences and walls, tiles and pebbles." Such nonsentient beings are intimately involved in the process of awakening practice for Dōgen.[20]

Yunyan Raises His Whisk

Returning to Dongshan's story, when he finally arrived at Yunyan's cave after leaving Guishan, he asked who was able to hear the Dharma expounded by nonsentient beings. The ensuing mind-bending dialogue began when Yunyan said, "Nonsentient beings are able to hear it." When asked if he could hear it, Yunyan told Dongshan that if he could, then Dongshan could not hear him, Yunyan. Then Dongshan asked why he could not hear it himself. Yunyan raised his fly-whisk, and then asked if Dongshan heard it yet. When Dongshan replied that he could not, Yunyan said, "You can't even hear when I expound the Dharma; how do you expect to hear when a nonsentient being expounds the Dharma?"[21]

Although there is no indication of any communication between Guishan and Yunyan aside from the person of Dongshan inquiring before them, Yunyan intriguingly performed the same action as Guishan, raising his fly-whisk. Rather than seeing this as an exotic example of mystical accord or extra-sensory perception between Guishan and Yunyan (they had no e-mail available), this exemplifies simply using what was at hand, literally. Such whisks were symbols of teaching authority and Dharma, commonly carried by Chan masters. But more directly, the whisk was the conventionally inanimate object most immediately at hand. If all nonsentient beings proclaim the Dharma, there was no need to look further.

After the above exchange, Yunyan gave as scriptural citation for Dongshan not the Huayan Sutra, as did Nanyang Huizhong, but, interestingly for a Chan teacher, from the Pure Land Amitābha Sutra, "Water birds, tree groves, all without exception recite the Buddha's name, recite the Dharma."[22] Dongshan reflected on Yunyan's response and composed a verse that he presented to Yunyan:

> How marvelous! How marvelous!
> The Dharma expounded by nonsentient beings is
>   inconceivable.
> Listening with your ears, no sound.
> Hearing with your eyes, you directly understand.[23]

This verse, as will be discussed in the next section, relates the teaching to be gleaned from the inanimate worldly environment to the processes of human perception.

A slightly different version of this exchange than the one from the *Recorded Sayings*, given above, occurs in the *Jingde Transmission of the Lamp*, the most prominent lamp transmission text, compiled by Daoyuan in 1004, and is cited by Dōgen in his *Extensive Record* with his own comment. In this version, the whisk and the citation to the Amitābha Sutra are not included, suggesting they might perhaps have been colorful accretions for the later *Recorded Sayings* text.[24] However, Yunyan initially states that if he could hear nonsentient beings, Dongshan would not hear him. But then

Dongshan, in this version, rather than asking why he himself could not hear them, responds that then he, Dongshan, could not hear Yunyan. This implies that Dongshan is admitting that he could indeed hear the expounding of nonsentient beings, contrary to the other version. Such hearing might have impelled Dongshan's related questions in the first place. Further, the awareness expressed by Dongshan as "Hearing with your eyes, you directly understand" might be seen as an example of going beyond self-clinging, our usual sense of self as related to and separate from the perceptual world, in accord with the traditional Buddhist teaching of non-self. Dongshan's awareness of inconceivable Dharma represented by the totalistic apprehension of sensations demonstrates both nonself and the experience of suchness discussed in the next chapter.

Dōgen comments at length on this story in his essay "Mujō Seppō," affirming the Dharma capacity of nonsentient beings and the depth of Dongshan's verse. Dōgen states, "Insentient beings hearing insentient beings speak dharma is essentially all buddhas hearing all buddhas speak dharma."[25] He allows no separation at all between nonsentient beings and buddhas. Dōgen also points to the underlying question in the story and in Dongshan's response as to the very nature of sentience, perception, and consciousness, and their relationship to the teaching. With his characteristically challenging wordplay, Dōgen proclaims that Dongshan "revealed his towering determination to speak dharma for insentient beings. He not only experienced insentient beings speaking dharma, but he thoroughly took hold of hearing and not hearing insentient beings speaking dharma."[26] In light of such clear affirmation, what does it mean to be a sentient being or a nonsentient being, and what is the difference? How do such beings connect to awareness of suchness?

Chan and Interacting Perceptions

In Dongshan's closing verse commentary, the same in both renditions of the story, he goes beyond merely inquiring into whether or how nonsentient beings might expound the Dharma and demonstrates his own comprehension of this Dharma. "Hearing with your eyes, you directly understand" provides a description of synesthesia, the mingling of senses so that sensation in one mode occurs from stimulus in another sense mode. This synesthesia has been described as a subtle and skillful mode of apprehension in a great number of contexts, both in Buddhism and in other human cultural traditions. Synesthesia might be correlated with the Buddhist *dhārani*, incantations commonly chanted in Sanskrit, or in East Asia with transliterations of the Sanskrit into Chinese or Sino-Japanese. While the meaning and functions of dhārani are complex, often the particular sounds in dhārani are supposed to have particular, beneficial spiritual results.[27] Signified meaning is not necessarily the point, but the active aural invoking of Dharma effects is useful. The actual ritual experience of proclaiming these sounds is said to have somatic benefits, and also to aid memory and analytic faculties, fostering eloquent expounding, and so to connect the senses of speech or sound with mind.[28]

A number of examples of sense mingling have appeared in Chan lore. One involves a story about Yunyan and his Dharma brother and biological brother Daowu Yuanzhi (769–835; Jpn.: Dōgo Enchi). Their relationship will be discussed in more detail in chapter 3, but many stories of dialogues between them are recorded. In one story, cited by Hongzhi as case 54 in what became the *Book of Serenity*, Yunyan asked what the bodhisattva of compassion does with so many hands and eyes, and Daowu responded, "It's like reaching back for your pillow in the middle of the night."[29] This image from Daowu expresses the active workings of compassion as immediately responsive and uncalculated, with the hand able to see even in total darkness. This is represented iconographically as one of the prominent forms of Avalokiteśvara, the bodhisattva of compassion, having one thousand hands, each with an eye in it.[30] Wansong comments on the *Book of Serenity* case, "When reaching for a pillow at night, there's an eye in the hand; when eating there's an eye on the tongue, when recognizing people on hearing them speak there's an eye in the ears."[31] Wansong goes on to tell of someone who wrote when conversing with a deaf man and was amused that he used his hands for a mouth while the deaf man used his eyes for ears. Wansong adds, "The Buddha spoke of the interchanging functions of the six senses—it is true without a doubt." Here we see a new model of apprehension for sentient beings, with awareness flowing through the interactivity of various senses.

A modern example of synesthesia is the nineteenth-century French symbolist poet Arthur Rimbaud seeing the sound of the vowels and consonants in his own writing as colors. For Rimbaud, particular sounds corresponded with particular colors. In his "Season in Hell," he writes, "I invented the color of the vowels!—*A* black, *E* white, *I* red, *O* blue, *U* green.—I regulated the form and movement of each consonant, and, with instinctive rhythms, I prided myself on inventing a poetic language accessible some day to all the senses. I reserved translation rights. It was at first a study. I wrote out silences, and the nights. I recorded the inexpressible."[32] But Rimbaud talks about this sensory mingling as one of his follies. He did not have a meditative practice tradition or psycho-spiritual container in which to explore or use beneficially this awareness. He had some experience of seeing the colors of the sounds of his poems, but this came in the context of his "season in hell," which he described as a kind of derangement. His rejection of such seeing and vision might have been part of his abandonment of his own poetry and writing after only a few intense, adolescent years.

Dongshan uses synesthesia to present experiential evidence of an awareness of suchness beyond the conventional limitations of sensation and the familiar routines of human conceptualization. Rather than a derangement, this description may also be taken as a meditation or samādhi instruction. A quality of presence is indicated, often defined in Zen practice traditions in terms of uprightness and qualities of *mudrā*, or postures. The practitioner's openness to the phenomenal world is not narrowly defined in terms of particular sense media or from verbal understanding based on "hearing" the Dharma, but, rather, awareness of phenomena occurs within a more primal wholeness, not separated into visual, aural, smell, taste, tactile, or thought. All of the senses might be seen as part of a single instrument for perceiving, engaging, and practicing suchness. This multifaceted embrace of sensation also suggests radical awareness and acceptance of the phenomenal world of karma, the causes and conditions that allow one's presence. The rejection of the sense perception world is sometimes promoted in Buddhist and Zen meditative teachings. However, Zen includes strong cautions against seeing ultimate awareness as a way of rejecting this world and all its suffering. The bodhisattva tradition, of which Zen is one expression, involves remaining present in the world, even while informed by deeper awareness. This also fits the Chinese, and perhaps even more the Japanese, cultural appreciation of the beauty of this world of phenomena.

While commenting on the Lotus Sutra, Dōgen offers testimony to the mingling of senses as a mode of communion with Buddha. About naturally accepting Buddha and entering his wisdom, Dōgen says, "Having heard the Buddha's teaching is like already seeing the Buddha's body. . . . Furthermore, seeing Buddha's body with your ears, hearing Buddha's preaching with your eyes, and similarly for all six sense objects, is also like entering and residing in Buddha's house, and entering buddhahood and arousing the vow, exactly the same as in the ancient vow, without any difference."[33]

The lengthy story about Dongshan's meeting with Yunyan, and its background, demonstrates aspects of the subtlety of teaching that is characteristic of the tradition that extends from Dongshan and on past Dōgen. Guishan's statement to Dongshan that, "It can never be explained to you by means of one born of mother and father," as well as the instructions by the national teacher and from Yunyan, all indicate that this realm of teaching is beyond the usual human conceptual categories, and challenges the student to his own experiential realization, beyond any theoretical explanations.

Speaking with Silence

There is a later story from Dongshan in his *Recorded Sayings* that is related to the story of hearing or not hearing nonsentient beings expounding Dharma through which he met Yunyan. This story also relates to the practice of receiving the awareness of suchness. Dongshan instructed his assembly, saying, "Experiencing the matter of going beyond Buddha, finally capable we can speak a little." An intrepid monk inquired, "What is speaking?" Dongshan said, "At the time of speaking you do not hear." The monk asked, "Master, do you hear or not?" And Dongshan replied, "Just when I do not speak, then I hear."[34]

Even though he previously recommended hearing with the eyes, Dongshan here recommends not using the tongue as a way to hear. This implies silence and the practice of silent meditation as the context for "going beyond Buddha." Such going beyond signifies not attaching to prior awareness or conceptions of awakening, but fully and ongoingly sensing and simply meeting the present suchness. And yet there is still the suggestion of eventually speaking "a little" to subtly convey this awareness. Silence alone is not sufficient to go beyond Buddha. And suchness is an unending and shifting, not static, reality.

Commenting on this dialogue from Dongshan later in Japan, Dōgen says in the koan verse commentaries in his *Extensive Record:*

Seeing words we know the person like seeing his face.
Three direct pointers are tongue, sharp wit, and writing.
Fulfilling the way, wings naturally appear on the body.
Since meeting myself, I deeply respect him.[35]

Dōgen here is praising Dongshan. Since meeting the constructed illusory self, his own "myself," Dōgen says he deeply respects this teaching, and the so-called other.

Dongshan's *Recorded Sayings* includes numerous subtle stories about how to convey this silence, or hearing with the eyes, that is the engagement and practice of suchness. Dongshan and Dōgen are both concerned here with how one meets this Dharma of suchness; how one might hear, taste, touch, enjoy its fragrance; and then how one engages this sensing of reality. Still, despite its illusiveness, Dongshan says one must "speak a little" to convey this reality. And Dōgen is even willing to praise "tongue, sharp wit, and writing."

In another reference to this story in his *Extensive Record*, Dōgen emphasizes the commonplace prevalence of the deep relationship between the nonsentient and the Dharma. After relating Dongshan's verse about hearing with the eyes, and Huizhong's dialogue about sages hearing the nonsentient teaching, Dōgen comments, "The National Teacher said that all the sages can hear it, and Yunyan said that nonsentient beings can hear it. Although they said it like that, why did they not say that ordinary beings can hear it?"[36] For Dōgen, this Dharma expounded by nonsentient beings that was so important to Dongshan is ever present and available, even to ordinary people and beings. When we consider the complexities of perception and sense faculties, and how awareness works through such sense gates, the very meaning of sentience and non-sentience opens and shifts.

CHAPTER TWO

Depicting This Reality

Recognizing the Companion

In an earlier story about Dongshan when he was still a young monk studying under Nanquan Puyuan (748–835; Jpn.: Nansen Fugan), the complex relationship of student and teacher is already prefigured. In the story, Nanquan was preparing for the memorial service for his own teacher, Mazu Daoyi (709–88; Jpn.: Baso Dōitsu), a great, important teacher sometimes said to have had 139 enlightened disciples. Nanquan said to his assembly, "Tomorrow we will pay homage to Mazu. Do you think he will return or not?" When nobody else responded, young Dongshan came forward and said, "He will come as soon as he has a companion."[1] Already Dongshan realized that the reality of a teacher was in the interaction with a worthy student.

Nanquan then complimented the young monk as being suitable for training. Dongshan said, "Master, do not crush what is good into something mean." Here Dongshan rejected the view of Zen teaching as being a matter of molding, perfecting, or improving the student. Of course, Zen practice ideally transforms and develops qualities of character, but the implication here is that insight and compassionate caring are fundamental capacities already present, perhaps fostered but not instilled by some fashioning from the teacher. In his later meeting with Yunyan, as we will see, Dongshan would realize the reality of teaching as the mutual recognition of suchness and the complex relationship that intimately expresses the full dynamic of the practice of suchness.

33

It Now Is Me; I Am Not It

Probably the most pivotal and emblematic story about Dongshan occurred with his departure from Yunyan, rather than in their first meeting discussed in the previous chapter, which was concerned with nonsentient beings expressing Dharma. After some period of practice with Yunyan (its duration unspecified in extant records, as far as I know), just before departing to visit other teachers, Dongshan asked Yunyan, "Later on, if I am asked to describe your reality [or teaching], how should I respond?"[2] After some pause, Yunyan said, "Just this is it."

The narration states that Dongshan was then lost in thought, and Yunyan said, "You are now in charge of this great matter; you must be most thoroughgoing." Dongshan departed without further comment. Later while wading across a stream, he looked down, saw his reflection, and "awakened to the meaning of the previous exchange."[3] He then wrote the following verse:

> Just don't seek from others, or you'll be far estranged from self.
> I now go on alone; everywhere I meet it.
> It now is me; I now am not it.
> One must understand in this way to merge with suchness.[4]

This story is highly revealing about the nature of this suchness, or reality, and also for the teaching about it. Yunyan's "Just this is it" evokes meditative or mindfulness practices of bare attention from early Buddhism.[5] "This" certainly might be envisioned in the context of their dialogue as referring simply to the presence together of Yunyan and Dongshan, that just the interactive presence of teacher and student is it. "This" might also refer to Dongshan's directly prior inquiry, that the student's asking about the teacher's reality is the point. But "just this" also refers more universally to the simplicity and immediacy of reality here now, beyond human conceptualizations. Such a sterling utterance of the ultimate neither requires nor suggests any quick rejoinder from Dongshan, and none was forthcoming. But Yunyan sealed his conveyance of the Dharma to Dongshan by then saying, "You are now in charge of this great matter; you must be most thoroughgoing."

Dongshan's subsequent revelation upon gazing at his reflection in the stream presents an inner dynamic overcoming the familiar subject-object division, a primary hindrance to the apprehension of suchness. His verse response does not merely concern discerning a description of some external reality. Dongshan speaks to the complex dialectic that goes beyond the estrangement of self and other and integrates his personhood with the omnipresence of the reality of suchness. This reality is unavoidable: "Everywhere I meet it." Saying, "Just don't seek from others, or you'll be far estranged from self," Dongshan understands that he needs to realize this for himself, that Yunyan cannot just tell him this, or give it to him. Similarly, just hearing about this, the present reader does not automatically realize its import.

The provocative and profound key line that suggests the inner nature of this interrelationship is "It now is me; I now am not it." This dynamic interaction may be viewed from many perspectives. Gazing at his reflection in the stream, Dongshan could see that this image was him, yet he could not be reduced to the representation in the water. The relationship of true reality to image, reflection, or depiction is at work in various ways here. These reflections are not themselves this ultimate reality, but suchness fully includes all images or depictions of it. Our experience of suchness and any expression of it can be in accord with suchness, but do not fully capture the suchness of the world.

The "it" of "just this" is totally inclusive, incorporating everything. So "it" truly was him, the totality of his being, yet he could not personally claim to encompass it all. This depicts the relationship of the limited "I," including its egoistic self-clinging, to the all-encompassing universal nature, of which any individual "I" is simply a particular partial expression. This dialectic echoes the Huayan Fourfold Dharmadhātu with its development of the universal, the particular, the mutual nonobstructive interaction of universal and particular, and finally the mutual nonobstructive interaction of particulars with "other" particulars.[6] This dialectic between universal and particular would be developed as the Caodong five degrees teaching, introduced by Dongshan in his "Jewel Mirror Samādhi." In that teaching poem, this line from Dongshan's awakening verse celebrating the stream reflection, "It now is me; I now am not it," would be echoed as "You are not it; it truly is you."

This story helps illuminate the traditional Buddhist teaching of non-self and the issue of identity. Non-self, or *anātman* in Sanskrit, is one of the most fundamental Buddhist teachings. The Buddha declared that all selves are illusory constructions, not real as separate entities but mutually interdependent. Our attachment to our cherished self and its patterns of grasping and confusion obstructs seeing into deeper reality and the possibility of an awakened awareness that compassionately expresses the deep interconnection of oneself and supposed "others." Dongshan's "It now is me; I now am not it" provides a rich tapestry with which to look at the subtle interrelationship of this self with the wholeness of totality, of which the small self is an integral part. While "I now am not it" informs about the teaching of non-self, "It now is me" provides a deeper context for seeing the full reality in which we engage phenomena and have capacity to act responsibly.

I Is an Other

The complex dynamic expressed in Dongshan's "It now is me; I now am not it" might be further illuminated with the similarly challenging statement made a millennium later in an 1871 letter from the French symbolist poet Arthur Rimbaud, already mentioned in the previous chapter in connection with synesthesia. Rimbaud claims, "Je est un autre," or "I is an other."[7] Rimbaud's "I is an other" provides a viewpoint into the axiomatic Buddhist teaching of anātman, or non-self. This teaching expresses the illusory, constructed nature of our conventional "self," based on the usual human way of thinking and seeing separation between self and other, between subject and object. This might be considered the Buddhist fundamental ignorance, or even the Buddhist version of "original sin." The world appears to be "out there," not connected to oneself, and the things out there are also seen as unconnected to each other, a mere collection of dead objects. Deep in our language and mode of thinking is the sense of separate self and others, in which one is a self verbing others, or else being verbed by others "out there." In the Yogācāra Buddhist psychological classification of eight levels of consciousness, this sense of separation between self and others is sometimes described in terms of *manas*, a seventh consciousness that acts to separate our self as observer from the objects of awareness, observed via our usual five sense objects but also in a sixth awareness of thoughts as sense objects.[8]

When Rimbaud says, "I is an other," he is describing experientially the construction of a self, necessary to survive the adolescence from which he speaks as a seventeen-year-old. He sees his own "I" as an other, just as any other "other" is an other. In fact, "I" is indeed an other when one sees clearly the process of the construction of an "I." Whenever we are not fully engaging the body of suchness, we have bunches of others, including this "I." Just as we see fences and walls as others, we can see "I" as an other; indeed, "I" becomes an other whenever we imagine an "I." One approach to practicing with anātman, or non-self, is gently to see though this construction—not to get rid of the "I," or ego, but to see its illusory quality. By holding on to it, by trying to define and limit it and see it in some rigid way, one shuts off the possibility of fully engaging the body and mind of self and other and of all things of this world in their context of the immediacy of suchness. In his letter, Rimbaud's "I is an other" follows upon his stating, "It is wrong to say: I think. One ought to say: people think me."[9] The constructed ego self is not one's own private property but is a co-creation by all events in the universe. Seeing this, one might well view his illusory self, created by everything, by the people who "think me," in terms of the mutual nonobstructive interaction of particulars with "other" particulars, with one's self as simply a reflection of it all.

Indeed, "It now is me." But probably Rimbaud, in his season in hell in process when he wrote this letter, saw only that "I am not it," as opposed to also appreciating that "it actually is me," and felt deeply the sense of estrangement between "I" and the world of "other."

The figure of Rimbaud appears as one of the characters inspired by the life of Bob Dylan in the 2007 movie *I'm Not There* by Todd Haynes, in which six different actors (including Cate Blanchett, Richard Gere, Heath Ledger, and Christian Bale) play complex figures expressed at seven different periods in the long, brilliant, and famously shifting career of Bob Dylan.[10] Dylan presents an example of the complexity of identity, which includes all his different forms of expressing himself and totally changing his persona, often contrary to the wishes of fans who wanted him to remain as some certain, definable "I." Dylan's whole life-work is a monument to the "I" constantly shifting to become an other, as the "I" is not It, even though Dylan seems to be ever searching for that It, or perhaps for the ultimate suchness, which actually is him. "I'm Not There," the Dylan song for which the movie is named, is an eerie, haunting, mysterious song drenched with yearning and regret, seemingly sung about a lost, abandoned love.[11] Apparently incomplete and recorded only once, in the basement tapes with The Band, the singer confesses in the final refrain, "I wish I was there to help her, but I'm not there, I'm gone." Yet even the lyrics of the song, hard to decipher amid the pathos of the singer, seem themselves to evaporate, are not there. As Greil Marcus comments, "As you listen, words are precisely as irretrievable as the plot of a fading dream, the moment of certainty offered by the title phrase when it occurs seems priceless; superseded in the next movement by a line that has no more shape than water in your hands, that certainly seems worthless."[12] Even as the identity of the song seems to hesitate into the ephemeral and is itself not there but gone, the mysterious intensity of the singing becomes a quality that actually is us, the listeners. And any identifiable "I" is indeed not there, a mere phantom.

Dylan has throughout his career often played with the illusion of identity, changing his persona as well as singing style, often changing his appearance, including performing in white face during his Rolling Thunder tour in the 70s. This concern with the unreality of identity is further apparent in his cinematic appearances—for example, playing a character called Alias in *Pat Garrett and Billy the Kid*. Then Dylan and his wife, Sarah, played Renaldo and Clara in the film of that name, in which two other actors play "Bob Dylan" and his wife. In his brilliant film *Masked and Anonymous*, Dylan displayed and celebrated the complex fluidity of personal identity in the context of the failure of our American societal identity.

Dongshan's "I now am not it" similarly reveals that there is no real "I" here—"I is an other." Rimbaud's "I is an other" and Dylan's "I'm not there I'm gone" both open up this teaching of non-self contained in Dongshan's "I am not it." But Dylan's explorations of the illusory nature of identity shares with Dongshan's "It now is me" a reflection on the other side from "I am not it," and the manner in which this illusory self indeed performs as a piece of suchness. Dongshan's "It now is me" balances the whole by indicating the inquiry into how one might care for the reality of suchness, the rich reality of the world that is us, and of which we are totally part.

The Self Carried Forward

Returning to traditional Caodong/Sōtō expressions of the complexity of identity, and its relationship to ultimate reality, one of the seminal writings of Eihei Dōgen includes a line that might be taken as a revealing commentary to Dongshan's "It now is me; I now am not it." In his essay "Genjōkōan" ("Actualizing the Fundamental Point") from one of his masterworks, *Shōbōgenzō* (*True Dharma Eye Treasury*), Dōgen says, "To carry the self forward and experience myriad things is delusion. That myriad things come forth and experience the self is awakening."[13] In this case the "You are not it" is amplified as the self carrying forward or projecting some constructed self on to one's experience, defined by Dōgen as delusion. The constructed "you" is not it, or true reality.

Dongshan's "It now is me," on the other hand, is expressed by Dōgen as the myriad things of the phenomenal world interdependently co-arising and mutually experiencing the self, identified as awakening. This mutual arising of all would, of course, include the particular self, but now seen as merely one of the ten thousand particular aspects of reality, rather than imposing its desires and human presuppositions onto reality. The total interconnected dependent co-arising is exactly you. This description from Dōgen of the dynamic process of self, the projection of the constructed egoistic self, and non-self as the wholeness of reality, including the provisional person, illuminates the dynamic of Dongshan's five degrees and its integration of the particular, including each and every self, with the ultimate universal, as will be further discussed later in this book. Dōgen, like Dongshan, realizes both sides of "I am not it" and "It now is me" in terms of carrying forward a self but then seeing all things, including the constructed self, as experiencing the larger self.

Dōgen, perhaps more explicitly than Dongshan, emphasizes not the theoretical aspect of this dynamic but its actual practice and application to meditative forms. Through meditative practice and its expression in everyday activity we may find some relationship of awareness of totality to the world of the senses, the phenomenal world. In upright meditative sitting we can become intimate with our human habit of carrying forward into our world the patterns and habits familiar to our constructed self. As we relax these habits, we can also glimpse the underlying reality of all things mutually arising together, and simply feel this open self. Dongshan, too, in his concern not to seek outside or become estranged from self but to merge with suchness, suggests that one may breathe in suchness and exhale suchness.

"Just this is it" is not static, but just this is alive. Just this is constantly changing. Even if you experience some thorough, deep realization about just this, you need to keep paying attention. Upright sitting is alive. Sometimes we feel inhale, sometimes exhale, sometimes the space after inhale, sometimes the space after exhale.

You are not it, but, honestly, it is you, and practicing it is dynamic. A danger in the phrase "Just this" is that it may sound passive, like if I just accept everything as it is, then that would be it. But that is one of the classic four traps of spiritual practice: Just accepting things as they are, just going with the flow, and then "whatever happens" is fine.[14] That does not work and is not the "Just this" that Dongshan is describing, because you are not it, but it actually is you, and involves and requires your response. In the stories about Dongshan to be discussed further on in this work he explores how practitioners receive and express intimations of suchness.

Meeting Him Everywhere

In addition to its relevance to issues concerning the nature of suchness and the self, Dongshan's verse and Yunyan's primary response pertain to the student-teacher relationship and the "intimate transmitting" of this truth. In both Yunyan's statement "Just this is it" and the middle lines in Dongshan's verse above, there is a different indefinite pronoun that could be read as either "it" or as a personal pronoun (e.g., "him"). So Yunyan's response to Dongshan about describing his teaching might be understood as "Just this person." And the reading of Dongshan's verse might be "I now go on alone, but everywhere I meet him. / He now is me; I now am not him."

Yunyan's statement and this verse are often translated in this way, and both the readings of "it" to imply "suchness" and of "him" as the teacher are certainly implicit and valid interpretations in these lines of Dongshan's verse, as well as in his "Jewel Mirror Samādhi."[15] The Chinese character in Yunyan's statement is more commonly read as "it," while the different character in Dongshan's "I am not him" is more often a personal pronoun, but each might be either "it" or "him." Clearly, some of the comments on this story by Dongshan himself imply reading this as a personal pronoun, indicating the intricacy of his relationship to his teacher. But whichever meaning Dongshan initially intended for this word, whether "it" or "him," both meanings can evoke rich, illuminating, and relevant interpretations. We are concerned here with the text itself as a revelatory, enduring inspiration attributed to the iconic characters Yunyan and Dongshan, not primarily with the historical figures supposed to have proclaimed these utterances, and whatever they might have intended.

In Dongshan's *Recorded Sayings*, in the story immediately preceding the narrative in which Yunyan tells Dongshan, "Just this is it" or "Just this person," Dongshan is already described as taking his leave from Yunyan. Yunyan said, "After your departure, it will be hard to meet again." Dongshan replied, "It will be hard not to meet."[16] Even before he gazed at his reflection in the stream, Dongshan felt the enduring imprint of his teacher Yunyan's presence: "everywhere I meet him." So in addition to subtly commenting on the suchness of reality, this story and Dongshan's verse response present a subtle expression of the role of the teacher. "Just this person" is also a variant of a phrase used in medieval China for a criminal formally to confess guilt in court, in Chan contexts implying taking thorough personal responsibility, here as a teacher to his student.

Whichever version of Yunyan's statement and the pronoun involved is considered, "Just this is it" or "Just this person," his follow-up comment refers to the process of conveying teaching about suchness. After that statement of reality to Dongshan, Yunyan paused and added, "You are now in charge of this great matter; you must be most thoroughgoing." This admonition to take care of and preserve this teaching is at the heart of the tradition of Zen Dharma transmission, ever since Dongshan. In some elemental sense, the teaching about suchness is itself inextricably involved with how this teaching is maintained and passed along. Issues of teaching style and the subtle process of conveying and sustaining this awareness of suchness are not separate from engagement with the suchness of reality. In the stories about Dongshan and in the "Jewel Mirror Samādhi" to be considered later in this book, approaches to revealing and imparting awareness of suchness are central concerns.

How Could He Be Willing?

The story that Hongzhi later used as case 49 of the koan collection that would become the *Book of Serenity* is a follow-up story commenting on Yunyan's stating, "Just this is it." In the *Book of Serenity* text, the original story and Dongshan's verse after seeing his reflection in the stream appear only in Wansong's later commentary on the case. The main story featured in the case, highly revealing of the relationship of the master and apprentice, involves Dongshan some time later as leader of an assembly making offerings to an image of Yunyan as his teacher. He may have been making offerings to Yunyan on the occasion of a monthly memorial service for a teacher or temple founder, still part of Sōtō ritual. A monk came forward and asked, "When Yunyan said 'Just this is it,' what did he mean?"

Dongshan responded, "At that time I nearly misunderstood my late teacher."

The monk then asked, somewhat impudently, "Did Yunyan himself know it is, or not?"

Dongshan said, "If he didn't know it is, how could he be able to say this? If he did know it is, how could he be willing to say this?"[17]

The first half of this comment is clear. Yunyan had to have personally experienced the suchness of "just this" in order to be able to state as the heart of his teaching, "Just this is it." However, rather than presuming, it is significant that Dongshan responded to the monk with a question, "If he didn't know it is, how could he be able to say this?" The other half of the question expresses the problem of stating this directly. To really see "just this" includes the awareness that such realization cannot be "intimately transmitted" simply through verbiage. Dongshan needed to himself gaze into the reflection in the stream to realize "It now is me; I now am not it." Dongshan asked that if Yunyan really knew just this, how could he have been willing to say "just this" so nakedly and explicitly? Dongshan presented an unanswerable question about whether Yunyan could really have known suchness. And this deep questioning is what is most helpful toward provoking the student's own realization of the dynamics of suchness. Dongshan refused to give any direct answer to the monk questioning about Yunyan. My comments on this story here similarly provide the reader with no simple solution.

In the *Recorded Sayings*, immediately after the preceding exchange, presumably on a different occasion of Dongshan making offerings for Yunyan, another monk inquired as to why Dongshan so honored Yunyan, who was fairly obscure, as opposed to other renowned teachers Dongshan had studied under, such as Nanquan. Dongshan replied, "I do not esteem my late teacher's virtues or his Buddhist teaching; I only value the fact that he didn't explain everything for me."[18] Here Dongshan strongly emphasizes a pedagogic style of indirectness, and the crucial importance of the student's personal experience rather than intellectual or ideological presentations of inner truth. At the end of this dialogue Dongshan evinced his own indirectness by replying to the monk's further questioning by saying that he only half agreed with Yunyan because, "If I completely agreed, then I would be unfaithful to my teacher."[19] Just as Yunyan did not explain everything (or especially the most important things) for Dongshan, Dongshan would not be willing to blindly agree with Yunyan about everything. This is a retrospective nonexplanation aimed toward and honoring the memory of his teacher. Even if Yunyan now is Dongshan, and Dongshan meets Yunyan everywhere, Dongshan cannot fully be, and indeed is not, Yunyan. Thus, in such a way, Dongshan becomes Dongshan.

The Jade Works

Hongzhi offers a provocative verse commentary to case 49 with Dongshan's "If he didn't know it is, how could he be able to say this? If he did know it is, how could he be willing to say this?" Hongzhi's verse commentary follows:

How could he be able to say this?
In the third watch the cock crows—Dawn for the forest of
  homes.
How could he be willing to say this? The thousand-year crane
  grows old with the pine in the clouds.
The jewel mirror, clear and bright, shows upright and inclined:
The jade works spin—see them both show up together.
The Way of the school is greatly influential, its regulated steps
  continuous and fine:
Father and son change and pass through—oceanic is their
  fame.[20]

The two key lines of the verse are "The jewel mirror, clear and
bright, shows upright and inclined: / the jade works spin—see them
both show up together." Here Hongzhi evokes Dongshan's later
"Jewel Mirror Samādhi," and the dynamic interaction of ultimate
and provisional, in the original literally upright and inclined. The
jewel mirror here refers not only to Dongshan's teaching poem,
but also and more deeply to the luminous insight expressed by
Dongshan. He balances and subtly integrates the universal, expressed as "upright," and the conventional phenomenal realm,
expressed as "inclined," as in the compassionate response of the
bodhisattva, leaning out to express sympathy and assistance to all
suffering beings trapped by the grasping, anger, and confusion of
the phenomenal world.

The "Jewel Mirror Samādhi" includes the line "Like facing a
jewel mirror; form and reflection behold each other." Facing the
jewel mirror is followed by the line "You are not it, but in truth it
is you," echoing Dongshan's verse after looking into the stream,
"It now is me; I now am not it." This evocative, pregnant line is
itself the potent jewel mirror, which Hongzhi clarifies as clear and
bright, displaying upright and inclined.

Hongzhi's next complex image of the jade works is intriguing,
and instructive. The highly complex Chinese character translated

here as "works," and by Cleary as "machine" (Ch.: *ji;* Jpn.: *ki*) also connotes energy, opportunity, function, capacity, occasion, a mechanism, a loom, or even the moving power of the universe. The "Jewel Mirror Samādhi" includes this character in the line "The meaning does not reside in the words, but a pivotal moment brings it forth." This pivotal moment is literally the "arrival" of this working, capacity, function, opportunity, or mechanism arising immediately in response to the student's intent inquiry. This is indeed a working pivot, turning with energy, curiosity, and potential.

Hongzhi's point is that this pivot is actually working, revolving, functioning effectively in the story and in Dongshan's utterances "It now is me; I now am not it" and "If he did know it is, how could he be willing to say this?" Thanks to the pivot of this precious jade device, Hongzhi proclaims, both upright and inclined, the universal and its particular phenomenal expressions "show up together" and immediately. This jade works is a great mystery that is working right now, in operation in the world, and in our life. In the following stories about Dongshan I will explore how they are effective in disclosing the suchness of this interaction between upright and inclined.

In the rest of Hongzhi's verse comment on case 49, he celebrates the depth and power of the transformative interaction between Dongshan and Yunyan, "Father and son change and pass through—oceanic is their fame." Hongzhi appreciates the legacy he has received. In response to Dongshan's intriguing question, "How could he be willing to say this?" Hongzhi states, "The thousand-year crane grows old with the pine in the clouds." Cranes are ancient Chinese symbols of wisdom and longevity, and Dongshan's legacy has indeed weathered a millennium, still up in the clouds, and studied by "clouds and water" monks and practitioners, ever pining for universal liberation.

Modern Turnings of the Pivot of Studying Self

Shunryū Suzuki (1904–71) was a Japanese monk who started the San Francisco Zen Center in the 1960s and founded Tassajara, the first Zen monastery in the West, thereby introducing the Dongshan and Dōgen lineage to America. Suzuki provided another reinterpretation of Dongshan's key verse after seeing his reflection in the stream. Various readings of the lines "Just don't seek from others, or you'll be far estranged from self. / I now go on alone; everywhere I meet it" are discussed above. Just as the final pronoun might be read as "everywhere I meet him," instead of meeting "it" or "just this," Suzuki discussed it as the practice of everywhere meeting oneself. In a talk to his students at Tassajara, he emphasized the importance of warm-hearted kindness, to oneself as well as others. He paraphrased the first two lines of Dongshan's verse upon crossing the stream, and about being far estranged from self, as Dongshan saying, "Don't try to figure out who you are. If you try to figure out who you are, what you understand will be far away from you. You will have just an image of yourself." Suzuki commented further, "Actually you are in the river. You may say that is just a shadow or a reflection of yourself, but if you look carefully with warm-hearted feeling, that is you."[21] Here is another spin on how the self is informed by its reflection, and how I am not it, or him, or even myself, but they actually are me, or "with warmhearted feeling, that is you." These are all approaches to deep study of the relationship between the illusion of self and the reality of non-self.

In another talk Suzuki criticizes his students' attitude of seeking some self-improvement from their practice. He quotes Dongshan as saying, "Don't try to see yourself objectively" and renders his lines after seeing his reflection as "I go my own way. Wherever I go, I meet myself."[22] Suzuki makes the Dongshan story personal and practical, about "meeting myself." Everywhere and everything in the universe, when we intimately engage it, is suchness, is the teacher, is actually yourself.

Suzuki's disciple Tenshin Reb Anderson has elaborated on this further. He reads Yunyan's saying as "Just this person" and Dongshan's verse as "Everywhere I meet him." But like Suzuki, Anderson uses this to point at the study of "myself." He comments, "When we wholeheartedly practice the teaching of 'just this person,' all beings come forth to meet us, and we realize that they are 'now no other than myself.'" He emphasizes this study as the heart of compassionate awareness. He adds, "Our compassionate ancestors studied, understood and taught completely how self-delusion arises and how it is the source of all our misery. Buddhas are those who deeply enter into learning about self-delusion and are greatly awakened in the midst of studying self-delusion."[23]

So this story about Yunyan saying, "Just this is it" (however the pronoun is read), and Dongshan's realization that "It now is me; I now am not it" provide a profound and practical entryway to studying the suchness of oneself, and of one's own experience.

CHAPTER THREE

Yunyan's Journey to Suchness

Yunyan's Role in Dongshan's Teaching

In the introduction to the "Jewel Mirror Samādhi" in Dongshan's *Recorded Sayings*, Dongshan says to his disciple Caoshan that Yunyan "secretly entrusted me with the Jewel Mirror Samādhi, thoroughly conveying its essence."[1] However, nowhere else in the writings about Dongshan or Yunyan is there any suggestion that the verse text itself of the "Jewel Mirror Samādhi" was composed by Yunyan. So this reference might well be taken as signifying Dongshan's appreciation of the heart of its teachings having been conveyed by Yunyan. As described in the introduction, no text of the "Jewel Mirror Samādhi" was published until the early twelfth century, and no extant copies date from before 1632.[2] Although its historical context is uncertain, this important teaching poem has long been studied and considered a product of Dongshan himself, rather than of Yunyan.

Yet Yunyan Tansheng is clearly an important figure, deeply appreciated by Dongshan, as revealed in the stories about Dongshan's training. Yunyan was not well known in his own time. We see in the later stories of Dongshan being questioned about Yunyan, on the occasions when Dongshan made offerings and honored him, that Yunyan was not highly regarded except by Dongshan. Before considering stories about Dongshan's teaching, an interlude to further consider a few significant stories about Yunyan's own studies and teaching is appropriate.

Yunyan as Chan Failure

Many stories about Yunyan include his Dharma brother and older biological brother, Daowu Yuanzhi. Daowu and Yunyan studied together under and became successors of Yaoshan Weiyan. However, there are different stories about Yunyan and Daowu studying together prior to Yaoshan. These include study with the very prominent Chan teacher Baizhang, the teacher of Guishan, who would direct Dongshan to Yunyan, as described in chapter 1, and then with Nanquan, whom Dongshan visited later on as a young monk, as related in the beginning of chapter 2. In both sets of stories, Yunyan is depicted as a complete failure, despite these eminent teachers' reputations for skillfulness.

Baizhang is renowned in Chan lore for many sayings and anecdotes. He reputedly originated the Chan monastic guidelines and said, "A day without work is a day without food," when he was old and his disciples hid his tools to prevent him from working in the fields.[3] Baizhang is also famous for giving a formal monk's funeral to a fox, a creature of malevolence in East Asia. Supposedly, the fox body was the remains of an ancient master who had incorrectly answered a question by dismissing the importance of karma, thereby incurring the destiny of becoming a fox for five hundred lifetimes, until Baizhang saved him.[4] In the story about Yunyan and Baizhang, Yunyan is said to have been Baizhang's personal attendant for twenty years without understanding Dharma. According to the Lamp Transmission literature, Daowu studied under Baizhang for only a year, then went to study with Yaoshan and strongly encouraged Yunyan to follow him.[5] Yunyan was finally persuaded by Daowu and departed to study with Yaoshan.

Yaoshan once asked Yunyan, "What do you do about the birth and death right in front of you?" Yunyan responded, "There is no birth and death in front of me." Yaoshan said, "You were with Baizhang for twenty years and still have not gotten rid of your commonness."[6] Yunyan here seems to be attached to some view of transcendence as separate from phenomenal reality, with birth and death merely nonexistent. Perhaps he had actually seen beyond birth and death and realized emptiness in some sense. This may indicate a worthy meditative accomplishment, but that is a very small part of true awakening practice. Expression of awakening cannot be separated from the causes and conditions that lead to spiritual practice, and that may trigger opening experiences. One can actually see through life and death and express something that goes beyond life and death, right in the midst of the situations of life and death, and within the particular times and conditions of the phenomenal world. Yunyan in this exchange seems to seek evasion from such worldly conditions, or even to be rid of birth and death altogether.

Another time Yaoshan inquired of Yunyan again about Baizhang's teaching. Yunyan mentioned how Baizhang once entered the hall to teach and drove the monks away with his staff, then called out, "O monks!" When they turned around, Baizhang asked abruptly, "What is it?" Hearing this, Yaoshan said to Yunyan, "Why didn't you say that before? Now thanks to you, I have finally seen brother [Baizhang Huai]hai." When Yaoshan said this, Yunyan finally awakened.[7] Yaoshan appreciated how Baizhang had been able to sharply elicit and bring forth the monks' attention. And Yunyan then realized what Baizhang had been pointing at. It is not that Yaoshan was a better teacher than Baizhang, or vice versa. And perhaps Yunyan had not wasted his twenty years with Baizhang. But conditions were finally right, and Yunyan was ready to really hear Baizhang's "What is it?" through Yaoshan's response.

Yunyan's Failure with Nanquan

In another story Yunyan and Daowu were studying with Nanquan before reaching Yaoshan. As is often the case with these accounts, any actual history is obscure. These may be two stories, perhaps written much later, intended to show how hopeless Yunyan was before awakening while studying with Yaoshan. But perhaps after leaving Baizhang, and after studying under Yaoshan for some period, Daowu and Yunyan went to practice with Nanquan for a while. Yaoshan's response to Yunyan indicating that Yunyan had returned from visiting Nanquan, discussed below, would seem to support that scenario. Aside from questions about their historical sequence, these narratives all point to Yunyan's ineptitude.

The story of Yunyan and Daowu studying with Nanquan appears in the commentary to case 69 of the *Book of Serenity* koan collection. Wansong's commentary states that later, after returning to Yaoshan's temple, Daowu was listening outside the abbot's room and was so mortified at his brother Yunyan's failure to understand his previous exchange with Nanquan that, "unconsciously [Daowu] bit his finger so hard it bled."[8] We will return to Daowu's bleeding finger as the ultimate statement of Yunyan's failure.

The main story of this case, selected by Hongzhi, is simply Nanquan proclaiming to his assembly, "The buddhas of past, present, and future do not know it is; cats and cows know it is."[9] The subject of this story, as in the story of Dongshan later departing from Yunyan, concerns the nature of suchness, just that "it is." Nanquan declares that cats and cows immediately know this suchness, but humans are confused by their discriminating consciousness. Even the buddhas do not know it, perhaps due to their very efforts to convey this truth to confused humans. Nanquan himself had a complicated relationship to both cats and cows. In a very famous and controversial Zen story, Nanquan is said to have cut a cat in two when the monks from the left and right sides of the hall had fought over it and then could not respond to Nanquan's request for an ultimate statement to save the cat.[10] Nanquan also once claimed that after his death he would become a cow or ox down the mountainside from his temple. He added that whoever wanted to follow him, "must come with a blade of grass in your mouth," perhaps to feed him.[11] Later, in the "Jewel Mirror Samādhi," Dongshan commented, "Because some [students] are wide-eyed, cats and white oxen."

In Wansong's commentary to this story about buddhas "not knowing it is" in the *Book of Serenity*, he relates a fairly complicated story about Yunyan and Daowu's practice with Nanquan, before they returned to Yaoshan.[12]

When Daowu arrived, Nanquan asked him, "What is your name?"

Daowu said, "Zongzhi" (Jpn.: Sōchi), another of his names, which means "source knowledge."

Nanquan asked, "Where knowledge doesn't reach, how can you take it as source?"

Daowu said, "Just don't speak of it."

Nanquan responded, "Clearly, if you speak of it, then horns grow on the head."

Here Daowu says, "Just don't speak of it," to indicate the source when knowledge does not work. Nanquan's "horns grow on the head" is a Chan expression for being less than human, a beastly animal, or even a demon, and therefore lacking capacity for understanding. Nanquan says this perhaps ironically, as he had proclaimed that cats and cows know it is, rather than buddhas and ancestors. In Buddhist imagery even horned demons are sometimes depicted as converted into guardians of the teaching. This whole story and set of dialogues concern how to speak without speaking and how we can say or express anything at all about suchness.

Three days later, Nanquan passed by Daowu and Yunyan as they were mending and asked Daowu, "The other day we said where knowledge doesn't reach, just don't speak of it. If you speak of it, horns grow on the head. How do you put it into practice?" He is asking how the inconceivable is truly practiced.

Daowu immediately got up and went into the meditation hall. He responded completely. And Nanquan just left.

This is a story about actually putting into practice understanding beyond mere knowledge, and about how to cut through speech with speech. These stories involve a different kind of language, beyond Chinese or English. And yet this language is pointing at something about the deep experience of suchness and how to express that in practice. So Daowu just went to take his seat, and Nanquan just got up and left. But Yunyan did not see Daowu's complete response.

A little later Yunyan asked Daowu, "Brother, why didn't you answer the teacher just then?" Daowu simply said, "You are so sharp." Yunyan still did not get it and instead went and asked the teacher, Nanquan, "Why didn't Daowu answer that issue just then?"

Nanquan said, "He is acting within different kinds."

Yunyan said, "What is acting within different kinds?"

Nanquan said, "Haven't you been told where knowledge doesn't reach, just don't speak? If you speak of it, then horns grow on the head. You must go act within different kinds."

This complicated story includes a number of aspects. But at this point, clearly Yunyan still did not understand. And if even the great Dongshan's teacher Yunyan did not understand, the reader need not feel bad to also fail to comprehend. All students of the Way may be encouraged hearing how much difficulty and how long it took for Yunyan to realize suchness. Daowu knew that Yunyan did not get the point, and he recognized that Yunyan's affinity was not with Nanquan, so they went back together to Yaoshan. Daowu was taking his brother around to different teachers to help him toward realization. And apparently, even after they had been back at Yaoshan's for a while, Yunyan still had not gotten it.

Acting within Different Kinds

There might well be different kinds of understandings of this phrase, but "acting within different kinds" can refer to activity while immersed in all the varied particularities and concrete phenomena of the conventional world. This is contrary to Yunyan's having told Yaoshan, "There is no birth and death in front of me." There is an appropriate time to just not speak of it. In that mode Daowu went back to the meditation hall, perhaps for more immersion in such a state of realizing sameness. But only not speaking, a practitioner might become stuck in sameness and attached to emptiness or abstractions, as seems to have been the case with Yunyan.

How do we act appropriately within different kinds, within the particularities of our own situation? How do we see the difference between situations, and between the particular person we are meeting with and some other person we may encounter? Each situation is a different kind. These teachers are discussing how to practice within the different kinds of difficulties in the world, too. This is language about going beyond language. Nanquan just responded. So when Yunyan asked again, "What is acting within different kinds?" Nanquan said, "Haven't you been told?" and he kindly added, "Where knowledge doesn't reach, just don't speak of it. If you speak of it, then horns grow on your head." Awakening practice requires activity within differences.

Nanquan and Daowu acted out a scene to demonstrate the usefulness of the fullness of this practice. Bodhisattva practice expresses the dynamic interaction of sameness and difference that Yaoshan's teacher Shitou had written about in his teaching poem "The Harmony of Difference and Sameness." There is a time when it is necessary to act in different kinds, and even allow horns to grow on the head. When the brothers went back to Yaoshan, Yunyan related this story of Nanquan speaking of acting within different kinds, which then was reenacted.

Yunyan's Failure with Yaoshan

When Yunyan related the story of the exchange with Nanquan, Yaoshan said, "How did you understand this time that you have come back?"

Right at that point Yunyan might have expressed something that would have shown that his returning was actually an understanding, a way of acting within different kinds. At any moment he might have somehow expressed that.

But Yunyan had no reply. Yaoshan then laughed.

Yunyan persisted and asked, "What is acting within different kinds?"

Yaoshan said, "I'm tired today, come ask another time." There are a number of stories like this, where a monk asks a teacher or another monk for some answer, and the teacher says, "I have a headache today, go ask so-and-so." Or perhaps he responds, "I'm sorry; I'm too sleepy now." The point is that the questioner has to see it for himself. These stories or dialogues are about pointing to something that you need to see yourself.

Yunyan said, "I have come back especially for this."

Yaoshan said, "Go away for now." So Yunyan simply departed.

It was during this exchange that Daowu was outside the abbot's room, listening in on Yunyan's failure. Unconsciously, he bit his finger so hard that it bled. The image of Daowu listening in to his brother's responses while lurking outside the teacher's room is somewhat comical. And yet the scene is also sad, even tragic. Poor Daowu was trying so hard to help Yunyan see for himself, aided by a few of the greatest teachers in Tang China. And Yunyan remained clueless. But Yaoshan and Daowu did not abandon him.

Later comes a fresh reenactment of the story with Nanquan. Daowu and Yunyan were attending to Yaoshan, and Yaoshan said, "Never speak of where wisdom doesn't reach. If you speak of it, horns will grow on your head. Practitioner [Daowu Yuan]zhi, what about this?"[13]

Daowu immediately left.

Yunyan asked Yaoshan, "Why did [Daowu] not respond to the teacher?"

Yaoshan replied, "My back hurts today. He understands; go and ask him."

Then Yunyan went and asked Daowu, "Brother, why didn't you respond to the teacher just now?"

Daowu just said, "I have a headache today. You should go ask the teacher."

According to this story, Yunyan apparently did not understand, even with Yaoshan. Yaoshan and Daowu were trying to get Yunyan to actually put his practice into active expression, to simply not speak of the place where knowledge does not reach. Sometimes in these stories there are responses with words, and sometimes there are complete responses with headaches and sore backs.

Much later, the story goes, after Yunyan had become a teacher and instructed Dongshan—when he was about to pass away, Yunyan sent someone with a letter of farewell to Daowu. (According to the traditionally accepted dates of their lives, Yunyan actually outlived Daowu, so either this anecdote is apocryphal, or the recorded dates are incorrect, which is less likely. Nevertheless, this is a revealing story about how Yunyan was viewed in the lore about him.) Supposedly, Daowu read the letter and said, "Yunyan did not know 'it is.' I regret I didn't tell him back then. Although this is so, actually, he was nonetheless a successor of Yaoshan."[14]

Of course, this does not fit with the story about Dongshan's departing from Yunyan, when Yunyan said clearly, "Just this is it." But as Dongshan said much later to an inquiring monk, as decribed in the previous chapter, "If [Yunyan] did know 'it is,' how could he be willing to say it?" Throughout the stories of Daowu trying to coax his brother Yunyan to awakening, as well as in the stories about Dongshan talking about his teacher Yunyan much later, the issue remains about Yunyan's relationship to suchness and how to express and enact its ineffability. If Daowu was correct in the story when he said, "Yunyan did not know 'it is'," how could Yunyan know to say, "Just this is it" to Dongshan? Even Daowu acknowledged that Yunyan was nevertheless a worthy successor to Yaoshan.

Yunyan remains an icon of a paradoxical enigma, a long-time failed student who became teacher of the founder of a major Chan lineage. Yunyan serves as a good example of how much sustained effort it may take to understand our own life and practice, and a good reminder of the practice of patience. He finally did awaken, when he heard Yaoshan's appreciation for Baizhang's ability to elicit his monks' attention by calling to them after driving them out of the hall with his staff. Eventually, while he did not become famous in his own age like Baizhang or Nanquan or Yaoshan (to a lesser extent), Yunyan did express the teaching of suchness and became the teacher of Dongshan, the founder of Caodong or Sōtō Zen.

Later Dōgen expressed a different view about the relationship of Daowu and Yunyan. In his *Shōbōgenzō* essay "Kannon," Dōgen discusses a dialogue between them (mentioned in chapter 1) concerning the bodhisattva of compassion and how he uses the thousand hands and eyes in one of his main iconographic forms. Daowu invokes the image of reaching back for a pillow in the middle of the night as an expression of the workings of that compassion. But rather than Daowu being awakened and Yunyan the clueless brother, Dōgen proclaims them as completely equal. "Yunyan and Daowu had practiced shoulder to shoulder as co-practitioners under Yaoshan, and after that they practiced together for forty years. . . . They cut off each other's understandings when these were not right and verified each other when their understandings were right."[15] For Dōgen the two Dharma brothers were simply working together to fully express the true teaching.

Yunyan's One Who Is Not Busy

The earlier stories established Yunyan in Chan lore as a notable "Chan failure" who, despite great teachers, took a very long time to realize the Way, if, indeed, he ever did. On the other hand, a number of other encounter dialogues establish Yunyan's keen, deep insight. Many of these anecdotes, enshrined in the koan collections, involve Yunyan and his brother Daowu. In the following story, Yunyan provides an extraordinary expression of going beyond mere theoretical nonduality.

Case 21 of the *Book of Serenity* starts with Yunyan sweeping the ground. Cleaning the temple is a common activity of monks, and apparently this was when Daowu and Yunyan were students together. Daowu saw Yunyan sweeping and said, presumably with a critical tone, "Too busy."

But Yunyan responded, "You should know there is one who is not busy."

Daowu said, "If so, then there's a second moon."

Yunyan held up the broom and said, "Which moon is this?"[16]

I've considered this brief story periodically for a great many years, and it remains one of my very favorites in all of Zen lore.[17] It is highly pertinent to current spiritual concerns. In our modern age many of us are preoccupied with multitasking. We can be inundated with information from all over the world, thanks to the Internet and other increasingly speedy technologies. And some contemporary occupations and activities require responding at a pace that is measured in nanoseconds. So we all can easily feel "too busy."

Of course, sweeping the ground is not something that can be accomplished once and for all. New dust or falling leaves land on our path, and it must be swept afresh. No end to dust, and no end to sweeping. We may be unbothered by the dust and allow it to pile up for a while. But eventually spring cleaning will come around, and we will need to pick through and brush away the detritus. And, hopefully, there will be another spring.

In our busy present-day context, we might consider sweeping the ground as a soothing, relaxing, and even pastoral pastime. We may all reflect on whether we are too busy to appreciate the natural, organic rhythms of our life, of the world, and of reality itself. Zen meditative attentiveness and settling offer communion with inherent, underlying deep awareness. The question is how to fully occupy and engage our lives. During our busy worldly life, we might check whether we also know that there is one who is not busy. The one not busy is not something to discover or create but is already right here.

Daowu was concerned that his brother monk was distracted by his work from inquiry into the great matter of life and death, and from expression of fundamental reality. However, Yunyan responded unhesitatingly to Daowu, "You should know there is one who is not busy." This is a brilliant utterance, expressing complete freedom and awareness. Even in the middle of engaging our active responsibilities, one may be somehow connected with something that is not "too busy" and serves as an ever-present inner resource.

We might see the primary work of Dongshan, and of Yunyan, as the full integration of awareness of underlying suchness with its compassionate expression in the midst of the world. In Wansong's commentary to this case, he says, "Yunyan and Daowu were illustrating the active conditions of the Dongshan progression." The one who is not busy need not be passive and dormant. Wansong instructs, "As you eat, boil tea, sew, and sweep, you should recognize the one not busy—then you will realize the union of mundane reality and enlightened reality; in the Dongshan progression this is called simultaneous inclusion, naturally not wasting any time."[18] Tenshin Reb Anderson has said that we waste time whenever we do not know that there is one who is not busy. But how does the one who is not busy function in the world?

The great American Zen pioneer Gary Snyder says that Zen comes down to two activities, meditation and cleaning the temple, and it is up to each of us to decide how widely the temple boundaries stretch. While not busy, still we may extend our aware, helpful activity to respond to a range of situations in the world, even beyond our immediate surroundings. Going back to the time of Yunyan and Dongshan, this is the challenge of all awakening bodhisattva activity; and in the present situation of our world, it is all the more challenging.

Yunyan's Moon

Daowu's response to the one who is not busy, "If so, then there's a second moon," expresses his concern that Yunyan is imagining a second, separate reality. Is the one not busy something special other than or outside of taking care of the practical responsibilities of phenomenal reality? Is our life bifurcated into calmness and busyness, with suchness as a secondary, separate event merely lurking in the background of everyday activities? Daowu wondered whether Yunyan might be establishing an alternate, peaceful experience, a second wholeness, as an escape from the world of phenomenal particularities. In terms of the previous story, was Yunyan busy acting within different kinds in a dualistic manner that was separated and estranged from just not speaking of it?

Yunyan met Daowu's challenge directly by holding out his broom, and asking, "Which moon is this?" Is Yunyan merely indulging in rhetoric, assuming that there is only one moon or that we cannot distinguish between various moons? It is skillful and appropriate that Yunyan responds with a question. He is not making any assertion, but posing an extraordinarily revealing inquiry. He does not take any side but provokes our deep investigation.

Wansong comments on Daowu's line "If so, then there's a second moon" with the added saying, "Only two? There's hundreds, thousands, myriads."[19] Once we enter the different kinds, there may be innumerable activities, and our lives can become fragmented. Might there be one not busy on each of those different moons? Wansong comments on Yunyan's response "Which moon is this?" with upraised broom by saying, "This expression originally comes from the *Heroic March Scripture* [Śūrāṅgama Samādhi Sūtra], which says, 'Like the second moon, who will say it is the moon, who will deny it? For Mañjuśri only one moon is real—in between there is naturally nothing that is or is not the moon.'"[20] The bodhisattva of wisdom, Mañjuśri, represents the teaching of emptiness, and the related teaching of oneness or sameness. Emptiness teaching is about the insubstantiality and the nonseparation of all entities or events. Another way to speak of this is in terms of the insight into wholeness or sameness, to see the true commonality and interconnectedness of all the different kinds.

In East Asia speaking of the moon usually refers to the full round moon, a glowing image of wholeness. As the moon reflects the light of the sun, it is also indicated as a reflection of the inner light of wholeness and the inner serenity of the Buddha, or of those who through meditative awareness have realized the one who is not caught up in busyness. Holding up his broom as a moon pointer, Yunyan is invoking the perfect round moon beyond all separation. Can there really be two moons? Is there even one moon? Are there any moons at all?

These questions are implied in a verse comment on this story by Dōgen as case 12 in his ninety-case koan collection in volume 9 of his *Extensive Record*. Interestingly, while citing the exact same dialogue as in Hongzhi's version in the *Book of Serenity*, Dōgen here identifies the questioner not as Daowu but as Guishan, the founder of one of the five houses, who had first directed Dongshan to Yunyan in the story about nonsentient beings expounding the Dharma. This alternate identification further exemplifies the confused history about the traditional koans or teaching stories in the Chan tradition. It is not uncommon to have similar stories or even, as here, the same story attributed to different characters from the iconic Chan pantheon. In another citation of this story, however, Dōgen does identify it with Daowu and Yunyan. At any rate, we have Dōgen's verse comment on the basic dialogue:

> Who sweeps the ground and also sees the moon?
> Holding up the moon, his sweeping is truly not in vain.
> Within tens of thousands of moons is placed this moon.
> Although called the second, how could there be a first?[21]

For Dōgen, Yunyan was clearly holding up the moon with his broom and saw the moon not busy as he swept. This moon exists within all the myriad different kinds of moons. And in reality, can any of these truly be labeled as a moon? Furthermore, it is impossible to segment the moon into pieces, slicing into it as if it were merely a big pizza pie.

Full and Crescent Moons

One of the commentaries to another *Book of Serenity* case contains a further illuminating story about Yunyan and Daowu and varied aspects of the moon. The featured main case, number 37, is not directly pertinent, but another story about Yunyan and Daowu and the moon appears in Wansong's commentary to the following verse commentary by Hongzhi:

One call and he turns his head—do you know the self or not?
Vaguely, like the moon through ivy, a crescent at that.
The child of riches, as soon as he falls
On the boundless road of destitution, has such sorrow.[22]

The last two lines refer to a famous parable from the Lotus Sutra that will be discussed in detail in chapter 5 of this work, concerning Dongshan's encounter with a white rabbit. The story of Dongshan and the white rabbit, which is the topic of *Book of Serenity* case 56, is also related in full by Wansong in his commentary to this verse.

Statements from Yunyan and Daowu about the moon are recorded by Wansong in response to Hongzhi's line about the self being known only "vaguely, like the moon through ivy, a crescent at that." In many East Asian paintings or poems depicting the moon, rather than a full, round moon, it is visible only partially, with wispy clouds, reed grasses, or a flying heron, for example, in front of the moon. An ancient, common practice in East Asia, still done, is to go out in the evening to gaze at the full moon. But the wondrous round moon is appreciated more completely when not quite fully revealed or when highlighted by some foreground phenomena. Wansong refers to Huayan school teachings about how highly advanced bodhisattvas "see nature like looking at the moon through a gauze net." But Wansong says that ivy provides a stronger image than gauze and quotes the great Chinese poet Li Bo (701–62), "There is the moon through the ivies crossing the mirror of the morning, a wind in the pines strumming the harpstrings of night."[23]

In addition to whether the full moon is seen completely, or through a faint screen of ivy, Wansong raises the issue about the full moon becoming partial through its monthly phases. He relates a story about Yangshan Huiji (807–83; Jpn.: Gyōsan Ejaku), subject of the main case and cofounder of one of the Chan five houses, along with Guishan, mentioned above.²⁴ Once Yangshan was gazing at the moon with Shishi Shandao (n.d.; Jpn.: Sekishitsu Zendō), a Dharma brother of Yunyan's teacher Yaoshan. Yangshan asked, "When the moon is a crescent, where does the round shape go? And when it is full, where does the crescent shape go?" These questions are about the phases of round wholeness signifying complete awakening and the partial state of the crescent moon implying incomplete realization of awakening, if not delusion. Through imagery of the moon, this question is really about the nature of enlightenment and of full realization of suchness. When the moon is full, what happens to delusion? When it is a crescent, or only partial realization, where is suchness, or awakening? Yangshan's inquiry concerns Buddha nature, and whether it is actually omnipresent in all beings or not, a major issue in Chinese Buddhism, as discussed in chapter 1.

Shandao responded to Yangshan, "When it's a crescent, the round shape is concealed; when it's full, the crescent shape remains." He is partial to the partial state, implying the prevalence of delusion. Amid delusion, no Buddha nature appears. When realization arises, still delusion ever lurks, ready to create harm. Shandao seems pessimistic about the manifestation of enlightenment.

Apparently, Daowu and Yunyan heard about this exchange, as Wansong presents their responses to Yangshan's question immediately after presenting that of Shandao. Daowu commented, "When it's a crescent, yet it is not a crescent; when it's full, it's still not round." Here Daowu emphasizes emptiness, and the conditioned, illusory nature of both enlightenment and delusion. Neither enlightenment nor delusion is absolute; both are interrelated and imply each other. Whether full or crescent, it is the same moon.

Yunyan's response was "When it's a crescent, the round shape remains; when it's full, the crescent does not exist." In this exchange, Dongshan's teacher Yunyan favors fullness, emphasizing the presence of awakening whether it is apparent or concealed. There is no secondary moon. The true, complete full moon is always present, in all phases of the moon. Of course, even when the moon is but a crescent, looking skyward we can still discern the faint outline of the full moon. We divide ourselves when we fall for and prefer some idealized version of the perfect round moon. Seeking or holding to some ideal of perfection, we miss the wholeness of the moon and of our practice, ever present in all aspects of the moon. Even partial awakening can be wonderful, and even amid incompleteness we can know the one who is not busy.

Dōgen's Appreciation of Yunyan Sweeping the Moon

Dōgen has an essay on the moon, "Tsuki," in his Shōbōgenzō. He says, "The moon is not one moon or two moons, not thousands of moons or myriads of moons. Even if the moon itself holds the view of one moon or two moons, that is merely the moon's view."[25] Here Dōgen discounts Daowu's concern about a second moon. The moon's radiance is beyond enumerations.

Dōgen comments specifically in a few places concerning the story about Yunyan's one who is not busy and the second moon. Traditionally, the mid-autumn October full moon is considered the most exquisite. In a 1249 Dharma hall discourse on the occasion of the mid-autumn full moon, Dōgen quotes a mid-autumn talk by Hongzhi, who said, "The clear body and mind disperses appearances and embraces the moon at midnight. It is spiritually self-illuminated, vast and always empty." Dōgen celebrates this as an incitement to sustained practice. He closes by saying, "Why has our ancestor Yunyan's 'Which moon is this?' suddenly appeared as a round sitting cushion?"[26] For Dōgen, the realization of total nonduality and wholeness, represented by the moon, glows when expressed in upright sitting practice.

On the occasion of the 1252 mid-autumn full moon, Dōgen's last before his passing, he celebrated at length the wholeness of the moon. He begins by asserting the power of the moon, whether full or crescent: "The moon is neither round nor lacking, how could it wax or wane?" He refers to a number of stories about the moon, including stating that "Yunyan's 'which is this?' moon does not flourish," before adding an old story about the Buddha preserving the moon. Dōgen closes by expressing his wish to support Buddha and "increase the radiance of the moon palace and illuminate the darkness of delusion." In a closing verse he proclaims,

> Because of Buddha's majestic power, the palace is bright,
> A thousand glorious rays appear at once.
> Even if humans love the moon in mid-autumn,
> The brightness of the half moon is boundless in the heavens.[27]

Here Dōgen agrees with Yunyan that the round moon remains, whether crescent or full. The whole Buddha nature is bright and boundless, even in the partial half moon.

Keizan's Second Moon

Keizan Jōkin (1264–1325)] was a Dharma successor three generations after Dōgen and is considered the second founder of Japanese Sōtō Zen, along with Dōgen. Keizan adds a new spin to the story of a second moon. Like Yangshan and Shandao almost five centuries earlier, once Keizan was out gazing at the full moon with one of his disciples, Gasan Jōseki (1276–1366). Keizan asked, "Do you know that there are two moons?" When Gasan said he didn't, Keizan told him, "If you don't know there are two moons, you are not a seedling of the Sōtō succession."[28] The story goes on that Gasan was perplexed but then went and sat with great determination "like an iron pole" for years, before finally realizing that there are two moons.

Almost all of the surviving Japanese Sōtō school derives from Keizan. He was an energetic and imaginative teacher who founded several monasteries, including Sōjiji, which remains one of the two headquarter temples of Sōtō Zen, along with Eiheiji, founded by Dōgen. Keizan and his successors in the next couple of generations helped spread Sōtō Zen in the Japanese countryside such that it became one of the most popular denominations of Japanese Buddhism. Gasan became one of Keizan's six major disciples, and of the two disciples whose lineages flourished and still survive, Gasan's is the more prominent.[29] Keizan's admonition to Gasan about the second moon illustrates how these old family stories remain vital in the Zen tradition and are developed and transformed at times. In this story Keizan turns around the image of the second moon critiqued by Daowu.

In traditional Buddhist terms, two moons may represent the two truths of Mādhyamika teaching, that reality includes the ultimate dimension but also conventional reality. Our conditioned conventional reality is a delusion, mere fantasy based on the web of causes and conditions. Nevertheless, this is a kind of reality, with beings fooled by conditions and thereby suffering. Those who are awake to suchness and yet willing to "act within different kinds" honor rather than ignore conventional reality and its effects, even if it may sometimes seem only a faint reflection of suchness.

Yunyan proclaimed that we should know there is one who is not busy. In the original case in the *Book of Serenity*, Hongzhi added a couple of commentaries by later masters about Yunyan's sweeping question "Which moon is this?" In one of these comments, Xuansha Shibei (835–908; Jpn.: Gensha Shibi) said, "This is truly the second moon." Xuansha was later celebrated by Dōgen for proclaiming, "The entire universe is one bright pearl," like the full moon.[30] And much later, Keizan indicated to his student Gasan that he must know there are two moons. Keizan thereby clarified that the one who is not busy must also know that there is one who is busy.

PART TWO Teachings of Suchness

CHAPTER FOUR

No Grass for Ten Thousand Miles

Among the numerous encounter dialogues or stories attributed to Dongshan in his *Recorded Sayings*, I will discuss a small selection that are revealing of his considerations of the nature of suchness and of skillful approaches to its teaching and presentation. Developing from these themes and their dynamics, some of the stories focus through varied situations on the interrelationship of the ultimate, unconditioned truth with the particulars of the phenomenal, conditioned world (the focus of the five degrees teaching), and approaches to the practice of that intricate relationship. The ensuing comments and partial exegeses of these koans, as well as of the stories discussed earlier, hardly explain much less exhaust the complexities and vital spiritual challenges they present. Readers might beneficially find their own way to explore further the various contexts for these stories in their own lives.

The Long Search

The following story occurred at the end of a traditional three-month summer monastic practice period led by Dongshan, called a time for peaceful abiding (*anju* in Chinese, *ango* in Japanese). Dongshan seems to criticize sensory engagement with suchness when he enigmatically recommends that his departing monks now go where there is no grass for ten thousand miles (*li*). This story appears as case 89 in the *Book of Serenity*, framed by Hongzhi Zhengjue with later comments from two other teachers:

Dongshan spoke to the assembly, "It's the beginning of autumn, the end of summer, and you brethren will go, some to the east, some west; you must go where there's not an inch of grass for ten thousand miles."

He also said, "But where there's not an inch of grass for ten thousand miles, how can you go?"

Later Shishuang said, "Going out the gate, immediately there's grass."

Dayang added, "I'd say, even not going out the gate, still the grass is boundless."[1]

This is an example of Dongshan's difficult, demanding teaching. What does it mean to go where there's not an inch of grass for ten thousand miles? Could the monks ever find such a place? The ten thousand grass-tips are a conventional Chan expression for the whole phenomenal world—all the myriad things of the world. All of the sense objects, our possessions, and all of our physical experiences are all just so much grass, or, in effect, weeds, as neatly trimmed grass lawns are not at all a feature of traditional East Asian culture.

Dongshan's instructions seem to imply a place beyond conditions, beyond karma, beyond this phenomenal world and its struggles. He apparently encourages travel into the realm of the unconditioned, beyond desires and aversion and habitual patterns of seeing things and of reacting. The unconditioned *nirvāṇic* realm is juxtaposed with the realities of the temporal world in which the grasses grow. But could one also see suchness as grasses, or grasses as suchness?

Dongshan asks how one could go where there is not an inch of grass for ten thousand miles. I am reminded of Joni Mitchell's refrain: "They paved paradise, and put up a parking lot."[2] That might be one way to get rid of all the grass. In our time the very mountains and rivers are under threat with climate change damage and mountaintop removal to harvest coal. But I do not think that is what Dongshan had in mind when he talked about this. He was concerned with suchness and how we meet the world. He and his students had just finished a three-month period of deep, peaceful abiding in the mountain monastery, presumably steeping in meditative awareness and calm. How would Dongshan's students fare as they proceeded out into the world?

The Growth Right Outside the Door

The version of this story in the *Recorded Sayings* includes the later response from Shishuang Qingzhu (807–88; Jpn.: Sekisō Keisho), a Dharma heir of Yunyan's Dharma brother Daowu, prominent in the previous chapter. In this version, Shishuang's statement criticizes Dongshan's monks, as he said, "Why didn't someone say, 'As soon as one goes out the door, there is grass'?" Of course, there is no place in the world without the thick grasses of conditioning and phenomena; weeds are sprouting everywhere. How could Dongshan's students not have said so promptly after his request? Dongshan heard of Shishuang's comment and approved, saying, "Within the country of the Great Tang such a man is rare." In a version in the *Book of Serenity* commentary Dongshan added, "These are the words of a teacher of fifteen hundred people."[3] Indeed, Shishuang eventually led a congregation of over a thousand monks who sat so still, upright as tree stumps, that his monastery was called the "Dead Tree Hall."

In his challenge to go where no grass grows for ten thousand miles, Dongshan is tricky, a challenging teacher. Even though students may glimpse or imagine a realm beyond the phenomenal sense world, his encouragement may help them to see that the unconditioned is not the whole reality of suchness that he saw in the stream after departing from Yunyan. Dongshan asks, "Where there's not an inch of grass for ten thousand miles, how can you go?" In all our activity, our whole practice, whether walking, driving, or bicycling, we inevitably move through the grasses of our life. Without such phenomena, how could anybody proceed on their way, or even express the path toward awakening?

Both Yunyan's statement "You are now in charge of this great matter; you must be most thoroughgoing" and Dongshan in his "Jewel Mirror Samādhi" conclusion, "Just to do this continuously is called the master among masters," to be discussed further in the last section of this work, are encouraging engagement with suchness to be sustained long term, right amid the realm of sense awareness and the unavoidable grasslands, but unobstructed by attachments. How to move through the grasses and weeds without being obstructed is a truly serious matter.

Overgrowth and Mowed Grass

As indicated in the *Book of Serenity* case 89, a later teacher in Dongshan's lineage, Dayang Qingxuan (d. 1027; Jpn.: Taiyō Kyōgen), commented, "Even not going out the gate, still the grass is boundless." The phenomenal world is ever present, even within the monastic container and its enterprise of turning within and going beyond to deepen our current self-awareness. One may sit in monastic seclusion in remote spaces with few distractions and a pristine setting designed for settling into serene meditative awareness, but even in such a place, through memories, patterns of attachments, awareness informed by all those we have ever met, as well as from our fellow practitioners, the wild grasses of the world may readily sprout and poke through our sitting platforms to intrude on inner calm. Sustained meditative engagement often confronts one with the patterns of conditioning, not allowing any escape from human limitations. And even finding a place of illumination may become a sterile trap. As Wansong, the commentator of the *Book of Serenity*, says, "Don't stay by the green of the unusual plants on the cold cliff; if you keep sitting in the clouds, the source is not marvelous."[4] Relief and some sense of space may come only from willingness to uprightly face the grasses of world-liness and step out from some imagined safety zone. It is necessary to engage the world.

The investigation and balancing of a fundamental practice polarity is implicit here. Intuitive insight or wisdom is usually seen in Mahāyāna or Chan practice as the product of meditative turning within, at least glimpsing the unconditioned realm, empty of all grasses, a realm beyond striving. Traditionally, this is balanced in practice at some point with going out into the realm of diverse suffering beings, the myriad grass-tips, extending awareness with compassion. Dongshan's initial admonition to the departing monks in this case might suggest that they retain their meditative insight as they travel. Is it really possible, or even desirable, to try to maintain some connection to clear awareness and the one not busy while venturing into the turmoil of the world? But if not, what is the value of immersion into serene awareness and communion with wholeness beyond attachments?

This story might be seen as Dongshan subtly suggesting the suchness that encompasses both luminous awareness beyond conditions and the many grasses sprouting in particular fields. Yet in another related story, Dongshan seems more emphatic about going where there is no grass. His disciple Huayan Xiujing (n.d.; Jpn.: Kegon Kyūjō) confessed to Dongshan that he was still caught by "the vicissitudes of feelings and discriminating consciousness," and that he wished to escape them. Dongshan told him to go to the place without an inch of grass for ten thousand miles. Xiujing humbly asked if it was all right to go to such a place, perhaps concerned not to disregard the grasses, or wondering if such was even possible. Yet Dongshan replied, "You should only go in such a way."[5] Here Dongshan uncompromisingly insists that his student experience fully on his own. He seems to urge that even while trudging through the tall grasses, Huayan proceed without being caught by discriminations.

The Spring Wind Fanning the Burning Scars

In the *Book of Serenity* case 89, in which Dongshan speaks at the end of the summer practice period, Hongzhi offers his verse comment to the story. He poses the challenge of setting out from meditative settling and entering the suffering of the world. Hongzhi says,

> Grass boundless;
> Inside the gate, outside the gate, you see by yourself.
> To set foot in the forest of thorns is easy,
> To turn the body outside the luminous screen is hard.
> Look! Look!
> How many kinds?
> For the while going along with the old tree, with the same
>   emaciation in the cold,
> About to follow the spring wind into the scars of the burning.[6]

The "forest of thorns" might be a reference to the monastic setting, sometimes referred to as a forest of monks (Ch.: *senglin*; Jpn.: *sōrin*), and here in context that seems indicated. But with thorns this image might also evoke the outside world with its painful barbs. Turning outside the luminous screen indicates leaving the vision of radiance from meditative immersion. Once leaving the monastery, the monk must confront the variety of the "different kinds," as discussed in the previous chapter. The old tree and the emaciation also reference the archetypal ascetic sitting of Śākyamuni Buddha preliminary to his awakening. But the challenge for the monks departing after their practice period involves how to follow and support the energy that has emerged as they enter into the world of suffering, vividly described as the "scars of the burning." Hongzhi seems to be encouraging practitioners to go ahead into the thick grasses, even while clarifying the tensions and challenges involved in this proceeding, but also in some way still informed by the experience of engagement with the luminous screen.

Grass Teachers

In the Chan background before Dongshan, as well as in the older Mahāyāna lore, we can find hints as to how to see the grasses outside the gate as well as inside the gate as entryways to the clear space for ten thousand miles. In the century before Dongshan, the famed Chan Layman Pang (d. 808) cited as an old saying, "The bright clear hundred grass-tips are the bright clear mind of the ancestral teachers."[7] Appropriately for an adept who chose to remain a layman amid the phenomenal world, and who saw his everyday activities of chopping wood and carrying water as his miraculous power, Pang saw the grass-tips themselves as the great ancestral teachers. The traditional Buddhist study of consciousness describes how awareness of the phenomenal world arises through the sense gates, through sights, eye function, and eye consciousness; sounds, ear function, and ear awareness; and similarly for smell, taste, touch, and mental objects, or thoughts. Layman Pang suggests that these sense objects and our gates of perception of them are exactly the bright clear mind of the buddhas, or all the teachers who have kept alive the teaching and practice of awakening and compassion. Thus, these sense gates are themselves Dharma gates, or entryways into reality. The third of the fundamental four vows of bodhisattvas is that Dharma gates are boundless; the bodhisattva vows to enter them all. Thus, the monastery gates involved in the story about Dongshan's departing monks become doorways swinging in both directions toward liberation.

Dōgen in his *Extensive Record* comments on Layman Pang's line about the hundred grass-tips and the ancestral teachers' minds. Dōgen's verse commentary clearly refers to this story about Dongshan:

Although wanting it all tied up, for tens of thousands of miles nothing holds.
Staying within the gate, do not wait for the brightness of others.

Without your caring, it is easy to lose the path of active
practice.
Even those hard of hearing are moved by the sound of evening
rain.[8]

Dōgen's first line suggests a possible reason for Dongshan telling
his departing monks to "go where there's not an inch of grass for
ten thousand miles." After a period of intensive meditation and
retreat, they might imagine or wish that they had their practice
and awakening "all tied up." But for ten thousand miles they cannot find a clear space without the wild grasses of desire and aversion growing. In much of his teaching, Dōgen encourages active
expression of practice in everyday activity, as well as in meditative
retreat. Here he warns practitioners who have completed a period
of intensive practice not to wait for or depend on the brightness
of others. This echoes Dongshan's line after leaving Yunyan and
seeing his reflection in the stream, "Just don't seek from others,
or you'll be far estranged from self." Dōgen emphasizes the need
for the practitioners' caring, or sustained intention. And finally he
proclaims the virtue of sound, a traditional, highly recommended
Buddhist meditation object. Listening to the world, and especially
even to the suffering of the world, whether inside or outside the
gates, is one definition of compassion in Buddhism, the meaning
of a name of the bodhisattva of compassion, Guanyin in Chinese,
Kannon or Kanzeon in Japanese. Dōgen says that even those who
cannot listen well, perhaps tired out from scouring the ground
for some grassless wasteland, are still moved and brought back to
awareness by the sound of rain in the evening, a familiar subject of
Chan/Zen poetry. Along with hearing with eyes, as Dongshan recommended, the wetness of raindrops can encourage deep listening.

In 1248, on the occasion of the annual memorial service for his
own Chinese teacher, Tiantong Rujing, Dōgen said to his assembly, "On this day Tiantong [Rujing] mistakenly made a pilgrimage,
not to Mount Tiantai or Wutai. How sad that for ten thousand
miles there is not an inch of grass."[9] Death is often referred to

as a pilgrimage in the Mahāyāna, and Mount Tiantai and Mount Wutai are two of the traditional Chinese sacred mountains, often the destination for pilgrims. But here Dōgen evokes this saying by Dongshan as heralding a pilgrimage by his monks departing the summer practice period and says that sadly, Rujing by dying has found the space without grass for ten thousand miles. But the path of active practice requires seeing that even within the gates there is no end to the grass. Dōgen another time referred to Dongshan's "not an inch of grass for ten thousand miles" in a talk at the very beginning of one of his summer monastic practice periods, encouraging the monks to stay put amid the assembly and not wander off on such a personal quest. "Our vitality must be the strength of the assembly."[10]

A Grass Shack in Dongshan's Background

One of Layman Pang's main teachers was Shitou Xiqian, teacher of Yunyan's teacher Yaoshan, and thus three generations before Dongshan. Shitou is best known for a teaching poem, "Harmony of Difference and Sameness," which describes the harmonizing interaction between sameness or oneness and differences or particularity. This verse is apparent as a precursor to Dongshan's "Jewel Mirror Samādhi" and its presentation of the dialectic between the universal and the phenomenal. Shitou also composed a long teaching verse called "The Song of the Grass Hut," which describes the dynamic of settling practice, as opposed to the more philosophical dynamic of the "Harmony of Difference and Sameness."[11] Dongshan would certainly have known both these poems, and Shitou's teachings may serve as a backdrop context for all of the Dongshan stories.

"The Song of the Grass Hut" starts with Shitou saying, "I have built a grass hut with nothing of value. After eating, I relax and enjoy a nap. When the hut was completed, fresh weeds appeared. Now it's been lived in—covered by weeds." Here is a teacher outside the monastery gate, though his grass hermitage was near the temple where he taught. But he is happily covered in grasses, nothing to avoid. He avows, "Though the hut is small, it includes the entire world." Shitou is not trying to pave over any of the grasses, as he recognizes the deep interconnectedness of all phenomena and their presence in each bit of phenomena. This clearly reflects his influence from Chinese Huayan Buddhism's philosophy of mutual interpenetration of all things, another manner of describing the truth of dependent co-origination and its deep implications. Later in this poem Shitou says, "Bind grasses to build a hut and don't give up. Let go of hundreds of years and relax completely." Shitou indicates that the goal is to let go of centuries of overgrown karma, and relax completely, or as Dōgen would describe it much later, to "drop body and mind." In the Zen tradition that would later be regarded as stern and stoic, or even expressed at times in martial or macho tones, Shitou's goal of practice as complete relaxation is notable. For Shitou the way to realize this complete letting go is fully to take on or bind up all the grasses of conditioning and not give up immersion in them.

Shitou ends his grass hut song, "If you want to know the undying person in the hut, don't separate from this skin bag here and now." The undying or totally unconditioned person, alive in the space where there is not an inch of grass for ten thousand miles, as Dongshan would put it, must not separate at all from this present skin bag and all its foibles. Perhaps Dongshan gave his admonition to find some grassless space because he did not want any of his departing monks to settle into a grass hut and get too comfortable. But he must have known that despite such efforts they could not avoid the grasses of the world and would find their own grass hut of practice out beyond the monastery gates.

Grasses and Medicine

There are images from Mahāyāna lore that help illuminate Dongshan's "not an inch of grass for ten thousand miles." Dōgen cites a story about Mañjuśri, the great legendary bodhisattva of wisdom, asking the pilgrim Sudhana to bring him one stalk of medicinal herb. Sudhana is the pilgrim hero of the Gaṇḍavyūha Sutra, which is the large final chapter of the massive, colorful Avataṃsaka Sūtra. But, although Mañjuśri is prominent therein as one of Sudhana's fifty-three great bodhisattva teachers, this particular story does not appear in any of the extant Chinese translations of this Sanskrit sutra. In the story, which also appears in a commentary in the *Blue Cliff Record* koan anthology, after Mañjuśri's request, Sudhana departed and searched through the entire earth, but he could find nothing that was *not* medicine. Sudhana returned to Mañjuśri and said, "The whole great earth is medicine. Which one should I pick and bring back to you?" Mañjuśri asked him to bring back one stalk, so Sudhana immediately plucked a blade of grass and handed it to Mañjuśri. Mañjuśri held up the grass for the assembly and announced, "This one blade of grass can both kill a person or give them life."[12]

Whereas Dongshan encouraged his monks to find a place without any grass for ten thousand miles, in this story Sudhana sees that there is no place, inside or outside any gate, where there is no grass. But Sudhana's quest is to look for a space where there is healing grass, and he sees that every grass stalk is also medicine, just as Layman Pang appreciated that every grass provides an entryway to the truth of the Dharma. Mañjuśri insists that Sudhana bring him some medicine, and so Sudhana plucks the blade of grass at hand. Mañjuśri holds up the grass and proclaims that this medicine can both kill and give life. Indeed, we know that good medicines are lethal when taken in overdose. So when Dongshan requested that his departing monks go where there was not an inch of grass for ten thousand miles, he probably knew that such a place could kill as well as give vital life, and also that the abundant grasses right outside the gate would be lethal if grasped as attachments but might also heal the monks from any attachment to emptiness.

A Grass Sanctuary

Another story about the power of a blade of grass reaches back all the way to the Buddha Śākyamuni. As related in case 4 of the *Book of Serenity,* one day the Buddha was out walking with his students. The Indian creator deity Indra was one of the heavenly beings who attended Buddha's teachings, along with many other kinds of beings, including ordinary humans. Buddha pointed to the ground and said, "This spot is good to build a temple." Indra reached down and picked a blade of grass, stuck it in the ground, and said, "The temple is built." Buddha smiled.[13]

In this story even a single blade of grass not only affords healing, as demonstrated by Sudhana, but can form an entire grass hut and a site for practice and total awakening. Any spot of ground and every blade of grass provide opportunity and nourishment for buddhas. Awakening is available everywhere. And yet Dongshan told his monks departing from such a temple, and a time of peaceful abiding, to go where there was not an inch of grass for ten thousand miles. Dongshan's admonition remains a challenge for all practitioners working to find their balance amid the weeds of the world.

CHAPTER FIVE

Beyond Heat or Cold

Beyond the Comfort Zone

Dongshan challenged his monks in an even more immediate, personal manner in another story, which appears in both the *Recorded Sayings* and as case 43 of the *Blue Cliff Record* koan collection. A monk inquired, "How does one escape hot and cold?" Dongshan retorted, "Why not go where it is neither hot nor cold?" When the monk asked where that place was, Dongshan confided, "When it's cold, you freeze to death; when it's hot, you swelter to death," or in another translation, "When it's cold, the cold kills you; when it's hot, the heat kills you."[1]

Here Dongshan is challenging his monks not merely to avoid all of the worldly affairs described somewhat abstractly via the metaphor of grasses, but to go beyond their own personal comfort zones. This is elemental and physical, not theoretical. First he says to go to a place with no heat or cold, both of which may have been intense at times at his monastery up in the mountains. Even more, Dongshan says, to accomplish this the monks must be willing to give up their very lives. Such letting go of self can be seen as an expression of the bodhisattva practice of generosity. In his commentary on the Saṃdhinirmocana Sūtra, Tenshin Reb Anderson says that bodhisattvas "give away everything they have before they can lose it. They give away their livelihood, their mind, their reputation, and their life. They can't lose them because they are constantly giving them away. Therefore they are not afraid."[2] After hearing Dongshan's response, "When it's cold, the cold kills you; when it's hot, the heat kills you," we might wonder how long it took for this monk to realize this radical generosity beyond self-clinging, if ever he did.

Although Dongshan does not engage in the shouts or blows famously employed by the closely contemporary Chan masters Linji Yixuan and Deshan Xuanjiang (780–865; Jpn.: Tokusan Senkan), Dongshan's subtler teaching of facing extreme hot or cold was no less challenging to his students. Also, this and previous stories should make clear the falseness of the stereotypical notion that Caodong does not engage in the encounter dialogues later cited as formal *gongan* (koans), as in the Linji tradition.[3]

Dongshan's challenge reflects the very narrow span of temperature in which human beings can survive. Even more limited is the small range of climate in which many feel comfortable. Similarly, we detect only a narrow scope of sound waves or smells, missing much of what dogs hear or sniff. Of course, some humans have adapted to live in arctic cold or equatorial heat. But for home-leaver monks, or perhaps for any spiritual practitioner who wishes to connect with suchness, going beyond or letting go of one's familiar, habitual comfort zone is essential. The intensity of Dongshan's story of a place with no hot or cold refers at least on one level to the familiarity of our weather patterns. I can personally attest to the power of what we are accustomed to, after relocating seven years ago to Chicago and its relatively severe temperatures, whether hot or cold. Just stepping outside the door here, I immediately feel the unmistakable physical difference in temperatures after almost three decades in the mild, usually comfortable San Francisco Bay Area climate, where this story from Dongshan may be harder to appreciate fully.

In his call to renounce personal comfort even to the death, Dongshan suggests the need to go beyond any attachment to personal survival, and thus beyond our limited notion of self. The practice he suggests is not only about one's self, our own personal physical comfort clearly apparent in terms of the weather. Rather, giving up personal comfort allows the possibility of deeper connection ·

with the wider breadth of all beings, sentient and nonsentient, the whole of which, as Dongshan has indicated, actually are us.

This story in particular opens to a number of possible areas of provocative interpretation and leads into a range of speculative and stimulating reflections. These include considering our inner emotional temperature and comfort along with the weather outdoors. From the perspective of the Caodong/Sōtō approach to koan practice, trying to find the one "correct" interpretation or explanation of the story would be frivolous and even counterproductive. We may well consider a number of modes suggested by Dongshan's response to the monk, and reflect on their potential usefulness.

Frozen to Death

In exploring Dongshan's challenge, we may consider vivid examples of the extremes of freezing or burning to death. While Dongshan is of course not literally recommending these, their literal impact informs the level of renunciation of comforts and endurance of extremes of pain intimated by Dongshan. Wholehearted engagement with extreme conditions, whether of meteorological or emotional temperatures, is how we loosen our individual identities and encounter suchness in the present situation.

The great early-twentieth-century American writer Jack London (1876–1916) was an explorer of sorts, who traveled to the well-below-freezing climate of gold-rush Alaska and sailed the equatorial South Seas, and wrote eloquently about both regions. Perhaps the iconic tale that most epitomizes cold and death is London's brilliant, unforgettable 1908 story, "To Build a Fire."[4] A relative newcomer to the Yukon is caught outside in perilous temperatures approaching 75 degrees below zero. But he is arrogantly ignorant of his danger and self-assured about reaching his destination, despite warnings he had received not to go out alone in such weather. He did not, London writes, "meditate upon his frailty as a creature of temperature, and upon man's frailty in general, able only to live within certain narrow limits of heat and cold; and from there on it did not lead him to the conjectural field of immortality and man's place in the universe."[5] As the nameless protagonist proceeds, with only a dog and one pack of matches, he finds increasing dangers. When he breaks through the ice and gets his feet wet, then burns up his matches, his inevitable demise and the stages of freezing are described graphically: "The man looked down at his hands in order to locate them, and found them hanging on the ends of his arms. It struck him as curious that one should have to use his eyes in order to find out where his hands were."[6] As depicted dramatically by London, the literal version of the freezing to death mentioned by Dongshan is a terrible prospect, even including the man's eventual acceptance of his fate, lying down in the snow to drowse off "into what seemed to him the most comfortable and satisfying sleep he had ever known."[7]

Scorched to Death, and Self-Immolation

As to burning to death, we can find fiery literal examples in Buddhism's own history and modern circumstances. Lotus Sutra chapter 23, "Previous Lives of the Medicine King Bodhisattva" (later to become the Medicine Buddha) describes one of this buddha's predecessors, the Bodhisattva Seen with Joy by All the Living, as he anoints himself with fragrant oil and sets fire to himself, an act of devotional self-sacrifice praised by many buddhas.[8] After rebirth, the same bodhisattva this time burns his arms as an offering, although as a consequence of his virtue, they are restored. While I otherwise deeply appreciate and esteem the Lotus Sutra, I have always been rather dismayed by this chapter, which perhaps is influenced by ancient Indian pre-Buddhist sacrificial offering practices. Based on cultural and cosmological assumptions alien to the modern and especially the Western world, the valuing of self-immolation as an acceptable offering in this chapter seems to encourage an unhelpful disdain for life and this world.

The image of self-burning in this Lotus Sutra chapter has inspired a sporadic historical practice in Chinese Buddhism of self-immolation, or sometimes burning of fingers or limbs, going back to the fourth century, preceding Dongshan by several centuries.[9] While only a very occasional phenomenon throughout Chinese Buddhist history, intermittent examples, seen as forms of legitimate devotional sacrifice to Buddha, have persisted up to modern times.

In modern times this practice has taken a twist in being used as a form of societal protest. My very first image of a Buddhist monk was the striking photograph, broadcast around the world, of the Vietnamese monk Thich Quang Duc (1897–1963) immolating himself in a public square in downtown Saigon as a protest of the Vietnam War then raging. Part of the great impact of that act was his utter calm demeanor as he sat upright while the flames consumed him. Sister Chan Khong, a Vietnamese nun and colleague of the eminent Vietnamese Zen master Thich Nhat Hanh, writes in her book *Learning True Love* of how she happened to arrive at the site just as Quang Duc set himself on fire.

> I witnessed him sitting bravely and peacefully, enveloped in flames. He was completely still, while those of us around him were crying and prostrating ourselves on the sidewalk. At that moment, a deep vow sprang forth in me: I too would do something for the respect of human rights in as beautiful and gentle a way as Thay Quang Duc.[10]

Clearly, his meditative stability and calm were powerful enough for him to follow literally Dongshan's suggestion to allow the heat to kill him amid the flames. Whether Thich Quang Duc's act was effective can certainly be questioned. His self-immolation inspired many Vietnamese to protest and raised questions in the United States about the war, helping to lead to a mass antiwar movement, but the horrors of that war would continue for another dozen years. Other concerned Vietnamese activists tried to follow his example, but most lacked his meditative experience as preparation for the searing pain and sometimes burned in panic. Sister Chan Khong writes movingly of a young woman friend who emulated Thich Quang Duc's sacrifice with difficulty several years later.[11]

The scars of the Vietnam War persist four dozen years after the American forces were compelled to flee Saigon. But now we have a new wave of Buddhist self-immolations. In response to the repression of Tibetan culture and Tibetan Buddhism by the Chinese government, recently many Tibetan monks have immolated themselves. This wave began in early 2009, when a young monk burned himself in protest of religious persecution, including the enforced cancellations of ceremonies at his monastery. From March 2009 to June 2012, at least thirty-five Tibetans committed self-immolation in protest. More than eight Tibetans immolated themselves in 2012—monks and nuns, but also farmers, students, and restaurant workers.[12] In some cases Chinese soldiers extinguished the flames and shot the monks instead or detained them, and the fate of some remains unknown.

The exiled head of a monastery where many of these incidents occurred commented, "With the Chinese government making arbitrary arrests and passing unimaginably harsh sentences on the basis of false representations and allegations, Kirti [monastery] has been turned into a virtual prison. . . . It has reached a point of desperation where people would choose to die rather than go on living."[13] These Tibetan self-immolations continue, but, again, the value and effectiveness of these actions are questionable. There is little likelihood that these theatrical, basically symbolic protests will effect changes in Chinese policies, under which the Chinese control virtually all of the economy and modernization in Tibet. Tibetan Buddhist leaders appreciate the selflessness of these actions, and the need for active response, while encouraging nonviolence and not holding on to hatred for the Chinese.[14] It is a sad situation. Such self-immolation protests are far from the escape from cold or heat sought by Dongshan's monk or encouraged by Dongshan. But in some situations, entering even literally into deadly cold or heat, as Dongshan suggests, may seem the only course available to the oppressed.

Our Damaged, Changing Heat and Cold

Considering the limited ranges of comfortable temperature, we may see this koan as particularly poignant and relevant in our own time. The challenge of human-induced climate change has affected many people all around the world and is already certain to be an increasing peril for all beings in our environment, sentient and "nonsentient," in the foreseeable future. Writing in May 2012, James Hansen, a leading climate scientist who directed the NASA Goddard Institute for Space Studies, says emphatically, "Global warming isn't a prediction. It is happening." Writing at a time when the "dirtiest" and most environmentally damaging of fuels, Canadian tar sands and American tar shale, were actively being promoted for exploitation, Hansen says that if this were to go forward,

> Concentrations of carbon dioxide in the atmosphere eventually would reach levels higher than in the Pliocene era, more than 2.5 million years ago, when sea level was at least 50 feet higher than it is now. . . . The disintegration of the ice sheets would accelerate out of control. . . . Global temperatures would become intolerable. Twenty to 50 percent of the planet's species would be driven to extinction.[15]

Not only students of suchness but all beings need to face extremes of heat or cold, or other extreme weather phenomena that threaten many forms of life, or at least our previous sense of how we live. As I write, the United States is encountering its worst drought since the 1950s, with 60 percent of the country affected. The strongest drivers of climate change, government policies and corporate practices that push greenhouse-gas emissions ever higher, need to be drastically altered to lessen the most damaging foreseeable effects, which even now can be somewhat mitigated with extensive development of alternative, sustainable energy sources. Yet the fossil fuel corporations, which are the worst polluters, are still subsidized with billions of taxpayer dollars.[16]

In his illuminating book *Eaarth: Making a Life on a Tough New Planet*, Bill McKibben, an environmental scholar and activist, describes clearly, with comprehensive scientific documentation, how our planet has changed physically just in the past two decades or so into a new world, transformed significantly from the place humans have inhabited since long before Dongshan.[17] He offers many detailed examples, such as this one: "Already the ocean is more acid than anytime in the last eight hundred thousand years, and at current rates by 2050 it will be more corrosive than anytime in the past 20 million years." He goes on to say that this will have numerous effects, such as, "Coral reefs will cease to exist as physical structures by 2100, perhaps 2050."[18] And, "The vast inland glaciers in the Andes and Himalayas, and the giant snowpack of the American West, are melting very fast, and within decades the supply of water to billions of people living downstream may dwindle. The great rainforest of the Amazon is drying on its margins and threatened at its core. The great boreal forest of North America is dying in a matter of years."[19] To denote the physical transformation of our world, McKibben renames it Eaarth, with an extra vowel.

However, in the second half of his book McKibben takes up the challenge of going beyond heat or cold, speculating, based on already existing social experiments, about how humans might survive and helpfully find constructive, innovative ways to live so as to make the best of the challenging new situation. His extensive, thoughtful suggestions involve finding ways to live on a smaller scale, working more closely in local communities, and developing regional agricultural and economic systems. This would require imagining sustainable approaches to livelihood, rather than being dependent on an economic system of endless, cancerous growth. Such a new vision would involve surviving, not thriving. Finding the place where there is no heat or cold will mean making radical changes in our way of life but could have many spiritual benefits, including fostering more cooperative, harmonious communities. Contrary to the comment famously attributed to Mark Twain, "Everybody talks about the weather, but nobody does anything about it," in recent history reckless human use of fossil fuels has done much to affect the weather. To respond to the resulting damage, we will all need to do more to transform ourselves and mitigate our damage to the weather.

Inner, Emotional Heat and Chill

Complaints about the meteorological situation or our new extreme weather may be evoked by the monk's question to Dongshan of how to escape heat and cold. However, taking the question metaphorically and perhaps more deeply, this monk may well have entered the contemplative life to escape the inner heat and intensity of human rage or passions. And he may also have realized that the icy chill of uncaring dullness or of lifelessness presents an equally pernicious alternative. The heat of burning passions, of craving, desire, or lust, is seen as the source of suffering going back to early Buddhism, as the twelve-fold causal chain of life and death is propelled by grasping after objects of desire. Such grasping causes harm, for others and oneself. The Buddha's teaching focused on ahimsa, or nonharming, and much of early Buddhist practice and meditative practice throughout Buddhist history has involved developing self-awareness and intimacy with one's own habit patterns, so as to cool the fires of desire and foster contentment rather than suffering.

Along with the heat of craving, we can feel the burning of anger, hatred, frustration, and fear. Rage can be a very powerful, energetic experience, which people sometimes indulge and turn into destructive grudges and hatred. All these heated, negative emotions obstruct the possibility of the open awareness and kindness that Dongshan saw as available even to nonsentient beings in his early explorations of Buddha nature. The Mahāratnakūta Sūtra provides an example of the Mahāyāna emphasis on the importance of sustaining openness to suffering beings as the primary value for those dedicated to universal liberation. The sutra compares the breaking of bodhisattva precepts out of desire and out of hatred and finds the former to be relatively minor, as those who break precepts through desire are at least still connected with sentient beings. Hatred is most damaging, since "a Bodhisattva who breaks precepts out of hatred forsakes sentient beings altogether," and so this is called "a gross, serious fault."[20] This perspective shows the danger of severe mental or emotional heat, as it becomes a hindrance to the primary practice, clearly central to Dongshan, of exploring suchness in order to convey it to sentient beings when possible.

However, the heat of craving or hatred cannot be escaped by turning to coldness. Emotional heat can burn with scorching intensity, but with the alternative we may feel that our life is barren and cold, with some inner deadness like a tree stump. When we try to live with such emotional cold, just as with hatred, we lose our connection with other beings, and part of our humanity dissolves. Spiritual practice requires basic caring and warm-heartedness about the quality of one's own awareness and about the well-being of creatures in the world. So this monk questioning Dongshan was likely looking for the place with no such emotional heat or chill. How can one become free of the passions of life without resorting to emotional frozenness, and not be obstructed by any emotional extremes when they appear?

Early Buddhist psychology suggests how to breathe into negative emotions and find a way not to run away from ourselves but to use constructively the energy of our heat and passions. We can transform anger or desires, our passions, rages, and frustrations. When engaged with awareness and patience, desire or lust can be transformed into devotion. Similarly, the energy of anger and hatred can be transformed into clear, penetrating understanding, and can be used to find the resolve and determination to address the situations that allow our feelings of anger.

Like the monk in this story, as human beings we can spend much of our time and energy trying to avoid inner emotional turmoil. In the middle of heat or cold we may fear some abrupt or unfortunate conditioned reaction. We do not know what we might do in an extreme situation. Meditative calm can support us just to be present amid heat or cold, without running away or trying to distract ourselves. Dongshan is pointing to the immediacy of just this. We cannot plan or control what will arise before us. Yet through practice we may develop the capacity to respond simply, to enact what appears helpful to this body mind and to what is happening in the world around. This requires much effort, or perhaps a reserve of trust and calm. Dongshan's suggestion to the monk to let the heat or the cold kill you may imply killing, or simply giving up, the narrow self, the "you" to which we habitually cling, thus going beyond to the wider self that is interconnected to all beings of our world, sentient or nonsentient. This emotional balance is a central aspect of Dongshan's response about heat and cold.

Blue Cliff Record *Comments on Dongshan's No Hot or Cold*

Returning to traditional Chan commentary, in his verse comment on this story in case 43 in the *Blue Cliff Record*, Xuedou, who selected the cases and wrote the primary verses that are the basis for this collection, refers in one of his four lines to Dongshan's five degrees teaching, asking, "Why must correct and biased be in an arrangement?"[21] Correct and biased are the two sides of the polarity whose interrelationship is elaborated in the five degrees or ranks. These two sides have also been designated as real and apparent, upright and inclined, universal and particular, ultimate and phenomenal, oneness and many, or absolute and relative; they are frequently suggested in Chan discourse by the metaphors of host and guest or lord and vassal.

Yuanwu wrote an introduction to the cases and commentary on the stories themselves and on Xuedou's verses, as well as interlinear comments on the stories and the verses, to create the final *Blue Cliff Record* collection. Yuanwu is a major, esteemed figure in Chan/Zen history, teacher of Dahui Zonggao (1089–1163; Jpn.: Daie Sōkō), who developed the influential approach to gongan/koan practice in the Linji/Rinzai tradition that encourages meditative concentration on "headwords," or *huatou*. Yuanwu was also a skilled poet and an insightful thinker, so it is somewhat disappointing that in his commentary to this case on the place with no heat or cold, he takes a reductionist approach, elaborating exclusively on Dongshan's fivefold arrangements of correct and biased. Analyzing the story only in terms of correct and biased, Yuanwu quotes in full Dongshan's own five verses on the five interactions toward the end of his *Recorded Sayings*. There Dongshan identifies the five as the biased within the correct; the correct within the biased; coming from within the correct; arrival within the biased; and arrival within both at once.[22]

These five degrees will be discussed in more detail in the final chapter of this book. We may appreciate Yuanwu citing Dongshan's five degrees verses and discussing this teaching. Through his commentary on this case, Yuanwu shared in the responsibility for bringing the five degrees teaching into the Linji tradition. These categories of universal and particular might indeed be employed analytically here, as for many dichotomies. But this story of hot and cold also simply informs Dongshan's expression of suchness with the intensities of hot and cold, and also with the transcending of the discomfort of hot and cold, whether from difficult climates or emotions. We have seen many facets in which the distress and intensity of heat and cold presented in this story provide substantial opportunity for consideration of personal physical practice, apart from abstract theoretical discourse. With all due respect to Yuanwu and his many other insightful and helpful commentaries in the *Blue Cliff Record,* in this case he may be ignoring the vividness and immediacy of heat and cold to which Dongshan responded. By reducing heat and cold into mere abstractions and simply another example of duality, he seems to miss the guts of this story.

We might see hot and cold as representative of extremes and thus consider them to some extent through the lens of Dongshan's dialectical synthesis of the extremes of the ultimate and provisional. Cold might express renunciation, perhaps representing one expression of the ultimate. Heat might reflect the intensity of helpful action in the world of phenomena. Yet we can readily consider the implications to practice of facing extremes of heat or cold, and renouncing personal comfort, without recourse to discussing universal and particular, or correct and biased.

Dōgen's Comments

Dōgen later devoted a whole essay called "Shunju" ("Spring and Autumn") to this dialogue of Dongshan in his *Shōbōgenzō*.[23] Kaz Tanahashi evocatively translates Dongshan's final line of the dialogue as "When it's cold, cold finishes the monk. When it is hot, heat demolishes the monk," suggesting the finality as well as the fullness of Dongshan's place without hot or cold, where these conditions are faced rather than evaded. Intriguingly, Dōgen uses for the title of his essay the seasons when heat or cold are least intense. Yet in his introduction he extols [his] cold or heat, saying, "When either comes, it comes from the summit of cold or the summit of heat, and manifests from the eyeball of cold itself, or heat itself. This summit is where there is no cold or heat. This eyeball is where there is no cold or heat." There is a meditation instruction here. Can we simply experience the full intensity of sensations, perceptions, feelings, and thoughts in this moment? We may give ourselves completely to our present life. This is to study the moment when cold comes, the moment when heat comes, beyond conditioned reactions and comparative evaluations. Dōgen adds, "Cold is the vital eye of the ancestor school. Heat is the warm skin and flesh of my late master."[24] This implies direct experience, beyond systematic, theoretical formulations such as the five degrees. Dōgen requires "understanding cold or heat in the everyday activities of Buddha ancestors."[25] Both Dongshan and Dōgen suggest that one face rather than avoid the reality of heat and ice.

In this essay Dōgen cites eight comments on the story by later masters and adds his own comments to these, most at least somewhat approving. A full discussion of all the comments is beyond the scope of this chapter. But the eight do include Xuedou's verse used in the *Blue Cliff Record* and a few others that reference the five degrees polarity. Dōgen strongly criticizes such analysis. He starts by citing the commentary by Kumu Facheng (1071–1128; Jpn.: Koboku Hōjō), a Caodong/Sōtō lineage master who says that to analyze this story in terms of differentiation or oneness "is to denigrate the ancient sage and lower yourself." Kumu offers a capping verse for the serene place of no cold or heat: "In the jade pavilion, a kingfisher builds a nest. In the gold palace, ducks are enclosed." Dōgen approves of Kumu and these instances of peaceful abiding. He adds, "If buddha-dharma had been transmitted merely through the investigation of differentiation and oneness, how could it have reached this day? Peasants or stray cats who have never understood the inner chamber of Dongshan . . . mistakenly say that Dongshan guided students with his theory of Five Ranks of differentiation and oneness. This is a confused view. Do not pay attention to it."[26]

A comment by Hongzhi, reviewed by Dōgen, emphasizes the byplay of Dongshan and this monk inquiring about hot and cold and thus their particular interrelationship. Hongzhi discusses the dialogue about hot and cold as if it were "like you and me playing a game of *go*. If you do not respond to my move, I'll swallow you up." Dōgen comments approvingly, "Who are the two players? If you say that you and I are playing *go*, it means you have a handicap of eight stones [a maximum handicap], it is no longer a game."[27] *Go* is an ancient Chinese (and then Japanese) game played on a board, both simple and highly subtle, to some extent analogous to chess. Two players take turns placing black and white stones on the board to delineate and mark off territory, although either player may at times use his stones to fully envelop and capture some of the other's stones, thus acquiring more territory. Dōgen references the equalizing handicaps that can be given to start the game and rejects seeing such an uneven discussion as a worthy contest. The monk has not realized at all Dongshan's place without heat or cold.

Hongzhi adds in his verse comment, "I see no cold or heat whatsoever. The great ocean has just dried up." Like Dongshan he is beyond heat or cold. Dōgen suggests, "You play *go* with yourself; the opponents become one." In response to Hongzhi's "If you do not respond to my move," Dōgen says, "That means *you* are not yet you." Some response is required to find one's own space beyond hot or cold, and in the original story, the monk remained silent. In reply to "I'll swallow you up," Dōgen adds, "Mud is within mud. . . . A jewel is within a jewel, illuminating other, illuminating the self." Hongzhi and Dōgen both see Dongshan as totally without resistance to the immediate situation, fully present and expressive, regardless of the climate.

Rather than Yuanwu's commentary in the *Blue Cliff Record*, discussed previously, Dōgen approvingly cites in "Shunju" a verse by Yuanwu that includes "A board rolls on a pearl and a pearl rolls on a board. Differentiation within oneness; oneness within differentiation."[28] Pearls rolling on a board, or in a bowl, is a not uncommon Chan image for the reality of things not abiding anywhere. But Dōgen states that Yuanwu's words, "'A board rolls on a pearl,' appear before the light and cut off the future—rarely heard in the past and present." This image implies, beyond the first image, the flexibility and inconceivability of the whole universe, any and all spaces, resting and rolling around on the particulars, a provocative viewpoint for the realm beyond heat or cold.

Dōgen does cite Xuedou's four-line verse for case 43 in the *Blue Cliff Record* and castigates Xuedou for even mentioning correct or biased, or in Tanahashi's translation differentiation and oneness. Dōgen states, "It seems that Xuedou could not deal with this matter without the view of differentiation and oneness," and then proclaims, "Do not mistakenly say that Dongshan's buddha-dharma is the five ranks of oneness and differentiation."[29] Dōgen rejects the five degrees theory as a reliable vehicle for any understanding of Dongshan's teaching.

Among the others, Dōgen mentions approvingly Yuanwu's successor Fuxing Fatai (n.d.; Jpn.: Busshō Hōtai), whose verse comment on this story includes "The place where there is no cold or heat leads to you. A decayed tree brings forth blossoms once again."[30] Dōgen praises this verse as having "some power of crushing the fundamental meaning underfoot while raising it overhead." Dongshan's place beyond cold or heat is not some external place out there but points back to you. How do we find some middle way, where we are not caught up in the heat of passions, rages, and frustrations, but breathe into them so as not to run away from ourselves but use the energy of our heat and passion? Further, just sitting quietly, upright and still, we must not settle for some inner deadness. Our own creative energy and vitality can emerge from stillness. The decayed tree bringing forth new blossoms expresses a strong theme in much of Zen poetry and imagery. In one *Shōbōgenzō* essay Dōgen discusses the saying "A dragon sings in a withered tree."[31] Elsewhere Dōgen invokes awakening liveliness emerging from the seemingly withered or decayed by saying, "The plum blossom opens afresh on the same branch as last year."[32]

As he concludes the citations about this story from Dongshan in "Spring and Autumn," Dōgen notes a verse by Heshan Shouxun (12th cent.; Jpn.: Kazan Shujun), which includes "Go for fire when it is cold, and cool yourself when it is hot. All your life you can avoid cold and heat."[33] Going for fire or wearing a warm coat in the cold and cooling oneself with a fan or perhaps even air conditioning in the heat seem to make good common sense. But Dōgen states that these words appear as child's talk. However, Dōgen appreciates Heshan's "All your life" as invoking one's entire life and calls his avoiding cold and heat "nothing other than dropping away body and mind," a phrase Dōgen commonly uses for total awakening, as well as everyday zazen practice. As Dōgen amplifies, Dongshan challenges us to completely give all of ourselves to burning up in the heat or freezing in the cold as a way of taking care of ourselves throughout the intensity of this world.

—

Aside from this *Shōbōgenzō* essay focusing on Dongshan's place with no heat or cold, Dōgen also uses this story as case 74 in his collection of ninety koan cases with his own verse comments in volume 9 of his *Extensive Record*.[34] Dōgen's verse begins "When hot and cold comes, let go and proceed." Dongshan encourages the monk to not hold back from the heat or cold but to sustain active practice. Dongshan concludes, "Great peace is basically caused by generals, but don't allow the generals to see great peace." In the Buddhist context great peace refers to *nirvāṇa*. Generals here refer to the spiritual warrior, a heroic image for bodhisattvas, dedicated to assisting all beings to awaken to liberation and relief from suffering. But as the bodhisattvas vow to remain for the sake of all beings in the realm of suffering, including its intense cold or heat, the generals must not realize and escape to full nirvāṇa themselves, except inasmuch as it abides right in the midst of suffering, here described as burning heat or freezing cold.

Traditional Buddhist depictions of hell realms, populated by beings led there by harmful karma, graphically describe these hells as either intensely hot or cold. But bodhisattvas willingly enter such spaces for the sake of those suffering. So we can see Dongshan's responses to the monk seeking to avoid heat and cold as simply instructions in how to engage the bodhisattva lifestyle. Totally immersing oneself in extreme heat or cold as Dongshan encourages represents the true practice of bodhisattvas, of not trying to escape the world's suffering.

Contemporary Comments on Dongshan's Hot and Cold

Shunryū Suzuki commented on this story to his students at Tassajara in summer 1969. Suzuki said, "When it is hot you should be hot buddha. When it is cold, you should be cold buddha." This turns Dongshan's image of burning to death or freezing to death into ultimate awakening in hot or cold, killing all delusions. The place where there is no hot or cold appears when we accept whatever arises, just as it is.

A month later, speaking at his temple in San Francisco, Suzuki added, "We say it is cold because we are so accustomed to warm weather. That is why it is cold. . . . There is no climate that is just cold or just warm. Cold and hot are simultaneous. Because you know how cold it is in winter, in summer you say, 'It is hot.'"[35] This clarifies the original story with the perspective of the relativity of extremes. We can only sense hot in contrast to some experience of cold, and vice versa. And what seems hot to some creatures is comfortable or even cold to others. Eskimos would probably be distressed in the tropics, as would Tahitians in polar regions.

In considering Suzuki's viewpoints on Dongshan's story about going to the place where there is neither hot nor cold, we can see such a place as beyond comparative thinking, and just call it buddhahood. In all the above considerations, from self-immolation to global warming, to the suffering of emotional extremes, to the serene palace where all experience is directly accepted as it is, we can see the depths of Dongshan's challenge to the monk in the original story. We can consider for ourselves the functions of Dongshan's suggestion, "When it's cold, freeze to death; when it's hot, swelter to death." This is an instruction for fully taking on the situation of just this life, as it is, including all our inner emotional turmoil, and including the turmoil of our physical world, and the suffering induced by our societal arrangements. Just being hot Buddha, cold Buddha, seeing the relativity of hot and cold, opening and responding as best we can to the suffering in the climate we presently inhabit, bodhisattva practitioners do not fear freezing or sweltering.

CHAPTER SIX

The White Rabbit

How High a Rabbit Jumps

Eight of the stories in Dongshan's *Recorded Sayings* include Shen-shan Sengmi (9th cent.; Jpn.: Shinzan Sōmitsu), who was a fellow student of Yunyan's, and thus was referred to later as "spiritual uncle" by Dongshan's students. In all of these stories Dongshan and Sengmi are traveling on pilgrimage visiting various teachers, apparently after finishing training with Yunyan but presumably before Dongshan settled down to become a teacher himself.[1] In several of these stories Dongshan chastises Sengmi for speaking foolishly despite his venerable age. In one of the stories Dongshan mentions that they had been traveling together for twenty years.

Hongzhi Zhengjue selected one of these stories with Sengmi to be case 56 in his koan collection that became the *Book of Serenity*. In this story Dongshan and Sengmi were walking on pilgrimage, and a white rabbit suddenly darted across their path. Sengmi said, "How swift." Dongshan asked him how so.

Sengmi said, "Just like a commoner becoming a high minister."

Dongshan retorted, "How can such a venerable person as you speak like that?"

When Sengmi asked for Dongshan's understanding, he said, "After generations of nobility, temporarily fallen into poverty."[2]

The differing viewpoints about the white rabbit in this story suggest two contrasting approaches to awakening, and to spiritual practice. In Sengmi's first statement about the rabbit, "How swift," Thomas Cleary translates the Chinese character as "swift,"

William Powell as "elegant," and it might also be translated as "eminent" or "refined." This white rabbit is impressive and grand, not just for his speed. The question is how the rabbit became so eminent. This dialogue about the white rabbit indicates also the issue of how buddhas or great bodhisattvas become elegant and refined.

Sengmi claimed the rabbit was "Just like a commoner becoming a high minister." This implies the path of cultivation of a deluded person achieving elevated wisdom through great exertion, often thought of in terms of self-improvement. Many Buddhist sutras and other teachings include various systems of specified stages of development and spiritual growth as guides for practitioners. Wansong in his commentary in the *Book of Serenity* says, "Usually we awaken by means of cultivation, entering sagehood from ordinariness—a commoner is directly appointed prime minister."[3] Not only in Buddhism, but in many spiritual and cultural traditions, eminence and achievement are often seen as only the outcome of long, arduous struggle.

On the other hand, Dongshan describes the white rabbit's situation as "generations of nobility, temporarily fallen into poverty." This implies that such eminence is a facet of inalienable, inherent buddha nature, not the attainment of some new status or of spiritual social climbing. The upright nobility of a buddha's awareness and kindness is a birthright already present, not some new state that needs to be discovered or achieved. But temporarily falling into poverty is a necessary aspect of the bodhisattva way of life. Bodhisattvas, awakening beings dedicated to universal liberation, join fully with suffering beings and become impoverished at least spiritually if not also materially, just so they can reenact and exemplify awakening to this innate nobility as an encouragement for others. They practice, sometimes strenuously, not to reach some new exalted state but to uncover something already deeply present. Wansong says, "If you're first enlightened and then cultivate afterwards, you enter ordinariness from sagehood—traditional nobility is originally honorable; though drifting destitute in myriad conditions, the basic constitution is still there."[4] And Dongshan suggests that the fall into suffering, when bodhisattva practice is engaged, is finally only temporary.

The Lotus Sutra and the Prodigal Son

Dongshan's response to Sengmi, "After generations of nobility, temporarily fallen into poverty," refers directly to a parable in the Lotus Sutra, arguably the most important Buddhist scripture in East Asia. In this prodigal son story, a son and father are separated. The son drifts aimlessly and becomes destitute, while the father moves to another city and becomes very wealthy and highly respected. Eventually, the son in his wandering happens upon the estate of the father. The father immediately recognizes his son and sends some assistants to bring him in, but seeing the wealthy, eminent man in front of his mansion, the son is frightened and runs away. The father understands the humble son's shame and dread and sends his assistants disguised as lowly menial workers to invite the son to come and take a job on the estate shoveling dung in the fields. After a while, when the son feels comfortable with this job, the father has his assistants steadily give the son more responsibilities, until gradually, after a very long period, the son is managing the estate. When the father is finally about to pass away, he calls for all of his friends and the nobles and citizens of the city and announces to them, and to his son, that this really is his son, that they were separated long before, but that "Now all of my wealth belongs entirely to my son." The sutra goes on to state explicitly that the very rich old man is the Buddha, and that "we are all like the Buddha's children."[5]

In the sutra this story is presented by four of the Buddha's ten major disciples, all fully awakened arhats, or venerable ones. The arhat is the model for practice in earlier, pre-bodhisattva Buddhism. Arhats have fully purified themselves of all personal karmic defilements from the three poisons of greed, hatred, and delusion. They are personally enlightened, remarkable beings who have achieved this state through extensive cultivation, often represented as engaged over many lifetimes, indeed "entering sagehood from ordinariness," like a commoner becoming prime minister. But the arhat disciples relating this prodigal son story have been inspired by hearing the Buddha's prediction that one of their fellow arhats, Śāriputra, will in the future certainly become a buddha. This counters the conventional or early Mahāyāna view that arhats, concerned only with their own salvation, cannot fully realize buddhahood.

Eventually in the Lotus Sutra, the Buddha proclaims that everyone who even hears a line of the sutra will eventually realize buddhahood: "Anyone who hears even a single verse or a single phrase of the Wonderful Dharma Flower Sutra, and responds in joy for even a single moment, I assure that one also of supreme awakening."[6] The prodigal son story implies that all in the Buddha's assembly are actually children of Buddha, like the prodigal son. The image of the *sangha* (Buddhist community) as the family of Buddha appears in many sutras. All share the birthright of Buddha and have entered "ordinariness from sagehood" and nobility. Even if one is now drifting amid worldly suffering and infected by craving, hatred, and ignorance, the basic quality of awakening lies dormant nearby, ever available. Dongshan referencing this story implies his view of the nature of bodhisattva action, and of awakening.

Earlier in his studies with Yunyan, Dongshan had said, "It would be untrue to say that I am not joyful. It is as though I have grasped a bright pearl [or jewel] in a pile of shit."[7] Dongshan states this as the culmination of a dialogue that begins with him confessing to Yunyan that he still has some karmic habits not yet eradicated. When Yunyan asks how he has been caring for them, Dongshan says that he had not even concerned himself with the Four Noble Truths. Yunyan then asked if Dongshan was joyful yet, and he made the response, "It would be untrue to say that I am not joyful. It is as though I have grasped a bright pearl in a pile of shit." This refers to the treasure realized by the prodigal son once he was willing to dig in the manure. But Dongshan here also acknowledges that despite the birthright of children of Buddha, still there are karmic attachments and afflictions that do need to be acknowledged and overcome. Realizing underlying awakening requires the hard work of seeing through habitual views and grasping. This manual labor or hard work is as necessary in bodhisattva practice as in the arhat model. The immediacy of generations of nobility and suchness does not negate the work on ethical conduct and the necessity of practicing in accord with precepts and engaging in helpful rather than harmful activity.

However, the prodigal son story also emphasizes Dongshan's disregard, even as a student, for the stages of accomplishment and the path implied by the Four Noble Truths. Dongshan's critique of the traditional view of the Buddhist path of cultivation will be discussed further in the following chapters. The image of the jewel in the pile of shit also recalls two other Lotus Sutra stories relevant to the situation of temporarily falling into poverty though inherently noble.

The Jewel in the Clothing and the Dragon Girl

Wansong in his commentary to the white rabbit story refers to a saying, "In the metaphor of the destitute son is illustrated the Path; in the verse on presenting the jewel is shown the net of salvation."[8] The long path of the destitute prodigal son involves realizing a birthright already present. "The verse on presenting the jewel" might refer to either of two other stories in the Lotus Sutra.

In the first story, two friends are up late drinking, and the guest falls asleep. The affluent host is called away but first sews a priceless jewel into the guest's robe as a gift to provide for him. Later the guest awakens and departs. In his travels he faces hardships and must struggle just to satisfy basic needs. The friends happen to meet later, and the disappointed former host tells his indigent friend about the jewel he still has in his clothing and that he had only suffered want due to ignorance of the jewel. Now he knows and may live at ease.[9] The implications of this story are quite similar to the prodigal son story. The host who provided for his friend is explicitly compared to the Buddha. Like the prodigal son story, the jewel in the clothing parable is related in the sutra by arhats, this time by five hundred arhat monks, joyful that the Buddha has predicted their future buddhahood, as well. The impoverished friend suffered only due to ignorance of the jewel, already in his pocket, so to speak, and is compared to arhats not aware of their bodhisattva capacity leading to total buddhahood.

The second Lotus Sutra story suggested by Wansong's commentary about presenting a jewel is more complex. A bodhisattva visiting from a different world system, what we might consider another solar system or galaxy or perhaps a different dimension of space and time, inquires of the bodhisattva of wisdom, Mañjuśri, if there are any beings who could quickly become a buddha through diligently and devotedly practicing the sutra. Mañjuśri mentions the dragon king's eight-year-old daughter, who soon appears. She presents an exceedingly precious jewel to the Buddha as an offering, and he immediately accepts it. She then proclaims that she can become a Buddha even more quickly than the Buddha accepted the jewel, and even though she is not human, like the white rabbit, only eight years of age, and in terms of the prejudices of Buddha's time, merely a defiled female, she proceeds instantly to become a buddha.[10] The complexities of this story have rightly been much discussed in contemporary Buddhist women's studies. But in the context of the story about Dongshan and the white rabbit, what is important is that the dragon girl, like the rabbit, is swift and becomes eminent, achieving buddhahood very quickly. In the context of the traditional path requiring ages of effort to achieve excellence, she is quite revolutionary.

The net of salvation demonstrated by both these presentations of jewels is also immediate, not a product of endeavoring to reach new heights. The path of arhats and even traditionally of bodhisattvas prior to the Lotus Sutra involves many lifetimes of arduous practice. Dongshan's statement "After generations of nobility, temporarily fallen into poverty" invokes these stories and the view of awakening as an omnipresent, available capacity, not some product created or achieved though stages of accomplishment.

Awakening Both Instantly and in Stages

In his verse commentary to this *Book of Serenity* case, Hongzhi begins, "Matching strength with snow and frost, / Walking evenly through clouds and sleet."[11] This connotes the ability of the inherently noble to proceed with equanimity even through formidable conditions, or temporary impoverishment. Hongzhi then cites a number of elaborate Chinese historical or literary references and concludes, "Favor and disgrace are disturbing—profoundly trust in yourself: / In the real state one mixes tracks with fishermen and woodcutters." The encouragement to profoundly trust oneself echoes the fact of the innate birthright of enlightenment, and therefore not seeking from others, as Dongshan realized upon seeing his reflection in the stream after departing from Yunyan. Mixing agreeably with fishermen and woodcutters, conventionally commoners, implies the helpful activity of bodhisattvas amid supposedly ordinary beings. But still, it is then necessary to practice diligently so as to develop and demonstrate awakening qualities.

In commenting on Hongzhi's last line of this verse, "In the real state one mixes tracks with fishermen and woodcutters," the *Book of Serenity* commentator Wansong claims, "For Tiantong [Hongzhi] this still falls within stages."[12] (Tiantong was another name for Hongzhi, as he taught at Tiantong Monastery, where Dōgen's teacher, Tiantong Rujing, would later teach.) We will see the issue of stages of practice in play in more of Dongshan's stories. Dongshan clearly prefers the style of not falling into stages of achievement, emphasizing the background generations of nobility. But Wansong points out that even in the real state one must mix tracks with stages of development. In another case in the *Book of Serenity*, he cites the story about Dongshan, Sengmi, and the white rabbit while commenting on two lines from Hongzhi's verse on that case,

"The child of riches, as soon as he falls / On the boundless road of destitution, has such sorrow."[13] Here Hongzhi indicates that despite innate generations of nobility, one cannot evade the sorrows on the road.

The White Rabbit in the Moon

What of the elegant white rabbit in the original story? Perhaps it is only white in parallelism with the white robe of commoners, as "white-robe" is a widespread Buddhist epithet for laypeople and the phrase used to indicate "commoner" in the original dialogue. Similarly, "patch-robed" conventionally refers to home-leaver monks who wear patched robes. If the white color of the rabbit only parallels the white-robed ones or commoners, this may be evidence that the story, or at least its polished written form, is indeed a later literary production rather than a literal account of an event on Dongshan and Sengmi's travels.

In East Asia a white rabbit is commonly seen in the moon, just as people in the Northern Hemisphere in the West see a man in the moon, going back to Plutarch and Greek lore, and perhaps also Norse mythology.[14] With the white rabbit representing the moon, a customary Buddhist image of wholeness and full enlightenment, we can see the original story afresh. Thus, Dongshan and Sengmi are talking not just about a small rabbit, but about Enlightenment itself, which somehow they had glimpsed passing quickly in front of them. Therefore, as we have seen, their comments reflect approaches and strategies to developing enlightened awareness.

Down the Hole of the White Rabbit

A more familiar white rabbit may be pertinent for the Dongshan story. In Lewis Carroll's famed mid-nineteenth-century fable, a white rabbit leads a young girl named Alice to dive down a very deep hole. This white rabbit, too, is quite elegant, wearing a waistcoat with a pocket watch and holding white kid gloves. This white rabbit is also swift, and seeks to be even swifter, as he worries, "Oh dear! Oh dear! I shall be too late!"[15] Such anxiety about the time might be considered more a reflection of Sengmi's "commoner becoming a high minister," the practitioner toiling to purify himself with great effort over time to climb to an elevated status, and hoping to get there fairly soon. Perhaps Dongshan's white rabbit, "after generations of nobility, temporarily fallen into poverty," might also be nervous about his pace, to the extent that the bodhisattva is fooled in his fallen state and "has such sorrow," before recalling his generations of noble awakened ancestors.

Interestingly, the white rabbit crossing Alice's path dives into a hole, and she unhesitatingly follows. Diving down the hole after the white rabbit, she must fall into distress in order to discover herself in a wonderland, where things become "curiouser and curiouser." All conventional sense of logic and proportion has fallen far away, just as logic and proportion are transformed in the depictions of wondrous buddha fields and pure lands in the Mahāyāna sutras. The sense of wonder and awe abundantly expressed by Alice is appropriate in these magnificent buddha realms, as well. But Alice did not arrive in her wonderland by climbing and struggling up to some elevated state. Rather, she comes to this by simply diving down, and her wonderland abides available under the ground, right beneath her feet. This is not other than the space under the ground from whence emerge the bodhisattvas in the "Springing Up from the Earth" chapter of the Lotus Sutra.[16] These bodhisattvas abide ever present underground, ready to spring forth as needed to express the reality of the Buddha's fundamental omnipresence, which is also celebrated by Dongshan in his response to the white rabbit.

White Rabbit Practice

In a more recent invocation, Grace Slick, in her 1967 anthem "White Rabbit" on the Jefferson Airplane's *Surrealistic Pillow* album, sings, "One pill makes you larger, and one pill makes you small, and the ones that mother gives you, don't do anything at all." Indeed, in the path of cultivation, for commoners working to become eminent, some practices make you larger, providing a lofty perspective that may lead to self-inflation, and some practices make you small, either via a narrow focus of concentration or through the humbling awareness of one's self-centeredness. Perhaps from Dongshan's viewpoint of the foundational generations of nobility and the stark immediacy of suchness, the practices that Buddha gives you also "don't do anything at all." Rather than producing dramatic elevation or diminishment, the practices of Dongshan's Buddha simply remind the practitioner of the inner uprightness, dignity, and nobility of intrinsic awakening.

The implications of his response to Sengmi after encountering the white rabbit include Dongshan's advocation of practices to immediately recognize the awakened qualities of kindness and awareness available presently, and recognize the reality of just this suchness. Seeking to escape to some loftier realm is not the point. Practices of cultivation, seeking advanced concentrations, or seeing through and purifying negative karmic qualities might well be engaged, and even necessary, but only from the perspective of awakening from the temporary obstructions to our generations of nobility.

CHAPTER SEVEN

The Bird's Path

Sighting the Bird's Path

One story in the *Recorded Sayings* concerns Dongshan's use of the image of the bird's path, which he encourages his students to follow, leaving no traces. When a monk asked him what was the bird path that he regularly recommended, Dongshan replied, "One does not encounter a single person."[1] Thus, Dongshan's bird path involves the solitary, not seeking from outside, as in his verse after seeing his reflection in the stream. But not encountering a single person also indicates the emptiness of a single self, of oneself or any other selves, and the bird flying away with no traces of itself as a remnant, going beyond all clinging to self. The monk continued by asking how one takes such a path. Dongshan said, "One proceeds with no self underfoot." An alternative version of the story says to advance with not a thread tied to your feet, not bound by anything.[2]

The monk then asked if following the bird's path equals seeing one's original face, a common Chan image for fundamental nature. But Dongshan replied that by so believing, the monk was turning things upside down. When the monk then asked what is the original face, Dongshan replied somewhat enigmatically that the original face is *not* to follow the bird's path. The true original face is beyond any path or technique to achieve it.

The bird's path is a provocative image for selfless practice, reminiscent of Dongshan's space with no grass for ten thousand miles or the place without heat or cold. It also recalls the practical Chan or Zen admonition not only not to litter or leave traces, but furthermore to leave a space more clean than you find it. The bird's path serves as an analog and commentary by Dongshan to the traditional Buddhist teaching of the Path, *mārga* in Sanskrit and *magga* in Pali. Both the early tradition of the arhat ideal, focusing on personal liberation, and later Mahāyāna Buddhism, based on the bodhisattva ideal of universal liberation, present a great array of expressions and systems for paths of practice, which can be seen as road maps with stages of spiritual development toward ultimate awakening.[3]

An early presentation of the path is the eightfold path, composed of right view, right consideration, right speech, right action, right livelihood, right effort, right mindfulness, and right concentration. This eightfold path is the fourth in Śākyamuni Buddha's early teaching of the Four Noble Truths.[4] But the eightfold path is not sequential; one does not attempt to master each of the eight in turn, but all pertain to practice simultaneously. So the path may be open and inclusive, rather than a step-by-step progression. Dongshan's view of the path is clarified by this distinction between general directions toward awakening and systematic schemes of stages of accomplishment.

The Chinese character for *path* is *dao*, as in Daoism and its classic text, the *Dao De Jing*, which starts by saying that the dao that can be indicated or followed is not the true or ultimate dao.[5] In the Chinese Buddhist context, *dao* was also commonly used to imply the whole of awakening, the Buddha Way as outcome, as well as the course toward it. But in the context of advocating the traceless bird's path, particular road maps of the path toward awakening might be questioned. While not specifically criticizing any of the traditional teachings, Dongshan, in his bird's path and elsewhere, clearly presents an alternative to the approach to spiritual practice as a path with demarcated stages.

The Original Face

The original face invoked by the monk in this story is a primary image in Chan lore, frequently used to express or call for fundamental truth or the true self, often via the question "What is your original face before your parents were born?" This image probably first appears in a story about the celebrated Chan Sixth Ancestor Dajian Huineng, who was five generations before Dongshan in the lineage, and from whom all later Chan and Zen derive. The story, in short, goes that Huineng was an illiterate woodcutter and layman from the boondocks of Southern China who awakened upon hearing a line from the Diamond Sutra, a Perfection of Wisdom text focused on emptiness teaching. He traveled to the large monastery complex of the Chan Fifth Ancestor Daman Hongren (602–75; Jpn.: Daiman Kōnin), who later secretly gave Huineng Dharma transmission to become the Sixth Ancestor. When he departed and headed south with the help of Hongren, some of the learned monks who had trained there for many years chased after Huineng, jealously believing he had tricked the Fifth Ancestor into giving him the robe and bowl insignia of the transmission. When one monk caught up with Huineng, the latter placed the robe on a rock, but this monk, a former general, was not able to lift it. Ashamed, he asked for Huineng's teaching. Huineng asked him to put aside all thoughts of good and bad and then see his original or primal face. At least some portions of the longer narrative about Huineng are polemical hagiography and counter verifiable history. The part of the story about the original face does not appear until later Song dynasty editions of the Platform Sutra, which relates a version of the Huineng story, and a collection of teachings attributed to him. This story of the original face also appears as case 23 in the important twelfth-century *Gateless Barrier* koan collection.[6]

Dongshan told the monk who inquired about the bird's path and the original face that to see the original face he must not follow the bird's path. Dongshan here implies that the original face of foundational true nature is more immediate and primal than any path or progression, even one so ephemeral as the bird's path. Apart from stages of any progressive path, this original face is beyond any conceptualization at all, not caught by the conventional human discriminating consciousness that is aware of the world in terms of objects. In the context of discussing objectless meditation, Tenshin Reb Anderson calls the original face "a face that relinquishes any concept of face, so there is no way to carry any meaning about what your face is." Immersed in suchness arising beyond conceptual mediation, and beyond mental categories, one is "open to your face without any concept by which you can understand your face."[7] While Dongshan may recommend the bird's path to his students, he also encourages them not to be caught by it, or try to turn it into some program upon which to rely.

Earlier Presentations of the Bird's Path

The bird path image is not original to Dongshan but is cited in various much older texts.[8] It appears in the classic Pali text *The Dhammapada*, in chapter 7, on the arhat: "Like the path of birds in the sky, It is hard to trace the path of those who do not hoard, who are judicious with their food, and whose field is the freedom of emptiness and signlessness. Like the path of birds in the sky, It is hard to trace the path of those who have destroyed their toxins, who are unattached to food, and whose field is the freedom of emptiness and signlessness."[9] The untraceable bird's path is a useful image for the signlessness as well as emptiness and nonattachment of the worthy arhats, and for their freedom. Signlessness refers to the illusory nature of all signifiers. The labels we place on portions of our experience in order to talk about them are not fundamentally real, as the arhats realize.

The later Perfection of Wisdom literature, *prajñāpāramitā*, correspondingly uses the bird's path image to describe the bodhisattva. For example, in the *Perfection of Wisdom in Eight Thousand Lines*, the bodhisattva shuns attachments, and, "having cognized the world as like a snare for wild beasts the wise roam about similar to the birds in space."[10] Here the bird's path indicates flying free of worldly needs or attachments. In discussing the emptiness of conventional designations, the *Large Sutra on Perfect Wisdom* states, "Nothing real is meant by the word 'Bodhisattva.'" As enlightenment and so-called enlightened beings, as well as any other entities, are ultimately unproduced, such a thing as a bodhisattva is a thing that "does not exist, that cannot be apprehended; just as in space, the track of a bird does not exist and cannot be apprehended."[11] Here again the bird's path is unmarked, empty beyond attachments, and thus represents liberated awareness and activity.

The Daśabhumika Sutra, or Ten Stages Sutra, one of the earliest Mahāyāna sutras, presents the epitome of the stages of bodhisattva development. Yet in its introduction to these stages it says that these stages, "realized by sages," are actually "unattainable by mind, intellectually inconceivable." Then it cites the bird's path image: "Just as the tracks of a bird in the sky cannot be described or seen even by the enlightened, in the same way all the stages cannot be told of, much less heard."[12] So the stages depicted in this sutra are acknowledged at the outset as merely shadows or reflections of reality, ephemeral as the bird's path. They are retold only partially and imperfectly as skillful means, out of compassion for those who might be encouraged thereby.

No Such Path

Many other stories about Dongshan provide forceful critiques of attachment to the path, and even denial of the reality of any path. In a story already partially recounted in chapter 4, Dongshan strongly urged his disciple Huayan Xiujing to go to the place without an inch of grass for ten thousand miles. That story begins with Huayan admitting, "I am without a proper path," and that he cannot "escape the vicissitudes of feelings and discriminating consciousness." Dongshan asks, "Do you still think there is such a path?" And Huayan realizes, "No I don't think there is any such path."[13] Dongshan's encouragement to find a place beyond conditioning, without an inch of grass for ten thousand miles, is here linked to what is sometimes notably called "sudden awakening," the unmediated awareness of suchness right here now, always present, not the result of traversing some prescribed path. Even when we feel beset by emotionality and discriminations, we may face suchness right there. No neat road map can rescue us from the reality of human sadness or confusion. The evanescent bird's path, with no discernible tracks or steps to follow, may serve as a subtle indicator to the realization of omnipresent suchness beyond any indicated path.

The story about Dongshan's passing away in 869 will be discussed further in chapter 11, but in his death verse, Dongshan says that he had numerous disciples, but "not one has gained enlightenment; they err in seeking it as a path taught by others."[14] In his final teaching, again Dongshan emphasizes not seeking awakening from others, outside. He further discourages seeking some path aimed at attaining an alternate experience, aside from awakened awareness of this present body-mind.

Dongshan's Three Roads

In the development of Dongshan's lineage both in the Chinese Caodong and Japanese Sōtō schools, some scholar monks offered interpretations of his teachings, often concentrated on the five degrees. The eighteenth-century revival of Japanese Sōtō scholarship focused on Dōgen but included accounts of Dongshan's teaching. Shigetsu E'in (1689–1764) presented Dongshan's bird's path in terms of "three roads."[15] Shigetsu refers to "This road," which I take to refer to the path of just this, or suchness, where there is no path, and nothing that is not a path. Shigetsu says, "'This road' means while dwelling in the present heap of sound and form, first getting rid of clinging to self, and attaining our former original state of selflessness. And furthermore, you must know that all things have no self. Once person and things are selfless, in your daily activities you walk in [emptiness]." He further describes this activity as to "not chew through a single grain of rice," so as not to arouse "mindfulness of tasting flavor." Thus, not being caught by self or sense objects, Shigetsu states, is traveling the bird's path.

Shigetsu equates this with a second road, after realizing and settling into the tracklessness of the bird's path. As this is a mysterious traceless realm without name or meaning, it is called a "hidden road," beyond any dwelling place. Shigetsu describes as a third road, or a third aspect of the bird's path, "extending the hands" to relieve others. While remaining on the hidden road, one inspires and unifies beings in order to teach them. Shigetsu says that this is not a separate road and does not violate the bird's path. "Traveling the bird's path by yourself, yet you extend your hands." So even if the bird's path implies the solitary, as Dongshan tells the inquiring monk, it also includes compassionate bodhisattva activity, extending oneself to help relieve suffering and liberate beings.

The Mystery of Migration

Humans cannot see any trace in the sky after birds fly by, unlike the trail left for a while by jet planes. Nevertheless, some bird species follow the exact same seasonal migratory paths for many centuries. There is a great range of approaches to migration among the approximately 18 percent of bird species that do long-distance migrations, and occasionally the migration route of a type of bird may shift due to environmental or other factors. Some birds travel as much as fourteen thousand miles each year. Even non-flying birds often migrate, most penguin species by swimming, and blue grouse, for example, perform altitudinal migration by walking. Scientists speculate that birds recognize their traditional migration paths due to a variety of factors including solar position, electromagnetic cues, heredity, and training from parents.[16]

Does some trail or perhaps another trace invisible to human perceptions remain for birds to sense and follow? Certainly a mystery remains, part of the relevance of the bird's path in Dongshan's evocation of it. The parallel is striking to "clouds and water" monks, who traditionally migrated between different teachers, traveling by foot. This was true for Dongshan himself, as he visited various masters before becoming a teacher himself. Such purposeful drifting has persisted throughout much of the history of Chinese Chan and Japanese Zen, and still today for many modern Zen practitioners who visit different centers and teachers.

Birds Fly the Whole Sky

In his important early essay "Genjōkōan," Dōgen invokes the practice of birds (along with fish) in an extended metaphor for bodhisattva practice. He notes,

> When a bird flies, no matter how high it flies, it cannot reach the end of the sky. When the bird's need . . . is great, the range is large. When the need is small, the range is small. In this way, . . . each bird uses the whole of space and vigorously acts in every place. However, if a bird departs from the sky, . . . it immediately dies. We should know that . . . [for a bird] sky is life.[17]

This provides a clear setting for what happens on the bird's path. The sky is totally necessary to birds' flight, just as the teachings of awakening and the activities of practice are the atmosphere for Dongshan's students on the bird's path.

Though he did not mention the bird path explicitly in "Genjōkōan," Dōgen was familiar with this image from Dongshan. For example, in the long *Shōbōgenzō* essay "Gyōji" ("Continuous Practice"), Dōgen comments on the encouragement by the great master Zhaozhou Congshen (778–897; Jpn.: Jōshu Jūshin) to "not leave the monastery in your [whole] lifetime." Clearly, in context this suggestion from Zhaozhou serves as a metaphor for the attitude of meditative awareness everywhere, in all activity, including after departing the monastery literally. Zhaozhou is noted for his own wandering around for many years between various teachers, like a migrating bird. Dōgen comments on Zhaozhou's not leaving the monastery, "Learn to treasure each moment of sustained practice. Do not assume that not to speak is useless. It is entering the monastery, leaving the monastery. The bird's path is the forest [a traditional image for a monastery, or forest of monks]. The entire world is the forest, the monastery."[18] Thus, following the bird's path, one is not caught anywhere but utilizes the entire world as a pathway for sustaining practice.

In "Genjōkōan," Dōgen states that a bird uses all of the surrounding sky as it flies, but also that no matter how high or far it flies, it cannot reach the end or boundary of the sky. Practitioners cannot reach the end or limit of their practice. A bird's range as it flies or migrates may be large or small, depending on its need. Our practice extends widely, depending on the need of beings around us, as well as our own capacity to expand it. But Dōgen warns that a bird dies if it departs from the sky, as if it could do such a thing. Similarly, Dongshan warns his disciples that they cannot abandon their practice. On the bird's path they must persist and find the place without any grass for ten thousand miles and where there is no heat or cold.

Are Birds Free from the Chains of the Sky?

To be "free as a bird" is a common expression that might be evoked by Dongshan's traceless bird's path and is echoed in the older Perfection of Wisdom use of the image. But Bob Dylan ends one of his songs, "My friends from the prison, they ask unto me, 'How good, how good does it feel to be free?' And I answer them most mysteriously 'Are birds free from the chains of the skyway?'"[19] Are birds caught in the chains of the sky? The bird's path is ephemeral, blowing in the wind. But are the birds free?

What does freedom mean in relation to a spiritual path? The bird's path image indicates freedom as spacious nonattachment, not setting down or becoming trapped by some record of progress. Dongshan's various other stories about a path suggest freedom or liberation not as the destination or goal of the path, but simply as the free, playful, wholehearted engagement of a path at any point anywhere along that path. At the same time, this is not freedom from or absence of the karmic entanglements of particular situations of time and season, or the causal conditions that lead one to the spiritual path in the first point. As Dōgen says, "If a bird flies beyond the sky it dies at once." So birds are still enmeshed in the chains of the sky, the particular wind currents and changing climates that condition their migrations.

Off the Path

In his modern Zen masterpiece *Practice of the Wild*, the American Zen patriarch and pioneer Gary Snyder discusses the value of the path, as well as of sauntering off the path. The image of the bird's path may be amplified by seeing it as a flexible guideline rather than as a roadway with restrictive barriers on either side. Similarly, the traditional Zen monastic regulations may be understood not as constraining rules to follow strictly but as forms to help foster awakening, compassionate practice. For example, in his standards for monastic practice, Dōgen cites exemplary figures whose attitude and actions express dedication to the practice and kindness to the community, rather than rigid obedience of regulations. He presents stories about classic personages filling the roles of the temple positions he highlights. But of the twenty anecdotes Dōgen narrates and praises, ten of them involve actions by the exemplars in which they do something in violation of the literal regulations, a few even being shunned or expelled from the monastery for a time.[20]

In his chapter "On the Path, Off the Trail" in *Practice of the Wild*, Gary Snyder paraphrases the outset of Laozi's Daoist classic the *Dao De Jing*, "A path that can be followed is not a spiritual path," and comments, "The actuality of things cannot be confined within so linear an image as a road."[21] Snyder's illuminating model of the path, and of Zen practice, embraces the wildness of actual lives, not confined to ruts, routines, or literalist instruction manuals, free in the style of the undomesticated birds' path. Such a path cannot be followed through systems of stages or through our imagined attainments. Snyder states, "The 'perfect way' is not a path that leads somewhere easily defined, to some goal that is at the end of a progression." The forms of spiritual practice and guidance of paths offer a valuable legacy conveyed from Zen ancestors such as Dongshan. But following the ritual forms and suggested paths perfectly is not the point of the Zen bodhisattva tradition.

Snyder suggests "Off the Trail" as a helpful name for the Way. He says, "Sauntering off the trail is the practice of the wild. This is also where—paradoxically—we do our best work. But we need paths and trails and will always be maintaining them. You first must be on the path, before you can turn and walk into the wild." All the systems of paths of practice may be helpful starting points for finding one's own way, or developing new paths. But these pathways of practice necessarily must engage the ever-changing situation as the Buddha Way is transported into new cultures and radically different historical periods.

Unobstructed by the Wide Sky

In the Caodong lineage in the century before Dongshan, his predecessor Shitou revealed a further context for flying on the bird's path. Shitou wrote the "Harmony of Difference and Sameness" verse that was the precursor to Dongshan's "Song of the Jewel Mirror Samādhi," and he was the teacher of Yaoshan, the teacher of Dongshan's teacher Yunyan. Shitou was once asked directly by one of his disciples for the essential meaning of Buddha Dharma. Shitou responded, "Not attaining, not knowing." When asked if there was any other pivotal point, Shitou affirmed, "The wide sky does not obstruct the white clouds drifting."[22]

The bird's path is not a progression toward some attainment. Birds traverse the sky without rational knowledge of their pathway and without apparent roadside markers. The ones who do not succumb to predators or accidents on the way reach their destinations naturally. While birds may be relieved and even happy to rest at the end of a migration, and also to rest along the way, they do not have any sense of pride or sense of attainment for reaching their breeding ground or wintering spot. That is just their lives, in harmony with the spaciousness of the sky. The sky does not obstruct the birds' flight, any more than the sky is opposed to drifting clouds. Birds do not reach the end of the sky, and for the birds the sky is life itself.

CHAPTER EIGHT

On the Mountaintop

Reaching the Peak

Dongshan's image of the bird's path and his other comments about the path emphasize flying freely in the sky as it is, not striving to arrive at some destination. In his stories and through much of the history of the Caodong and Sōtō lineage, and still, the perspective prevails of the path starting on the top of the mountain. Perhaps some may also arrive back on the peak, again and again. But from the viewpoint of sudden awakening, suchness is omnipresent and can ever be realized immediately. Though dramatic experiences of this reality are not the point of practice, such realization is not trivial.

In another story in the *Recorded Sayings*, a monk demonstrates the subtlety of realization of suchness that Dongshan encourages. This unnamed monk has incorporated the ultimate in his own experience and engages in appropriate expression to confirm it with Dongshan.

Dongshan asked the monk, "Where have you come from?" and the monk responded, "From wandering in the mountains." Dongshan asked, "Did you reach the peak?" and the monk said, "Yes."

Dongshan asked if there was anyone on the peak. The monk replied, "No, there was not."

Dongshan said, "If so, then you did not reach the peak."

Here Dongshan indicates that if nobody was there, then neither was the monk, by definition. If this peak experience was true emptiness, in which not a thing exists, then neither could this monk exist there.

But the indomitable monk replied clearly, "If I did not reach the peak, how could I have known there was no one there?"

After this revelation, Dongshan asked why this monk had not remained on the mountaintop, and the monk replied honestly that he would have been so inclined, but there was someone from the West, probably referring to the Buddha or Bodhidharma, who would not have approved. Dongshan then praised the monk, saying, "I had wondered about this fellow."[1]

When Dongshan asked if there was anyone up on the peak, the monk said, "No, there was not." At its apex, reality can be described as not a single thing with no person existent there. A fascinating relevant story featured in the *Book of Serenity*, case 32, concerns Dongshan's contemporary Yangshan (born the same year), whose gazing at the moon was discussed in chapter 3. Yangshan once requested a monk to reverse his thought to think of the thinking mind, a fundamental meditation instruction. Yangshan then asked if there were many things there. The monk said, "When I get here, I don't see any existence at all." Although the commentary to the case lavishly praises the attainment of this monk, in the case itself Yangshan responds, "This is right for the stage of faith, but not yet right for the stage of person."[2] True practice necessarily goes beyond reaching the mountaintop.

Returning to the story of Dongshan and the monk who had reached the peak, Dongshan said if nobody was there, then neither was the monk. But the monk replied, "If I did not reach the peak, how could I have known there was no one there?" This is a true person. He did not hesitate or fade away but indicated that he was indeed present as a witness to the space without a blade of grass and without heat or cold. His presence and response demonstrate the subtlety of Dongshan's teaching of suchness. His engagement with the ultimate aspect of the suchness of the phenomenal world of causes and conditions through his own experience beyond conditioning was verified in his "speaking a little" with Dongshan. The monk also understood that the buddhas do not approve of settling in on some peaceful mountaintop. The bodhisattva path requires not remaining devotedly immersed in nirvāṇa, but taking personal responsibility and returning from the peak to share the awareness from this experience.

There is a provocative paradox in the monk's response "If I did not reach the peak, how could I have known there was no one there?" This paradox is reminiscent of the enigma in Dongshan's response to the monk who inquired about Yunyan's "Just this is it," as discussed in chapter 2. Dongshan was asked if Yunyan himself knew "Just this is it." Dongshan responded in part, that if Yunyan knew "just this," then "How could he be willing to say it?" If one sees suchness, how could there be any way to really say anything about it? If one truly reaches the peak, how could he or she actually exist there? But how could we know that without a reliable witness?

One of Dongshan's principal disciples, and the successor of Dongshan whose lineage was transmitted to Japan and still survives today, was Yunju Daoying (d. 902; Jpn.: Ungo Dōyō). Yunju and his teaching about suchness will be the focus of chapter 9. Once Dongshan asked Yunju where he had been, and he replied that he had been walking in the mountains. When Dongshan asked if he had found a mountain to reside on, Yunju said categorically that none was suitable for residing. Dongshan inquired if Yunju had visited all of the mountains in the country, but Yunju said he had not.

Dongshan commented that Yunju "must have found an entry path."

Yunju proclaimed emphatically, "No, there is no path."

Dongshan said, "If there is no path, I wonder how you have come to lay eyes on this old monk."

Then Yunju replied, "If there were a path, then a mountain would stand between us." Dongshan approved this, saying that henceforth not even ten thousand people could hold down Yunju.[3]

The very idea of a path implies some separation, and that some distance in space or time needs to be traversed to get to a particular destination. Yunju thus disdains any path and affirms his present communion with Dongshan. Though Yunju is not Dongshan, Dongshan actually is him, with no need to travel to some meeting place somewhere else. With any sequential path of progress, implying separation from some goal, one can never be fully present in this, the current situation. Of course, practice does involve transformation. And becoming familiar with one's tendencies based on the three karmic poisons of grasping, hatred, and confusion and thereby not being obstructed by them is a necessary part of awakening practice. But for Yunju, and Dongshan, some sequential systematized scheme of attainment necessarily implies separation from suchness.

Krishnamurti's Pathless Truth

A modern example of resisting all expressions of paths to the ultimate comes from the Indian sage Jiddu Krishnamurti (1895–1986). He was acclaimed in his early teens as an exalted spiritual figure by the Theosophical Society, a dedicated British occultist group highly influenced by Indian spirituality. They named the youth to become the leader of their worldwide Order of the Star of the East. But as a result of a series of mystical experiences, in 1929 Krishnamurti completely disbanded the order of which he was head. In his speech dissolving the order, "Truth Is a Pathless Land," he said, "I maintain that Truth is a pathless land, and you cannot approach it by any path whatsoever, by any religion, by any sect. That is my point of view, and I adhere to that absolutely and unconditionally. Truth, being limitless, unconditioned, unapproachable by any path whatsoever, cannot be organized."[4] Krishnamurti throughout his long life thereafter continued presenting insightful and incisive expressions of reality but adamantly challenged any systemic or institutional programs for achieving it.

Krishnamurti's approach to pathless suchness in his 1929 speech perhaps varies somewhat from that of Dongshan and Yunju. He does emphasize the need to reach the peak, although the monk conversing with Dongshan in the initial story above also needed to reach the peak. Krishnamurti said, "You cannot bring the mountain-top to the valley. If you would attain to the mountain-top you must pass through the valley, climb the steeps, unafraid of the danger-ous precipices." Dongshan and Yunju were concerned with how to convey their awareness of suchness and had disciples who founded practice lineages. Krishnamurti also traveled and spoke to many about his understanding, but he refused all followers. In the 1929 speech he said, "Because I am free, unconditioned, whole, not the part, not the relative, but the whole Truth that is eternal, I desire those, who seek to understand me, to be free, not to follow me, not to make out of me a cage which will become a religion, a sect. Rather should they be free from all fears—from the fear of religion, from the fear of salvation, from the fear of spirituality, from the fear of love, from the fear of death, from the fear of life itself." Here Krishnamurti may present a modern lens with which to compare and consider Dongshan's radical approach to suchness.

Starkness at the Top

The sudden awakening often spoken of in Zen implies the starkness at the top of the mountain. Suchness is not created or mediated by some intricate understanding or meditative accomplishment but actually is simply this immediate present reality. Sudden awaken-ing is not about suddenly obtaining some flashy experience in the future, after which one becomes an enlightened person. Certainly, however, realization of suchness, of the fullness, tenderness, and fragility of reality, may sometimes arise quite abruptly.

Dongshan's stories imply starting practice at the top, like the generations of nobility of the white rabbit, despite any temporary impoverishment. The traditional teaching known in Sanskrit as *bodhicitta*, or awakening mind, often is used to refer to the first thought of enlightenment. Paul Williams says, "*Bodhicitta* results from deep compassion for the suffering of others.... Truly generating this deep compassion and the resultant *bodhicitta* is a completely life-transforming experience; one ceases to be an ordinary being and becomes a 'Son or Daughter of the Buddhas.'"[5] In some mysterious way the first impulse toward awakening practice and caring about the quality of one's own and the world's being encompasses all of awakening. And yet this awareness calls out for endless development and unfolding expression. When you realize you are on the mountaintop, how do you proceed? As Yunyan told Dongshan, "You are now in charge of this great matter; you must be most thoroughgoing."

Our culture takes as axiomatic that it is "lonely at the top." In societal contexts this refers to those who are most powerful or successful. As Randy Newman sings ironically, "You'd think I'd be happy / But I'm not / Everybody knows my name / But it's just a crazy game / Oh, it's lonely at the top."[6] Those at the peak of worldly power or fame may well feel estranged from the rest of humanity and from the paltriness of the common, ordinary world.

In Buddhist and other self-reflective traditions, loneliness at the top may apply to those on the pathless path of expressing peak awareness. For these adepts there are often few if any with whom to share the joys and challenges of such experience. A venerable genre of expressions of loneliness at the peak has been bequeathed by brilliant Zen hermit poets such as Hanshan (8th cent.) and the Sōtō monk Ryōkan (1758–1831), as well as numerous other East Asian poets. Though reclusive, Ryōkan was friendly and loved to play with village children. But he also expressed a sense of loneliness. With spiritual insight, he writes, "In reality, / as in dreams, / I expect no visitor— / but old age / keeps calling."[7]

Filling in the Pathways

The meditation practice that expresses and enacts the awareness of the peak of suchness was especially articulated in the Dongshan lineage by later teachers such as Hongzhi and Dōgen. This practice can be described as objectless meditation. Focused on suchness itself, and whatever arises in awareness from suchness, this meditation does not concentrate on particular objects or limited objectives. Many traditional Buddhist and other meditation programs do involve focusing on a great variety of concentration objects; Buddhist literature includes libraries full of instructions about meditative objects and techniques. But the direct apprehension of suchness is objectless and open, spacious and panoramic in scope.

In most Zen and other Buddhist meditation, this objectless meditation is included, but only at a very exalted stage. A master of the Tibetan Gelukpa school, the tradition led by His Holiness the Dalai Lama, was very surprised to hear about the objectless meditation practice of a Western Sōtō temple when visiting there. Gelukpa monks are required to study for many years before attempting such practice.[8]

Even starting from the mountaintop, most practitioners eventually engage in practices that fill in the pathways from below to the peak of suchness. Often when the mind is groggy, or drifting along amid thoughts and feelings, it is helpful and settling to focus on particular objects for a while. And practically speaking, meditation involving objects, such as breathing, sound, phrases from the teachings or koans, or recitation of mantras, may be very useful for some students to approach suchness or return to it. Practitioners of suchness may naturally learn more limited practices just to help share such awareness with others who would benefit from these practices.

From the perspective of objectless meditation and suchness, it is perfectly fine to indulge in more limited meditation on objects, including stages of progress and attainment, as long as one does not get fooled or caught by such programs. With the background of suchness one need not become attached to a particular object or technique as the point of practice, or be obsessed with attaining some partial goal or objective. One may even joyfully engage with such objects and stages as the awakened play and background adornments of the practice of suchness. Particular practices are the beneficial, practical expressions of the ultimate truth of suchness within the limited phenomenal world. The willingness of Dongshan, as depicted in his *Recorded Sayings*, to engage with stages of progression appears in one of his descriptions of the five degrees, to be discussed in the final chapter.

Tenshin Reb Anderson describes such limited practices as the activity of the *nirmāṇakāya*, or manifestation body of Buddha, incarnated in historical human times. The reality body, or *dharmakāya* Buddha, whose presence is equivalent to the entire universe, on the other hand, engages in stageless activity while immersed in suchness.[9] Both aspects are connected and are among the three bodies of Buddha, to be discussed further in chapter 10 in relation to another Dongshan dialogue.

Overcoming Emptiness

Bodhisattvas recognize and investigate emptiness, the insubstantiality of all things, and realize that all beings are empty of inherent, unchanging identity. This awareness supports nonattachment, release from obsessions and craving, which can foster great peacefulness. But then bodhisattvas overcome attachment to emptiness, as well. Masters of emptiness teaching warn that the most dangerous attachment is exactly the attachment to emptiness or nonattachment itself, and to the bliss of ultimate awareness that may arise with realization of emptiness. Thus, the monk who told Dongshan that he had been to the mountaintop confessed that his inclination or desire was to remain and enjoy this realm. However, he heard the call of the ancestral teachers that he return and express this experience in the lowlands.

This dynamic of the shifting awareness of reality in terms of mountaintops, and entire mountains, was famously expressed by Qingyuan Weixin (9th cent.; Jpn.: Seigen Ishin):

> Thirty years ago, before I practiced Chan, I saw that mountains are mountains, and rivers are rivers. However, after having achieved intimate knowledge and having gotten a way in, I saw that mountains are not mountains, and rivers are not rivers. But now that I have found rest, as before I see mountains as mountains, and rivers as rivers.[10]

Before engaging with suchness beyond fabricated categories, one sees only the conventional, material view of mountains, rivers, and the phenomenal order. Once immersed in the mystery of the deeper reality of emptiness, mountains, rivers, and all things are no longer merely their superficial appearance. Mountains are no longer just mountains but fields of wonder and dedication, acutely interdependent with all beings. But after having fully engaged mountains and rivers in their suchness, one appreciates mountains and rivers as simply mountains and rivers, wondrous as they are in their stark reality.

Qingyuan's discernment was expressed more concisely, and perhaps more eloquently, by the Scottish mystic songwriter Donovan, when he sang, "First there is a mountain, then there is no mountain, then there is." Donovan says this song arose from his meditation practice, fusing his interest in Zen with Caribbean music.[11] This old saying reveals that even a mountain has no fixed mountain identity, but then transcends its own emptiness to realize a mountainous stage of personhood. Donovan's song adds two separate introductory lines as evocative, illuminating metaphors for the mountain's surpassing of limited self. "The lock upon my garden gate's a snail, that's what it is" exposes the limitation of our conventional perception of the mountain. For the revelation of the total glory of the realized mountain, Donovan sings, "The caterpillar sheds his skin to find a butterfly within. First there is a mountain, then there is no mountain, then there is."

Mountains Constantly Walking

Dongshan came to his teacher Yunyan through his question about whether nonsentient beings express the Dharma. How mountains provide teaching is an ongoing topic in the Dongshan lineage. With the initial conventional view of mountains as mountains, one might assume that the top of the mountain is the ultimate, supreme, fixed state. One might also imagine suchness itself as steady and unchanging. However, a Dharma descendant of Dongshan, Furong Daokai (1043–1118; Jpn.: Fuyo Dōkai), who was also known for reinvigorating Caodong monastic standards, once proclaimed that green mountains are constantly walking. Mountains may seem the very epitome of unmoving permanence. How can they be constantly walking?

Dōgen focused on Furong's saying in one of the most memorable essays in his *Shōbōgenzō* collection, "Sansuikyō" ("The Mountains and Water Sutra"). Among Dōgen's many writings, this is the only one he designates as a sutra, equal to the words of Buddha himself. This long essay treats many aspects of mountains, water, and walking and reveals the limitations of usual human perceptions about all three. Among Dōgen's comments:

> Though the walking of the green mountains is fast as wind and even faster, people in the mountains are unaware, uncognizant . . . . People who do not have the eyes to see the mountains do not notice, do not know, they do not see, do not hear. . . . If one knew one's own walking, one would know the walking of the green mountains. The green mountains are not animate; not inanimate; the self is not animate; not inanimate. One should not doubt this walking of the green mountains.[12]

One point is simply that humans cannot fully see the mountains, especially when they are in the mountains. In this essay Dōgen makes this point especially clear in terms of water. Certainly people see water differently than do fish, for whom water is simply the atmosphere; they would drown outside water, whereas we drown in the water. Dōgen poetically adds talk of how dragons see water and how some beings see water as pavilions or as jewels.

Mountains walking might be seen via geological time, wider than our usual sense of time span. We can readily understand that over geological time some mountains are older, like the Appalachians, or younger like the Himalayas, and mountains may erupt in volcanoes or settle, shifting over time. But Dōgen also talks about not knowing walking itself. The Chinese character for *walking* also means "conduct." So the walking of the green mountains, or of people, also refers to how they conduct or perform their own way of being. To really see how to conduct ourselves, Dōgen suggests we study the present performance of the upright mountains.

This leads back to Dongshan's fundamental question of how nonsentient, inanimate beings express the Dharma. And Dōgen proclaims that neither the mountains nor the self is caught in being either animate or inanimate. Our usual sense of consciousness and of life itself is challenged here. In the realm of suchness, all beings are alive. This certainly bears not only on how the teaching may be conveyed, but also on our deep interrelationship with the entirety of our phenomenal environment. "Mountains and water" as a compound in Chinese and Japanese simply means "landscape," so the whole natural world is implicated in this deep interconnectedness. Indigenous peoples around our planet see the world as alive, and even conscious. Some peoples—for example, the Native American Cheyenne—believe rocks have consciousness. Though this must certainly be a different order and manner of consciousness than our own, if you look at the rocks in some Japanese gardens, some have obviously been through a lot.

In the "Mountains and Water Sutra" essay, Dōgen says, "Although mountains belong to the nation, mountains belong to people who love them. When mountains love their master, such a virtuous sage or wise person enters the mountains."[13] Thus, the relationship of mountains with people dedicated to exploring suchness is deep and intimate. Such intimacy is required to fully enter the mountains and appreciate their walking. The suchness at the top of the mountain is not necessarily evident. Study of suchness involves studying the complexity of how the present suchness appears to be hidden from us. With his characteristic complex wordplay, Dōgen notes near the end of the essay,

> There are mountains concealed in jewels, there are mountains concealed in marshes, there are mountains concealed in the sky, there are mountains concealed in mountains. There is study which conceals mountains in concealment.
>
> An ancient Buddha said, "Mountains are mountains, waters are waters." This saying does not say that "mountains" are mountains; it says mountains are mountains. . . . If you investigate the mountains, that is meditation in the mountains.[14]

Awareness of how mountains are mountains, or not, is the practice of suchness of people who love mountains. Maybe it is not necessary to reach the peak of suchness, but in just enjoying the walkways here and there around the sides of the mountains, suchness is right there, as well. This suchness applies to the walking performed by the entire landscape.

Zen talk of mountains and rivers, and of green mountains walking, fits well in the terrain of Dongshan's China, in Japan, and in California, where I mostly trained. But now that I teach in the heartland of Chicago, I will add that as well as green mountains, green prairies and great lakes are constantly walking. The skyscrapers and avenues, too, are constantly walking, or sometimes driving along. And suchness is ever available, whether on the mountaintop, at the foot of the mountain, by the side of a lake, or out on a prairie, and even on a busy street corner.

CHAPTER NINE

A Person of Suchness

Already Such a Person

The wandering in the mountains of Yunju Daoying, and his declaration that there is no path, was discussed in the previous chapter. While Dongshan had many prominent disciples, none other is included in more than three anecdotes in his *Recorded Sayings*, and only one other appears in as many as three stories. But Yunju is featured with Dongshan in thirteen accounts. Although the actual history is obscure, it seems that only Yunju's lineage survived more than a few generations.[1] Further, it was Yunju's lineage that was transmitted to Japan by Dōgen, and which survives today.

Yunju once proclaimed, "If you want such a thing, you must be such a person. Already being such a person, why trouble about such a thing?" The first sentence of this utterance also might be read, "If you want suchness, you must be a person of suchness." This important teaching about suchness informs the whole Dongshan lineage and its practice of suchness. The fuller quote includes "One who has comprehended has a mind like a fan in winter, has a mouth growing moldy (from disuse). This is not something you force—it is naturally so. If you want to attain such a thing, you must be such a person. Since you are such a person, why trouble about such a thing."[2] When the present reality of suchness is realized, the discriminating mind and the expounding mouth need not be employed, like a fan in winter or a moldy tongue. Then a person of suchness lets go of all striving, with no need to deliberate via thought or speech about how to proceed. Engaging such a situation, one naturally just responds, with nothing to force or worry about. Still, we may wonder about this quality of natural response and function while fully enacting suchness.

Dōgen's Comments on Yunju's Suchness

Dōgen discussed Yunju's statement a number of times, and his comments illuminate the practice of suchness conveyed by Dongshan. In one of Dōgen's earliest writings, "Fukanzazengi" ("Universally Recommended Instructions for Zazen"), he cites Yunju's saying. Dōgen states, "Put aside the intellectual practice of investigating words and chasing phrases and learn to take the backward step that turns the light and shines it inward. Body and mind of themselves will drop away, and your original face will manifest. If you want to attain suchness, practice suchness immediately."[3] Here is a distillation of the practice that leads to Yunju's person of suchness, although Dōgen's encouragement to "practice suchness immediately" is a somewhat more active expression of Yunju's "be such a person." Body and mind dropped away is an expression Dōgen uses commonly for meditation praxis, and also for complete awakening, perhaps akin to Yunju's mind like a fan in winter and mouth grown moldy. This is the pristine original face of suchness, discussed previously in chapter 7 on the bird's path.

In the essay "Immo" ("Suchness") in his *Shōbōgenzō*, Dōgen elaborates at great length on suchness, starting with Yunju's words "If you want such a thing, you must be such a person. Already being such a person, why trouble about such a thing?" The initial section makes a significant point about the nature of the person of suchness, albeit in Dōgen's characteristically intricate and challenging prose.[4] He says that Yunju's statement means that "one who aspires to experience thusness is immediately a person of thusness."[5] ("Thusness" or "thus" is used interchangeably with "suchness" or "such" in English.) Dōgen emphasizes Yunju's implied point that simply the interest and aspiration to realize suchness is itself veri-fication of the reality of suchness. Dōgen proclaims that the entire phenomenal world is just a small portion of unsurpassable enlight-enment. We know suchness exists because the self is not limited to body and mind, and is constantly passing along. Suchness is dy-namic and active, not at all static. Dōgen says:

> Life is borne along by the passage of time, hardly to be kept for even a moment. Rosy cheeks have gone away somewhere—as they vanish, there are no traces. When we look carefully, there are many things gone which we can never see again. The red heart doesn't stay either—it comes and goes bit by bit.[6]

Dōgen adds that this truth has nothing to do with the realm of self or egoism. A person of suchness is spontaneously inspired to seek for suchness. This invokes the bodhicitta, or mind of enlighten-ment, mentioned in the previous chapter, which somehow arises from suchness itself and verifies suchness. One so inspired by such-ness "gives up what they had hitherto been fascinated with" and seeks to realize something fresh, exactly because they are such a person. "We know one is such a person because one wants to attain such a thing."[7] Already being such a person, as Yunju says, there is no need to trouble about suchness, even though it may seem strange or surprising. Suchness cannot be measured or assessed in terms of usual phenomena or principles, or even in terms of buddhas.

In the rest of the essay, Dōgen discusses several other evocative stories from Indian and Chinese Buddhist lore that relate to such-ness. I will mention one more, which involves Shitou and his suc-cessor, Yaoshan. Yaoshan was a lecturer who had mastered all the Buddhist canonical teachings. But he heard that the Chan people pointed directly at the mind to become buddhas, so he journeyed to sincerely inquire about this from Shitou. Shitou responded to Yaoshan, "Suchness is ungraspable, and it cannot be grasped beyond suchness. As such or non-such, it cannot be grasped at all. What about you?" Dōgen comments that suchness should be studied in nongrasping, and one may inquire into ungraspability within suchness. Suchness is the realization of ungraspability as such.[8]

This suchness that Yunju celebrates as such a person, and which is a crux of Dongshan's teaching, is elusive and ultimately ungraspable, even if one need not trouble about it. Yunyan instructed Dongshan that it is just this. Just this is simple and direct, nothing to make a fuss about. And yet actually engaging in the practice of just this suchness is a dynamic and subtle affair.

No Such Thing as Suchness, The Ten Suchnesses, and Other Such Teachings

While discussing Dōgen's writing *Shōbōgenzō* "Immo," the scholar Thomas Kasulis translates the particular term used by Dōgen, *immo*, as adverbial—literally, "being such (as it is)." He adds, "This term is often improperly construed substantially and metaphysically as 'Suchness.' *Immo*, though, is not a thing; it is a *way* things are experienced."[9] As discussed in the introduction, "suchness" is not actually an entity but a convenient designation for a way of seeing reality, just as with "emptiness." The danger of designating or reifying suchness or emptiness as nouns or objects is that practitioners might imagine they could grasp or attain them. Shitou in his statement above and Dōgen in his comments emphasize the ungraspability of suchness. And yet, being such a person, why trouble about such a thing?

While from the point of view of ultimate reality there may be no such thing as suchness, this way of speaking does go back to the Sanskrit category *tathatā*, and it became a significant subject of East Asian Buddhist discourse. Chapter 2 of the Lotus Sutra, a foundational scripture in East Asian Buddhism, refers to ten suchnesses, or ten reality aspects. These can also be translated as ten such qualities. This list of ten appears right after the sutra states that only buddhas, or a buddha together with a buddha, can fathom the depths of reality. Leon Hurvitz, in his respected academic translation, uses the word *suchness* in his list: "the suchness of the dharmas, the suchness of their marks, the suchness of their nature, the suchness of their substance, the suchness of their powers, the suchness of their functions, the suchness of their causes, the suchness of their conditions, the suchness of their effects, the suchness of their retributions, and the absolute identity of their beginning and end."[10] Gene Reeves in his excellent modern translation manages to render this list without designating anything as a suchness: "Every existing thing has such characteristics, such a nature, such an embodiment, such powers, such actions, such causes, such conditions, such effects, such rewards and retributions, and yet such a complete fundamental coherence."[11]

The variance between the two versions might reflect in part the difference between Sanskrit and Chinese. In his translation, Hurvitz references the original Sanskrit Lotus Sutra along with the Chinese. Unlike the common Chinese term used for *such*, the Sanskrit word *tathatā* is definitely a noun. But in the generally accepted Chinese rendition from the great translator Kumārajīva (344–413), the character used is read as an adjective.[12] However, in that particular passage the list of ten such things is completely omitted in the extant Sanskrit versions.[13]

This list of ten suchnesses or ten reality aspects, and various other theoretical doctrines concerning suchness, became important in the philosophy of the Chinese Tiantai school. Foundational to Chinese Buddhism before Dongshan and the Chan movement, Tiantai was originated by the brilliant Zhiyi (538–97), who creatively synthesized all Mahāyāna teachings with the Lotus Sutra as preeminent. Zhiyi cited as the textual basis for his system that integrated all Buddhist teachings exactly the Lotus Sutra passage on the ten suchnesses.[14] Later, during Dongshan's lifetime, Tiantai was transmitted to Japan as the Tendai school. Tendai was influential to all later Japanese Buddhism, including Sōtō, formally descended from Dongshan, as Dōgen and many of his leading disciples were previously Tendai monks.

The great Chinese Huayan patriarch Fazang, mentioned in chapter 1, discussed two major aspects of suchness, a suchness that is absolute or unchanging, and also suchness shifting to accord with phenomenal conditions.[15] Fazang and Huayan teaching were important precursors for Shitou, Dongshan, and Caodong/Sōtō philosophy. But Fazang was also influential for Japanese Tendai founder Saichō (767–822), who studied in China with Tiantai masters informed by Huayan as well as Tiantai teachings. Saichō agreed with Fazang that suchness has a dynamic as well as a calm, inactive aspect, and that in its dynamic quality suchness expresses itself through all phenomena, including providing the capacity for realization.[16] This was important in the view of Buddha nature as present in nonsentient beings, as discussed in chapter 1.

Saichō went beyond Huayan or Tiantai to state a preference for the dynamic aspect of suchness expressed as the phenomenal world, which Jacqueline Stone, a leading scholar of Japanese medieval Buddhism, sees as representing "a crucial step toward the profound valorization of empirical reality found in medieval Tendai."[17] This reflects an aesthetic preference of much of Japanese culture and spirituality for valuing suchness in the phenomenal and ephemeral world, rather than in its transcendence. In terms of the Dongshan story of seeking a place with no grass for ten thousand miles, this favors appreciating the grass present in every step, or even before going out the gate.

In a more problematic example of the application of suchness teaching, a twelfth-century Tendai text called *Shinnyo kan* (*The Contemplation of Suchness*) discusses the immediate realization of buddhahood that is available by simply awakening to the suchness of universal reality.[18] "If you think that suchness, which pervades the dharma realm, is your own person, you are at once equivalent to the dharma realm. . . . Because one contemplates suchness, one can quickly realize even buddhahood."[19] This text claims that all worldly phenomena from insentient beings to worldly passions are none other than suchness and enlightenment, and that the Lotus Sutra teaches that the bodies and minds of all living beings are precisely suchness.[20] Simply this realization is said to transform ordinary life into awakening.

Dōgen and other Japanese Zen teachers strongly criticized this kind of perspective as extreme for negating the need for actual practice and for at least implying dismissal of ethical or beneficial conduct. Clearly, the quality of suchness and its practice was a significant and sometimes contested concern in various East Asian Buddhist realms beyond Dongshan and his lineage. In accord with Dōgen, certainly Dongshan himself, and most of his lineage, did not sanction abandoning active practice or bodhisattva ethics. However, the criticism leveled against some of Hongzhi's successors during the Song period by Dahui and his followers was exactly that their practice was quietist or passive. While complacency is certainly an ever-present hazard for all long-time meditative practitioners, meditatively induced passivity was clearly not true of the teaching of Hongzhi himself.[21]

Can You Say Such a Thing?

Returning to Yunju, Dōgen refers to Yunju's statement of the person of suchness numbers of times in his writings, including various instances in *Eihei Kōroku*. In a talk therein from 1241, Dōgen begins,

> Studying the way has been difficult to accomplish for a thousand ages. How difficult is this? Ordinary people cannot be compared to the seven wise and seven holy ones. The ten holy and three wise ones cannot see the great way of all buddhas, even in a dream. Seeing in this way, one [Yunju] immediately said, "If you want to attain such a thing, you should be such a person. Already being such a person, why worry about such a thing?"[22]

According to conventional views, ordinary people cannot compare to bodhisattvas at various advanced stages of development. Yet Yunju cuts through all these accomplishments with an encouragement to be a person of suchness, to be willing to stop and face your life as it is. It is okay to be the person you are, this body and mind, right now, in this inhale and this exhale. This is how all Buddhas are. Already being such a person, why worry about such a thing? Seen thus, at any moment, this matter of suchness is available. Just be present and actually face the situation of this body and mind, the reality of suchness present right now. Already just the fact that you are reading this indicates that you are a person of suchness. It takes a while to be willing to actively face ourselves and the world, and this situation. But by returning again and again and facing the wall and ourselves, we may have some sense of just this. It is hard to see, like trying to see our own eyeballs, but it is that close, and that available. Active practice is still important, however.

Dōgen adds,

> Can you say such a thing or not? If you can say this, you attain the skin and marrow. If you cannot say this, still you attain the skin and marrow. Put aside for now whether you can say this or not, and whether you attain the skin and marrow or not. How is this suchness? Vipaśyin Buddha early on kept this in mind, and up until now has not grasped this mystery.

Can you say such a thing or not, Dōgen asks. "If you can say this, you attain the skin and marrow" is a reference to the founder of Zen in China, Bodhidharma, who said to two of his disciples, you have my marrow, and you have my bones. Then he said to another, you have my skin. Dōgen emphasizes that it does not matter how deep is our experience of suchness, but simply, can you now say such a thing as being such a person, or seeing just this? Humans spend most of our time trying to get more of this, or less of that, trying to accomplish things. Life in the world is about that, even if aimed at wholesome things, such as becoming more highly developed spiritually. But suchness is always present, beyond personal ambitions. Even if you cannot say such a thing, Dōgen says that skin and marrow are already attained. And yet there is still the challenge: Can you say such a thing?

Vipaśyin Buddha, who is mentioned in the last sentence of the extract above, is the first of the mythological seven buddhas leading up to Śākyamuni Buddha, said to be buddhas of past ages. Śākyamuni is said to have studied in a previous life under the previous buddha before him. This lineage of buddhas represents the beginningless and endless ages of thoroughly awakened ones in the universe. But in the context of the suchness discussed here, even this immeasurably ancient Vipaśyin Buddha, described as still present, has not yet grasped the mystery of suchness.

Such a Practice

In another talk in *Eihei Kōroku*, Dōgen relates a story about Yunju that appears in Dongshan's *Recorded Sayings* and comments on it in terms of the active practice of such a person.[23] In the version Dōgen cites, "Dongshan said to the assembly, 'Who is this person who, even when among a thousand or ten thousand people, does not face a single person and does not turn his back on a single person?'" In the *Recorded Sayings* at this point Dongshan adds, "Now you tell me, what face does this person have?"

Thereupon, in both versions, Yunju left the assembly saying, "This person is going to the hall to practice."

Dongshan's question inquires about the active practice of the person of suchness in the world, amid the myriad people. Not facing a single person even while not turning his back on anyone, not being attached to anybody but also without abandoning anyone, is reminiscent of the line in the "Jewel Mirror Samādhi" verse "Turning away and touching are both wrong, for it is like a massive fire." This is sometimes referred to as being in the world but not of it, and echoes going to the place where there is no grass for ten thousand miles. But it also concerns how to meet the sprouting grasses, how to engage other persons freely.

The response of Yunju, already such a person, is simply to go to the hall to practice. Presumably, this indicates Yunju is going to the monks' hall to meditate, since the rest of the assembly is in the Dharma hall with Dongshan, although perhaps Yunju may be going to chant or do some other practice activity. Yunju's response may seem like turning his back, or even seem antisocial, retreating to his meditation seat. Is he turning his back on the assembly, or on the thousand or ten thousand people in the world? Yunju might seem to be ignoring the suffering of beings in the world, but he is going to practice uprightly facing such reality, to give his attention to the question.

After relating the story from Dongshan's record, Dōgen comments further:

> When you can see like such [a person], then all the buddhas appear in the world, and this person goes to the hall; and then also eating gruel and rice, speaking one phrase, and coming from within the universal and particular are all this person going to the hall; and that you should be like such [a person] is also this person going to the hall. How could you say a phrase that is not practicing together with Yunju?
>
> *After a pause Dōgen said:* All of you monks, go to the hall and practice.[24]

"Coming from within the universal and particular" is a reference to the five degrees teaching initiated by Dongshan. "Universal and particular" could also be translated as "true and partial," "upright and inclined," or "ultimate and phenomenal."[25] Here this signifies that Yunju's practice had integrated the turning within of meditative awareness with engagement with the world, not turning his back on anybody right in his everyday activity with the other monks. Both ultimate suchness and the suchness in accord with changing phenomena are present for such a person in such a practice. After his comments, Dōgen simply asks his monks to go and continue such practice themselves.

CHAPTER TEN

Always Close

Beyond Categories

A brief dialogue appearing fairly late in the *Recorded Sayings* is included as case 98 in the *Book of Serenity* and also appears in the *Transmission of the Lamp* excerpt on Dongshan. A monk asked, "Which of the three bodies [of buddhas] does not fall into any category?" Dongshan responded, "I am always close to this."¹ The final "this" may refer to such a buddha body, but also to the whole question of not falling into any category, or not falling into a merely conditioned reality. The question might be interpreted as which body does not fall among the numerous discriminations of the phenomenal world. His simple response presents deep insights into Dongshan's perspective.

William Powell reads the *Recorded Sayings* version, the earliest extant version of which did not appear until some five hundred years after Hongzhi's citation in the *Book of Serenity*, as "I was once [or formerly] concerned with this." The variant reading basically differs only in putting Dongshan's concern or closeness in past tense, as opposed to being ever present, and abiding.² But Powell notes that he is using a more recent version of the text for "later" and that the earlier version of the *Recorded Sayings* says "always."³ So we may read Dongshan's concern about falling into categories, enumerations, or into the conditioned as ongoing.

The three bodies of buddhas in the monk's question is a teaching that was used to describe different aspects of what "buddha" came to signify in the development of the Mahāyāna. First, the *dharmakāya*, or reality body is the Buddha as the nature of reality itself, also seen as the body of the whole phenomenal universe, regarded from the ultimate viewpoint. Second is the *sāṃbhogakāya*, the reward or fruit of meditative practice, also known as the bliss body of Buddha, referring to buddhas who reside in meditative pure lands. One prominent example, among many, is the Buddha highly venerated in East Asian devotion, Amitābha (Ch.: Amitofo; Jpn.: Amida). The third body is the nirmāṇakāya, the incarnate or manifested body of a buddha appearing in history, such as Śākyamuni Buddha, the historical personage who lived in sixth or fifth century B.C.E. in what is now Northeastern India, although distant future and past *nirmāṇakāya* buddhas also emerge incarnated in history. This incarnate body of Buddha is the primary subject of early Buddhist views of Buddha. The teaching of three bodies, or at least that of the dharmakāya, appeared in early Perfection of Wisdom texts and later was articulated as three or sometimes more bodies in texts associated with the Cittamātra branch of teachings, also called Yogācāra.[4] As Mahāyāna sutras and commentaries proliferated, many more facets of Buddha were understood, as well as complex combinations of these three aspects.

This question asked of Dongshan is ironic. Even to distinguish bodies of Buddha is to create categories. One point of the question is the search for that which might go beyond categories, conditions, or limitations, like the place without a blade of grass for ten thousand miles. As we have seen, many of the stories about Dongshan involve realizing a practice that is not caught by stages of progress on some path of spiritual achievement, or dividing "just this" into any classifications of suchness. Dongshan's response successfully avoids grasping onto any category or explanation that might settle this monk's questioning. Yet Dongshan acknowledges the importance of the question by saying "I am always close to this," which might also be interpreted as "I am always intimate with this." The quality of not focusing on categories or stages of practice vibrates through Dongshan's teaching.

The Nation's Taboo

Wansong's commentary to this story in the *Book of Serenity* commences by reflecting on Dongshan's inclination to not respond directly. Wansong represents Dongshan's subtlety with other stories of indirectness by members of his colorful lineage. One of Dongshan's noted successors, Sushan Kuangren (837–909; Jpn.: Sozan Kyōnin), was a curious character known in part for his great intellect and meditative power. But Sushan was also very short and considered ugly and thus received the demeaning nickname "Uncle Dwarf." One story relates how Sushan used his small size to hide under Dongshan's chair and improperly listen in while he was giving Dharma transmission to Caoshan.[5] Despite Dongshan's displeasure on that occasion, Sushan eventually became one of his successors. In the commentary to the story about Dongshan and the buddha body beyond any category, Wansong relates how Sushan once asked Dongshan for a phrase that did not yet exist.[6] Dongshan refused, saying nobody would agree, and asked Sushan if he could approach it. Reflecting Dongshan's spirit, Sushan responded, "Still there's no way to avoid it." Like Dongshan, he remained close to the question.

Later a monk asked Caoshan about the meaning of Dongshan's "I am always close to this," and Caoshan would only reply, "If you want my head, cut it off and take it." Then the monk asked Xuefeng, who hit him with his staff and said, "I too have been to Dongshan." Xuefeng Yicun (822–908; Jpn.: Seppō Gison) was a prominent teacher with many disciples who was considered the successor of the forceful teacher Deshan, known for his shouts and blows. But Xuefeng had indeed been to Dongshan. Before he was a teacher, Xuefeng had worked in the kitchen at Dongshan's monastery, and once when he was washing rice, Dongshan asked if he sifted out the sand from the rice or the rice from the sand. When Xuefeng said he sifted them both out at the same time, Dongshan asked what the community would eat. Xuefeng melodramatically overturned the rice bowl. Dongshan said he should go find himself a more suitable teacher, which he apparently did with the less subtle Deshan.[7] But Xuefeng had experienced enough of Dongshan to know better than to respond with more than a hit of his staff to the monk asking about Dongshan's "always close to this."

Wansong brings up several other examples of descendants of Yaoshan, the teacher of Dongshan's teacher Yunyan, all of whom "brought it up indirectly, protecting taboo."[8] These include Jiufeng Daojian (9th cent.; Jpn.: Kyūhō Dōken), who said, "I'd rather bite off my tongue than violate the nation's taboo." Jiufeng was a student of Shishuang Qingzhu, a Dharma successor of Yunyan's brother Daowu. Shishuang's assembly sat so still that it was known as the dead stump hall. "The nation's taboo" refers to the traditional Chinese cultural taboo against saying the emperor's personal name. This image is used regularly in the Caodong lineage as a metaphor for the tradition's understood taboo against explicitly speaking of inner or ultimate truth. This directive goes back to Dongshan saying that he only valued his teacher because he didn't explain everything for him, and also saying that if Yunyan knew "just this," how could he be willing to say it? Each student must see for himself, without seeking from others.

The Technique to Help

Before presenting the main dialogue, Wansong introduces the case in the *Book of Serenity* with "Jiufeng, cutting off his tongue, made a sequel to Shishuang; Caoshan, cutting off his head, didn't turn away from Dongshan. The ancients' sayings were so subtle—where is the technique to help people?"[9] Here Wansong references two of his later exemplars of indirect response, akin to Dongshan. But he ends with the prime question, what does such subtle response and speaking indirectly have to do with relieving suffering and helping people awaken?

All of the enigmatic Chan imagery and rhetoric developed by Dongshan and the other Tang masters (or their later compilers or perhaps even formulators in the Song) arose squarely in the context of Mahāyāna Buddhism and bodhisattva practice. The point of the exploration of suchness, and its practice, is to help awaken people to liberation from conditioned, confused self-grasping. The subtle responses of Dongshan and his successors are not just some clever linguistic or mental game. How do the stories about Dongshan exemplify compassion, and how are they helpful?

From this perspective, we might look again at the monk asking the original question. He asks which body, or which quality of buddha or of awakening itself, does not merely fall into yet some further classification or worldly distinction. This questions how to find real freedom from the pain of worldly choices and striving. How might Dongshan's closeness be helpful to such a problem? Is such closeness a mere mechanical technique? And how is this particular issue, the body of Buddha that goes beyond categories, worthy of staying close with? We might also consider which issues in practice or the teaching would we each be willing to always be close with.

The Ultimate Familiarity

In his commentary to the case, following on the examples of those protecting the nation's taboo, Wansong cites a verse by Baoming Renyong (11th cent.; Jpn.: Honei Ninyu) commenting on this story about Dongshan's being always close to this question. Baoming wrote,

> This closeness is heartrending if you search outside;
> Why does ultimate familiarity seem like enmity?
> From beginning to end, the whole face has no color or shape,
> Still your head is asked for by Caoshan.[10]

"This closeness is heartrending if you search outside," says Baoming, as Dongshan had warned in his verse after seeing his reflection in the stream not to seek outside, "or you will be far estranged from self." If we get close to ourselves, or to our inner problem or truth, turning away or trying to evade the situation can be truly "heartrending." This is pointing to a kind of intimacy, or perhaps various kinds of intimacy, where we are vulnerable to having our hearts broken. Staying close, remaining present in the middle of uncertainty, discomfort, and vulnerability, requires a patience and a capacity that can be empowering if it is sustained. And yet the pain may not abate. Dongshan abides always close to this. As he says in the "Jewel Mirror Samādhi" about the practice of suchness, "Turning away and touching are both wrong, for it is like a massive fire."

In such intimacy, indeed "ultimate familiarity" may come to "seem like enmity." When we are truly close to someone, whether it is a spouse or romantic partner, or a child or parent, or a spiritual teacher, or a disciple, often we feel this tension. In any intimate relationship, the "other" may feel closer than oneself, and yet right in that intimacy we may feel enmity, a slightly more polite word for hostility or animosity. Such love-hate tension is all too human. Staying close is not easy, whomever our familiar.

In the context of Dongshan's teaching and the challenge of conveying the practice of suchness, certainly one focus of ultimate familiarity and this tender and troubling closeness is the engagement of the teacher-student relationship. Testing is apparent and often uncomfortable in Dongshan's encounter dialogues, going back to his questions to his teachers, and then to his instructions and examinations of his students. Both teacher and student must risk something, whether what we have is a failure to communicate in the present situation or a failure of the relationship itself. And yet sometimes the student matches or even surpasses the teacher. Sometimes the closeness just fits together, a true match, even when the process of meeting may seem like enmity.

The intimacy and ultimate familiarity in this story also applies to the study of the self. Even when not searching outside, we may feel as if we are caught somewhere outside ourselves. We often seek to avoid true closeness with that which is most true, or most troubling, about ourselves. Our individual karmic patterns of greed, anger, and confusion, and habits of grasping after some conditioned image of self, are deeply ingrained. But for the body of buddha that does not fall into any category at all, "the whole face has no color or shape," not a single identifying mark can be discerned. We might see through the vanity of our assessments of the face reflected back at us in the mirror. This deeper buddha nature beyond our stories of separate, isolated self, beset by categories and distinctions, may present a quality available when we are willing to risk true closeness and intimacy with that which goes beyond our limited characteristics. This closeness of Dongshan is about the nature of true intimacy itself. Such intimacy has its own value and helpfulness. What emerges when we are willing to simply stay close?

In his early song "All I Really Want to Do," Bob Dylan poses an alternative mode of ultimate familiarity that does not fall into categories. He sings,

I ain't lookin' to block you up
Shock or knock or lock you up
Analyze you, categorize you
Finalize you or advertise you

Then he presents his refrain as another option, "All I really want to do is, baby, be friends with you."[11]

Throughout the song Dylan simply presents an extended catalog of all the things he does *not* want to do, including not simplifying or classifying, and not wanting to select, dissect, inspect, or reject the person he really just wants to be friends with. This truly being friends suggests the closeness Dongshan also implies, whether it is with a student or teacher. The notion of the good spiritual friend, in Sanskrit *kalyāna mitra*, is indeed one traditional model for a teacher in Buddhism. But Dongshan's closeness and this simple friendship may also be with one's own deepest self, or even with Buddha. Staying close presents the challenge of how to become ultimately familiar, and become friends, with one's own sense of a limited self, even while seeing through all the attachments that lead children of Buddha to temporarily fall into poverty.

A Legacy from an Empty Pot

Hongzhi, the leading teacher in Dongshan's lineage in twelfth-century China, selected and arranged the cases and provided the main verse comments in what became the *Book of Serenity*. His verse for this story about Dongshan's closeness is particularly rich and evocative.

> Not entering the world,
> Not following conditions;
> In the emptiness of the pot of ages there's a family tradition.
> White duckweeds, breeze gentle—evening on an autumn river;
> An ancient embankment, the boat returns—a single stretch
>   of haze.[12]

The monk's question in this story invokes the unconditioned as a theme when he asks about not falling into categories or enumerations. Hongzhi begins, presumably describing Dongshan, with "Not entering the world, not following conditions." This not entering the world and its worldliness echoes Dongshan's calls to his students to go where there is no grass for ten thousand miles, or to find the place beyond hot or cold, or to follow the traceless bird's path. Dongshan repeatedly presents this challenge. This can only be based on some deep, meditative experience of suchness, of just this. His repeated challenges to his students reveal that he has somehow been able to convey some sense of this experience for them, as well. A feeling of wholeness and even purity is evident, but then, as Wansong asks, where is the technique to help people? Not following or being caught by conditions is to know there is one who is not busy, as Dongshan's teacher Yunyan expressed it. But just stepping outside the monastery gate, and even within the gates, the grasses and weeds of the world shoot up. Even so,

Dongshan has been pointing to a closeness or intimacy with one's own experience that allows familiarity with the one not busy. Moreover, as the examples presented by Wansong indicate, a whole lineage emerging from Yunyan and Dongshan has preserved and sustained this intimate engagement with suchness. From his vantage point nine generations after Dongshan, Hongzhi celebrates this living tradition in the next line of his verse, "In the emptiness of the pot of ages there's a family tradition," or "transmission," as the character used here is the one used for Dharma transmission. This empty pot of ages, or of a *kalpa* in Sanskrit, is a complex, stimulating image. Somehow from this empty food pot, a family tradition or legacy has been bequeathed, extending down over the generations.

One facet of this image is the difficulty of finding nourishment from a food pot that is literally empty. In a Buddhist context perhaps this pot is replete with emptiness. Hongzhi might be implying here that what sustains this transmission is the teaching of emptiness, clearly seeing the nonseparation and interconnectedness of all entities. While emptiness and suchness are flip sides of the same coin, Dongshan's teaching usually focuses on the more positive language of suchness. But both emptiness and suchness offer connection to the unconditioned, that which goes beyond categories and distinctions. The Chinese character for *empty* also means "space," so we might read this line as "In the spaciousness of the pot of kalpas there is a family tradition, or legacy." This family tradition celebrated by Hongzhi reflects the spaciousness opened up by the engagement with suchness. Dongshan's lineage is clearly encouraged in this story by the willingness to simply stay close to this question of going beyond categories.

This family legacy recalls the generations of nobility, whether or not temporarily fallen into poverty. How does one come to receive and renew the teaching of suchness and realize one's inheritance as a child of Buddha? Although Hongzhi's verse is set in autumn, in his *Eihei Kōroku* Dōgen cites this pot of ages twice in the context of springtime. He concludes a Dharma hall discourse from

1247 by saying, "Outside the window, plum blossoms open in secret, encompassing spring. [You] can catch the moon in the pot of ages in the sky."[13] In the context of catching the moon, these same three characters of the empty pot of ages are more aptly read as a kalpa pot in the sky, as "sky" is another meaning for the character for *empty* or *space*. This reading recalls an old Daoist fable about a venerable sage and healer who regularly returned home to his ancient vessel that contained a wondrous palace providing unending feasts. With this reference, Dōgen encourages the reading of this line from Hongzhi's verse as "In the pot of ages in the sky there's a family tradition." This pot of ages is also invoked with the image of the plum blossom, the first sign of spring in late winter, opening in secret, encompassing spring. This implies that Dongshan's family legacy may spring forth, again and again, from the stillness of the unconditioned and the immersion in suchness, becoming a container for the very moon in the sky.

Dōgen again raised this empty kalpa pot as looking toward the onset of spring, ending a verse on the occasion of the full moon day of the first month of 1252, "A single plum flower in the cold with fragrant heart blossoming, calls for the arising of spring in the emptiness of the pot of ages."[14] The renewal of a spiritual lineage, the meaning of Dongshan's ongoing practice of suchness, can occur only as it is conveyed anew in each new situation, in each age and new culture. Even as it revives within the world, it must go beyond the current fashions and conventions to some depth shared in the primal experience of those who commune with just this and gaze into its spacious vessel. Just then some new flower can blossom as such.

The Ancient Embankment

In the third line of his verse comment, Hongzhi sets an autumnal scene with "White duckweeds, breeze gentle, evening on an autumn river." In the dusk, white duckweed blossoms float on the surface of the stream, their drift depending on the sway of soft breezes, as well as the current. In such a scene of fading light and the year passing, sadness may be available, and yet it can be tinged with sweetness in memories of engagement of the way. Still, in Hongzhi's next line, the other shore is in sight: "An ancient embankment, the boat returns—a single stretch of haze." This other shore is the traditional, olden image for nirvāṇa, or salvation, in Buddhism. In the pre-Mahāyāna tradition, nirvāṇa, which literally means "cessation," was seen as a complete escape from rebirth into this conditioned, phenomenal world of striving. The yearning for relief from the suffering of the world is indeed primeval, predating Buddhism. But in the bodhisattva practice that is the context for Chan and Zen, one does not forsake the suffering beings in the world but remains to help all beings enter the path toward liberation. Nirvāṇa is seen as being upright and patiently helpful, staying close to the one not busy even while amid the world of conditions and confused beings. Dongshan encouraged his students to look for a place with no grass for ten thousand miles, even as he saw grasses sprouting right outside the gate and within it.

In Hongzhi's verse the boat returns. This vessel has visited the far bank many times before. I imagine a weary boatman poling the ferry across the river gladly, not at all for the first time. The bodhisattva carries others to the far shore yet again. How does it feel on this other shore, this liberation beyond conditions, though always close? In the hazy mist, a single line stretching out might simply denote a fleeting exhale in the chill evening air. Or perhaps this refers to the hazy lineage of transmission, the ephemeral family tradition sometimes barely surviving another generation. From Dongshan's efforts to remain close to what flows beyond categories emerges a way of seeing suchness with the ears, or perhaps with the soft touch on the skin of the cool haze of an autumn evening.

Somehow this family tradition continues to flower anew out of sometimes seemingly broken or at least cracked old pots, even today. In the twentieth century, Shunryū Suzuki was one of the descendants of the line of Dongshan and Dōgen who helped bring this family tradition to the West. Suzuki used to ask his students to find out "What is the most important thing?" Dongshan said he was always close to the body of Buddha that did not fall into any categories. How shall we each express that to which we are willing to remain always close?

CHAPTER ELEVEN

Caring for the One Not Ill

Dongshan's Passing

The story of Dongshan's passing away and a few intriguing pre-liminary dialogues appear in the *Recorded Sayings* and in the *Transmission of the Lamp*, and one of the dialogues is featured as case 94 in the *Book of Serenity*.[1] The basic story relates how Dongshan had been unwell. After some discussions he bathed, put on fresh robes, struck the bell, and announced his departure to the assembly. Sitting upright, he began to pass away, but his disciples wept loudly without cease. Dongshan opened his eyes and chastised them for lamenting and for attachment to life over death. He intentionally delayed his passing and arranged a "delusion banquet" to appease them. From one perspective, although Dongshan criticized their delusions, he still provided his students a feast with which to celebrate delusions.

Seven days later, after providing a festive last supper, he told the monks they "had made a great commotion over nothing" and asked that this time they not "make a noisy fuss."[2] Then he sat still and passed away. This story indicates Dongshan's ability to control the timing and manner of his own death and use it as a teaching.

The overall tone of the story might be taken as a hagiographic exaltation of Dongshan, and, again, we have no historical verification for these accounts. But there is a tradition of Chan and Zen monks dying intentionally, writing a verse, then dying sitting up, so we cannot simply discount this story. The narrative ends with the historical information that he passed away in the third lunar month of the year we know as 869, and that he was given the post-humous name Wuben (Awakening Source) and his stupa was designated "Wisdom Awakening."[3]

Yunju and the Uninterrupted Transmission

In a prelude to his passing, Dongshan asked a monk to take a message to his disciple Yunju and tell him that the transmission from Yunyan was about to be cut off. But Dongshan warned the messenger monk to stand back from Yunju while relaying this message.

However, when the monk arrived at Yunju and had just begun to speak, before he could finish, Yunju struck the monk.[4]

Perhaps Dongshan was testing his successor Yunju. If so, Yunju forcefully affirmed that the succession would continue. And indeed the transmission from Yunyan to Dongshan has continued to the present from Yunju. Or perhaps Dongshan and Yunju were together providing a teaching for the unnamed monk who visited Yunju.

A Worthless Name and the One Not Ill

When he was ready to pass away into nirvāṇa, Dongshan said to the assembly, "I have had a worthless name in this world. Who will remove it for me?" A novice stepped forward and asked Dongshan for his Dharma name. Dongshan responded that it had faded away.[5] One's worldly name indicates reputation or even fame in the world. It is also the fundamental signifier of identity and self. In nirvāṇa, and in death, there remains no individual self or status, nothing at all to grasp after. Dongshan was asking for release, and for permission from his students for the ultimate letting go of self. It took a novice monk to ask, "What name?" and free Dongshan. All names, reputation, status are finally so much dust.

Immediately thereafter in the *Recorded Sayings* and the *Lamp Transmission*, in the dialogue Hongzhi selected for case 94 in what became the *Book of Serenity*, another monk inquired of Dongshan, "You are ill, teacher, but is there anyone who is not ill?"

When Dongshan said there is, the monk asked, "Does the one who is not ill look after you?"

Dongshan responded, "I have the opportunity to look after him."

The monk asked, "How is it when you look after him?"

Dongshan said, "Then I see there is not any illness."[6]

We might assume that the one not ill would care for the one not well. But counterintuitively, Dongshan said that, although he was ill, he had the opportunity or responsibility to care for the one not ill. Dongshan's "one who is not ill" recalls Yunyan's "one who is not busy." In different ways, each may represent the ultimate unconditioned nature of reality. While body-mind is not at all separate, one not ill apparently emphasizes total physical well-being, health, or wholeness. The one not busy indicates more the side of awareness, no preoccupations but total mental presence, with attention given to just this. Even unwell, in his last fatal illness, Dongshan is looking after the one not ill, just as Yunyan remembered to know there was one not busy even while he was fully engaged in sweeping up the temple debris.

At the beginning of his comments to this dialogue in the *Book of Serenity* case, Wansong claims that before his passing Dongshan had only manifested "a slight illness" but then "everyone came to look in on him." He adds, "When the ancients were about to go, they frolicked in the realm of old age, sickness, and death." But Wansong rightly claims that Dongshan was unusual among them. This story is part of a customary genre concerning the manner in which Zen masters play with their upcoming deaths. There are many stories concerning teachers' sayings, activities, or death verses when about to pass away. Probably none could surpass in eccentricity the disciple of Mazu, Wutai Yinfeng (d. 9th cent.; Jpn.: Godai Impō), who, seeking to be unique, died while standing on his head.[7]

But the dying Dongshan turns the situation inside out by caring for the one who is well. Of course, awareness of eventual mortality always greatly assists full appreciation of our time of health and living. Dongshan's concluding statement is that when he looks after the one not ill, he does not see any illness at all. Wansong comments, "This is where everyday practice empowers you when you're dying."[8] The training in attending fully to awareness of life allows a calm awareness of death, we are told by teachers as they are preparing to die themselves. Then even death is not any illness, but an expression of the wholeness of life.

Diligent Practice in the Empty Realm

After this exchange about the one not ill, Dongshan recited this *gātha*, which might be taken as his death poem, as no later ones are given.

> Though the students are many, not one is enlightened:
> The mistake lies in pursuing the paths of others' tongues.
> If you want to be able to forget physical form and obliterate tracks,
> Work hard to diligently walk in the void.[9]

As mentioned in chapter 7 about the bird's path, Dongshan here says that none of his disciples are awakened, inasmuch as they still pursue some path described by others. Through such pursuits, seeking a path to some future destination, they have separated themselves from full presence and awareness in this life. In the last two lines, Dongshan suggests that to let go of the forms of this life and freely enter death, one must proceed and somehow practice sincerely even amid the emptiness beyond material forms. It was after reciting this gātha that he prepared to pass away, only to be forced to postpone the event for a week by his wailing disciples.

Life and Death and the Great Matter

The wooden sounding block hit with a mallet to signal meditation or other communal events in Zen monasteries is calligraphed with an inscription about life and death. A simple version reads, "Life and death is the great matter; don't waste time." A longer version includes two more lines, "Life and death are the great matter. Be watchful of your time. All is impermanent and passes swiftly away. Time waits for no one."[10]

I am not certain whether this wooden sounding block (*pan* in Chinese; *han* in Japanese) was used in Tang monasteries. But it was in use by the early Song, including this longer version of the verse inscribed on it:

> Let me respectfully remind you
> Life and death are of supreme importance.
> Time swiftly passes by
> And opportunity is lost.
> Each of us should strive to awaken.
> Awaken, take heed,
> Do not squander your life.

This verse and the custom of writing it on the *pan* reportedly goes back to monastic codes published in the early twelfth century and imported to Japan in the seventeenth century.[11]

Aside from this verse inscription, seen by all who visit Chan temples, the concern with seeing through the great matter of life and death is a central topic going back to the origins of Chan. For example, in chapter 7 it was recounted that the Chan Sixth Ancestor Huineng recommended that students see their original face before their parents were born. Considering life and death, and what precedes and follows life, is a strong encouragement to fully engage the practice of this life.

The Skin Bag

In his verse commentary on Dongshan's dialogue in case 94 of the *Book of Serenity*, Hongzhi does not speak about the one not ill, or the end of all illness. Rather, he discusses how life actually dries out and expires. He simply talks about the practice of dying:

Taking off the smelly skin bag,
Casting away the mass of red flesh;
Directly, the nose is straight,
Immediately, the skull is dry.
The old doctor doesn't see the indigestion from before—
The little one looks in on him, but it's hard to approach.
When the meadow streams are thin, the autumn ponds
    recede;
Where the white clouds end, the old mountains are cold.
You must cut off absolutely.
Don't be big-headed.
Evolving to the utmost effortlessness, he attains the state;
The lone stand-out is not in the same class as you.[12]

Wansong comments on Hongzhi's poem, citing direct references for several of the lines. "Taking off the smelly skin bag" refers to the "Song of the Grass Hut" by Shitou. That poem describes the space of practice using the metaphor of the teacher's small hermitage. It ends, "If you want to know the undying person in the hut, don't separate from this skin bag here and now."[13] In life the unconditioned is not separate from the phenomenal world. But for Hongzhi, Dongshan in passing away has gone beyond the undying, unconditioned person and dropped off his skin bag. Similarly cast off is the mass of red flesh, which refers to a famous story about Linji. Cited in *Book of Serenity* case 38, Linji said that within the mass of red flesh is a true person of no rank, always going in and out of the portals of your face.[14] But here, Wansong states, Hongzhi has us remove the mass of red flesh. Dongshan had seen there was no illness, but then he gave up the ghostly skin bag and fleshy mass. Death is just death.

"The skull is dry" refers to a story to be told in more detail in the next chapter about the "Jewel Mirror Samādhi." The provocative line in that poem, "The wooden man starts to sing; the stone woman gets up dancing," invokes life arising from stillness or seeming death. A teacher similarly once said, "A dragon sings in

a withered tree," and added that there was "an eyeball in a skull."
Dongshan's successor Caoshan later commented about this eyeball, "It doesn't dry up." But here, in relation to Dongshan's passing, Hongzhi simply says, "Immediately, the skull is dry." Instead
of a wooden man or stone woman springing to life, here a lively
dragon has leaped into stillness.

As to "the old doctor not seeing indigestion," Wansong comments that an old doctor becomes perceptive and skillful because
he seldom administers diagnoses or treatments. Wansong claims
this as the reason for Dongshan not seeing any illness. But perhaps
Dongshan sees something about the health and wholeness of the
world that is apparent only from the vantage point and advantage
of finality.

Hongzhi sees the autumn ponds recede and the old mountains
growing cold but insists, to Dongshan, or perhaps to all of us as we
fade away, "Don't be big-headed." The ultimate sickness is simply
this illusion of a separate, cherished "me" that we can spend our
time thinking about or protecting. The utmost effortlessness, the
final attainment, is simply letting go of this skin bag here and now.
Though this state awaits us all, right now we can still enjoy taking
care of the one not ill.

PART THREE   The Fivefold Suchness

CHAPTER TWELVE

The Jewel Mirror Samādhi

Background, and the Whole Poem

The "Jewel Mirror Samādhi" is a long teaching poem, one of a number of this genre in the Chan/Zen tradition. Like the five degrees in the chapter to follow, this text is certainly worthy of a full book-length commentary of its own. Here I offer only a brief commentary on each in the context of the whole teaching of Dongshan as presented in some of his key stories.[1] This poem is traditionally attributed to Dongshan, although in the *Recorded Sayings* Dongshan presents it to one of his main successors, Caoshan, and tells him that this teaching was secretly entrusted to Dongshan by his teacher Yunyan.[2] This may be a way of recognizing his teacher's inspiration, as there exists no other indication that the text itself was drafted by Yunyan. Of course, it is possible that aspects of the text's contents, or even many of its lines, were received from Yunyan during Dongshan's study with him.

From an academic scholarly perspective, this text is of questionable historical origin. It was said to have been transmitted orally from Dongshan's time, but no record of it appears until the early twelfth century. It was disseminated then by the scholar monk Juefan Huihong, and it has been described from an academic historical viewpoint as "different in style and character from the early Caodong records."[3] Nevertheless, since the early twelfth century the "Jewel Mirror Samādhi" has been studied in the Zen tradition as a work of Dongshan, and it does relate in various ways to issues of the study of suchness that appear in the stories about Dongshan previously discussed. Further, as will be discussed in the comments to the first line of the text below, if it was a text used in Caodong lineage teacher authorization, then reliable oral transmission even over centuries is not at all unreasonable.

The poem presents many suggestions about the reality of suchness and its teaching, and fairly cryptically incorporates the five degrees. The issues of the nature of suchness and how it is intimately transmitted that are the focus of this book are highlighted in the first line of the poem. Other featured themes include the relationship of teacher and student and the use of language in the process of conveying the teaching.

Several of the lines and images in the poem present challenging issues of translation and pose multiple possible interpretations. Often Chinese characters and compounds have numerous meanings, sometimes strikingly diverse. In the comments below I present significant or useful alternative interpretations, although I believe the main translation given here is meaningful and reasonable in the context of Dongshan's teaching. This is not necessarily only a matter of the meaning intended by Dongshan, or whoever originally composed this poem. As stated in the text itself, the meaning does not reside in the words, and yet suchness and its significance do respond to our own sincere spiritual inquiry. The images and metaphors herein are evocative, not didactic, and certainly multiple layers of implication and overtone may be suggested and informative.

The Chinese text is called in full the "Song of the Jewel Mirror Samādhi." Students thus occasionally ask if the poem originally had a tune or melody. I do not know; if so, it has long been lost. But it might be helpful to think of it as a song lyric, with its own rhythm and tones. Before commenting on groupings of the lines, I present here this song attributed to Dongshan in its entirety:

Song of the Jewel Mirror Samādhi
The Dharma of suchness is intimately transmitted by buddhas
    and ancestors;

Now you have it; preserve it well.
A silver bowl filled with snow; a heron hidden in the moon.
Taken as similar, they are not the same; not distinguished, their
places are known.
The meaning does not reside in the words, but a pivotal moment
brings it forth.
Move and you are trapped; miss and you fall into doubt and
vacillation.
Turning away and touching are both wrong, for it is like a
massive fire.
Just to portray it in literary form is to stain it with defilement.
In darkest night it is perfectly clear; in the light of dawn it is
hidden.
It is a standard for all things; its use removes all suffering.
Although it is not constructed, it is not beyond words.
Like facing a jewel mirror; form and reflection behold each other.
You are not it, but in truth it is you.
Like a newborn child, it is fully endowed with five aspects:
No going, no coming, no arising, no abiding;
"Baba wawa"—is anything said or not?
In the end it says nothing, for the words are not yet right.
In the illumination hexagram, inclined and upright interact,
Piled up they become three, the permutations make five,
Like the taste of the five-flavored herb, like the five-pronged vajra.
Wondrously embraced within the real, drumming and singing
begin together.
Penetrate the source and travel the pathways; embrace the
territory and treasure the roads.
You would do well to respect this; do not neglect it.
Natural and wondrous, it is not a matter of delusion or
enlightenment.
Within causes and conditions, time and season, it is serene and
illuminating.
So minute it enters where there is no gap, so vast it transcends
dimension.

A hairsbreadth's deviation, and you are out of tune.
Now there are sudden and gradual, in which teachings and
approaches arise.
When teachings and approaches are distinguished, each has its
standard.
Whether teachings and approaches are mastered or not, reality
constantly flows.
Outside still and inside trembling, like tethered colts or cowering
rats,
The ancient sages grieved for them, and offered them the dharma.
Led by their inverted views, they take black for white.
When inverted thinking stops, the affirming mind naturally
accords.
If you want to follow in the ancient tracks, please observe the
sages of the past.
One on the verge of realizing the Buddha Way contemplated a
tree for ten kalpas,
Like a battle-scarred tiger, like a horse with shanks gone gray.
Because some are common, jeweled tables and ornate robes;
Because some are wide-eyed, cats and white oxen.
With his archer's skill Yi hit the mark at a hundred paces,
But when arrows meet head-on, how could it be a matter of skill?
The wooden man starts to sing; the stone woman gets up
dancing.
It is not reached by feelings or consciousness, how could it involve
deliberation?
Ministers serve their lords, children obey their parents;
Not obeying is not filial, failure to serve is no help.
With practice hidden, function secretly, like a fool, like an idiot;
Just to do this continuously is called the master among masters.[4]

Along with suggestions about how to practice and convey the
teaching of suchness, the "Jewel Mirror Samādhi" introduces the
fivefold nature of the interaction between the universal and particular aspects of the truth, which is the topic of the five degree

teaching, the focus of the following chapter. This stimulating text includes many colorful images and references to Chinese cultural lore as well as to Buddhist traditions. The image of a jeweled or precious mirror implies that this text is about a samādhi, or meditative state, in which something precious about our self or the world is revealed when we look into it. Following are discussions of the lines grouped in sequence.

—

The Dharma of suchness is intimately transmitted by buddhas and ancestors;
Now you have it; preserve it well.

The "Jewel Mirror Samādhi" starts with the Dharma of suchness, and here *Dharma* can mean "reality" or "truth," and *suchness* itself is a way of seeing the nature of the present reality. *Dharma* also means "teaching," so this refers to the depths of reality, to teachings about this reality, and to how to engage it. This is what has been intimately and carefully transmitted and conveyed by all the buddhas and ancestral teachers. The poem says about the Dharma of suchness, "You now have it," with the admonition to "preserve it well." This expresses that the reality of suchness is not something that needs to be calculated or acquired. It is already present but needs to be personally discerned, realized, expressed, and carefully sustained.

The first two lines obviously echo Dongshan's parting from his teacher, as described in chapter 2, with Yunyan's teaching of suchness, "Just this is it," and then his follow-up, "You are now in charge of this great matter; you must be most thoroughgoing." An implication of preserving it well is to intimately transmit this Dharma of suchness to others. Although this is not in the *Recorded Sayings*, the version in the commentary to the *Book of Serenity* case 80 relates that Dongshan, when imparting the "Jewel Mirror Samādhi" to Caoshan, said, "Keep it well, and don't let it be cut off. Later, if you meet a true vessel of Dharma, only then should you pass it on. It should be kept hidden, not revealed in words—I think that if it's relegated to current conventions, it will be hard to contact people later."[5] If we credit that the "Jewel Mirror Samādhi" was used as a Dharma transmission document in the Caodong lineage, it would be easily understandable that it could have been orally transmitted reliably and unpublished for centuries. The poem is short enough to be readily memorized, and its importance as a transmission document would have made that a priority. Indeed, there are teachings about the five degrees, not included in this book, that are still part of Dharma transmission in the current Sōtō school.

However, at the point when the "Jewel Mirror Samādhi" became used as a communal chant in the Sōtō liturgy, the meaning of these first lines shifted somewhat. Regular chanting of the "Jewel Mirror Samādhi" was initiated by Menzan Zuihō (1683–1769). Menzan was a leader of a major Sōtō revival that featured Dōgen scholarship but also included five degrees commentary and Caodong study. Thereafter, not just Dongshan and his lineage of authorized personal successors, but in some subtle sense all who chant this poem "now have it" and implicitly receive the gift of suchness. The teachings are intimately transmitted so thoroughly by the buddhas and ancestors that our experience of suchness in this moment may be an encounter with them now, like Dongshan seeing Yunyan everywhere. Hopefully, it will not be relegated or dismissed by anyone as merely conventional poetry or philosophy. Some range of awareness of suchness may be a consequence of meditative practice. Thus, the poem suggests that all practitioners somehow preserve and care for whatever experience of suchness has been intimately conveyed from the practice and teaching.

The whole rest of this poem may be interpreted in terms of how it comments on this teaching or reality of suchness, on how it is intimately transmitted, and on how it may be watchfully preserved and carried forward. Many lines in the long poem refer to this teaching of suchness, the topic and theme of the poem, and elaborate on the meaning and function of suchness in various ways.

A silver bowl filled with snow; a heron hidden in the moon.
Taken as similar, they are not the same; not distinguished, their
places are known.

The issue of sameness and difference addressed here recalls the teaching poem by Dongshan's eighth-century predecessor Shitou, "The Harmony of Difference and Sameness."[6] That poem in many ways served as precursor to the "Jewel Mirror Samādhi" and frames its dialectic between universal and particular, named here as sameness and difference. With both glistening snow filling up a silver bowl, and an auspicious white heron flying in front of the full round moon, foreground and background blend and may seem alike. And yet one can easily distinguish snow from silver and the heron from the moon.

An underlying theme of the whole poem is the interaction and integration between these two aspects of awareness. The background ultimate or universal reality starts to become visible in meditative awareness. This can be seen as sameness, oneness, or emptiness, where distinctions are seen as illusory. That reality balances with the foreground highlighted phenomenal reality of differences and distinctions, the conventional realm of discriminating consciousness.

A silver bowl filled with snow is a reference to an old story reaching back to India. Nāgārjuna (150–250?; Ch.: Longshu; Jpn.: Ryūjū), the great Indian teacher and philosopher of the Mādhyamika school and master of emptiness teaching, is traditionally considered the fourteenth ancestor after Śākyamuni in the Chan/Zen lineage. We know that historically the names in the Indian Zen lineage were connected later in China, yet we do not know accurately who personally conveyed the practice over the generations in India. But the famed Nāgārjuna is claimed as an ancestral teacher in the lineage of all the later Mahāyāna schools. In the Chan lineage that was officially adopted in the major lamp transmission texts, the successor of Nāgārjuna is considered to be Kānadeva (n.d.; Ch.:

Dipo; Jpn.: Kanadaiba). Snow in a silver bowl refers to the legendary story of Kānadeva's meeting with Nāgārjuna in which he received Nāgārjuna's approval, recounted, for example, in the *Jingde
Transmission of the Lamp;* later as case 13 of the *Blue Cliff Record*
koan anthology; and still later, in fourteenth-century Japan, by the
early Sōtō teacher Keizan in his account of the lineage, *Denkōroku.*[7]
The story relates that when Kānadeva arrived to see Nāgārjuna,
the teacher placed a bowl full of water before Kānadeva, who put
a needle in it. Nāgārjuna was pleased and gave Kānadeva his approval, according to the *Blue Cliff Record* thereupon "transmitting
the Buddha Mind School to him."[8] In the *Blue Cliff Record* case
for which this story is cited in the commentary, a monk asked the
teacher Baling Haojian (10th cent.; Jpn.: Haryō Kōkan), "What
is the school of Kānadeva?" Baling responded, "Snow in a silver
bowl." This was said to be one of the three turning phrases by
which Baling received transmission from Yunmen. The commentary describes Kānadeva's skill in debate, as he colorfully bested all
adversaries. Thus, the great teacher Mazu Daoyi said that the school
of Kānadeva consisted of using words and phrases. But Kānadeva's
eloquence in placing a needle in Nāgārjuna's bowl of water was
performed in silence. Some translations say he thrust the needle
to the bottom of the water, some that it floated on the surface.
Needles in that period in India were likely made of silver, though
perhaps wood, but a needle for mending their robes was one of
the objects that all monks traditionally carried on their travels.
Whether or not it was silver, Kānadeva inserted a particular thin
sliver of phenomena into a calm round body of water. And Nāgārjuna was greatly pleased. Each particular is a unique expression of
the universal whole. But this particulate seems to have crystallized
all the water in the silver bowl into snow, and here manifests the
theme of the particular in the universal and their interaction in
the "Song of the Jewel Mirror Samādhi."

The meaning does not reside in the words, but a pivotal moment
brings it forth.

Many Zen/Chan sayings attest to the fact that the full reality of any event is beyond the capacity of words to satisfactorily define or describe. Anything that can be stated in words does not express the immediacy and tenderness of the open, genuine flowing that transpires in just this situation. Even Kānadeva could not resort to mere words. Nevertheless, this line indicates that, despite the inadequacy of language for conveying suchness, a pivotal moment can indeed arouse its meaning.

This "pivotal moment" is literally the arrival of *ki* in Sino-Japanese, a complex character that includes among its meanings: function, operation, workings, mechanism, pivot, opportunity, energy, capacity, student, loom (as in weaving), or even the moving power of the universe. Thus, this phrase might be translated in various renderings, such as the arrival or workings of energy or of inquiry. Suchness is not meaningless, albeit indefinable and sometimes incoherent. Its import does come forth to operate and function in the world. With the energetic, pivotal opportunity occasioned by the inquiring impulse or the questioning student's sincere effort, the reality of suchness does respond.

—

Move and you are trapped; miss and you fall into doubt and
vacillation.
Turning away and touching are both wrong, for it is like a massive
fire.

To realize such an opportunity for response one must settle and abide, observing patiently, and remaining ready for the pivotal moment to engage this suchness. Along with some lines further along in the poem, this could easily be applied as a meditation instruction. Remaining upright and still, one may sense the inner workings of the practice, or somehow experience it even beyond conscious recognition. But trying to squirm away from it, one may fall into a hole or trap and then collapse into regret for having missed out on this reality. In everyday activity, as well, we may easily be caught in anxiety and then hesitate from just meeting and responding to the situation in front of us.

"Turning away and touching are both wrong." First, turning away, or literally turning one's back on suchness, does not work. "Just this" cannot be ignored or evaded. Although we may live in denial for a while, that is not sustainable as the events of life confront us. But also this cannot be grabbed or grasped, other meanings of the character here translated as "touching." "Can't live with it, can't live without it," as is said. Here suchness is compared with a massive fire. Get too close, and you may be burned; but ignore it, and the flames may blaze out of control.

This "massive fire" recalls Dongshan's advice to the monk who wanted to escape hot and cold to just freeze in the cold or burn up in the heat. The Chan master Xuefeng said that all buddhas throughout all times abide in the middle of flames and turn the great Dharma wheel.[9] Xuefeng was the monk who overturned the rice bowl when he was still a student working in the kitchen at Dongshan's monastery, as described in chapter 10. Xuefeng's buddhas sitting amid flames are not like the self-immolating monks making offerings historically in China or the modern Vietnamese or Tibetan monks committing self-immolation as protest. These flames are vivid metaphors for the suffering of the world burning within and without us, whether from our own emotional pain or the anguish of people facing societal misery. All buddhas must sit and settle in patiently and with awareness amid the flames of suchness, the flames of the world, without vainly attempting to either escape or control or manipulate these searing circumstances. As one abides in this situation, the Dharma can be expressed and shared.

Dōgen offers an illuminating comment on "turning away and touching are both wrong" in his *Shōbōgenzō* essay "Kūge" ("Flowers in the Sky"). Commenting on a line from a poem by a Chan adept, "Aiming toward suchness is wrong," Dōgen says that turning away from suchness is wrong, and that aiming toward suchness is also wrong. But then he adds, "Aiming toward suchness and turning away from suchness are also both just suchness. Moreover, even being wrong is also itself suchness."[10] Even when jumping in or running away, one can never escape the fire and ashes of suchness.

—

Just to portray it in literary form is to stain it with defilement.

This is quite an ironic line, coming amid the literary event of this poem. But simultaneously it acknowledges that its aesthetic merits are not what is important. The practice of suchness is not just another concept but must actually be engaged and enacted. And its purpose, its meaning that resides beyond the ephemeral felicity of its words and phrases, is not merely trivial but is something precious like a jewel, not to be defiled or besmirched.

—

In darkest night it is perfectly clear; in the light of dawn it is hidden.
It is a standard for all things; its use removes all suffering.
Although it is not constructed, it is not beyond words.

Shitou's "Harmony of Difference and Sameness" uses the imagery of dark and light to point, respectively, to the universal and particular. "Darkest night" is an image for merging, for the ultimate nondifferentiation in a blackness where no particulars can be distinguished, indicating the absolute universal background reality. In darkest night the ultimate reality is perfectly clear. "Light" is an image, on the other hand, for the brightness where all the particulars can be clearly discriminated and discerned, and thus the ultimate reality of suchness is hidden. However, when seen in the context of the five degrees, as stated below, this line might also indicate the particulars emerging in dawn from the darkness of the ultimate.

The poem states that suchness and its teaching provide a universal standard, and its "use removes all suffering." The very nature of reality is a soteriological agent. When fully engaged, it can help to liberate beings from suffering, from the whole range of distress. The concern with the nature of reality is not a merely academic, theoretical affair. Chan/Zen is a form of Mahāyāna practice, based in the bodhisattva practice dedicated to relieving suffering and the liberation of all beings.

Some literalist Chan interpretations use the slogan "direct pointing to the mind, beyond words and letters" as an anti-intellectual discouragement from study of any written or verbal expression. However, in the line "Although it is not constructed, it is not beyond words" Dongshan avows that it is indeed possible for the teaching of suchness to be effectively taught or discussed. This line also acknowledges that suchness is not a mere fabricated object, or a conditioned product or a construction. Rather, reality is a dynamic, healing, vital process worthy of our efforts to express, in words or otherwise. Indeed, this needs to be expressed and conveyed to remove suffering.

—

Like facing a jewel mirror; form and reflection behold each other.
You are not it, but in truth it is you.

Like the first two lines of the "Jewel Mirror Samādhi," these two lines refer to the occasion of Dongshan's parting from Yunyan, here to Dongshan looking at his reflection in the stream soon after his departure. The stream or the reflecting surface is described as a jeweled mirror, which gives this poem its title. The relationship between form and reflection stands in for the encounter between Dongshan and suchness itself, as well as for the relationship between student and teacher. Both sides actively behold each other in intersubjectivity, as the stream looks back at Dongshan.

In the original witness in the stream, Dongshan said, "It now is me; I now am not it." Here in this poem, one difference in the line "You are not it, but in truth it is you" is that the word "now" has been omitted. Another variation is that the two sides are reversed, the subject being "not it" moved up from the end to the start, seemingly as simply a more appropriate fit poetically. More significantly, the second person "you" is substituted for the first person "me" or "I," with the effect of emphasizing the situation of the reader or listener. The "it" is the same character in both the "Jewel Mirror Samādhi" and in Dongshan's verse after he looked in the stream in the *Recorded Sayings*. As discussed in chapter 2, this pronoun might refer to either "it" as the suchness of Yunyan's utterance, "Just this is it," or else to "him," the teacher. In the context of the "Jewel Mirror Samādhi" and the Dharma of suchness, this is likely "it" rather than "him," and most of the translations use "it," referring to suchness. However, Powell translates the pronoun as "him," and the "Jewel Mirror Samādhi" certainly involves the role of teaching and teachers of suchness, as well as the reality itself of the Dharma of suchness.

In the discussion in chapter 2 in the context of Dongshan's looking into the stream, the nature of the self is set in relation to the ultimate reality of suchness or just this. This dynamic between self and suchness helps illuminate the greater non-self in which the limited constructed self is also implicated. Here in the "Jewel Mirror Samādhi" this "You are not it, but in truth it is you" is framed in terms of the mutuality of form and reflection beholding each other. Whether seen as the teacher and student sitting face to face, or the jewel mirror facing your constructed self, here a pivotal moment is bringing forth as a focus the important and intimate interrelationship between form and reflection. You and it are in a deeply interactive relationship, and the integration between it

and you becomes an important subtext that develops throughout
the poem.

—

Like a newborn child, it is fully endowed with five aspects:
No going, no coming, no arising, no abiding;
"Baba wawa"—is anything said or not?
In the end it says nothing, for the words are not yet right.

In these lines one awakened to suchness and its full reality is compared to an infant. Just as a completely awakened buddha is not
fooled by the segmentation of discriminating consciousness, an infant has not yet distinguished particular entities, seeing only a uni-
fied sense field. But the baby still needs nourishment and quickly
fixes on the mother as the source of nurture, and the process of
discrimination begins. The baby does not yet have an ego, while a
buddha must overcome the egoistic construction of a sense of separate self and the discriminations required to survive adolescence,
in order to then again see the possibility of non-estrangement. It
is as if infants have the full openness to reality, but then this must
be realized further in the context of having developed a self. Non-
self is about seeing through the constructed self, not about getting
rid of the self.

The parallel between infant and the awakened one is described
in terms of five qualities, the first of an explicit series of fives in
the poem that establish the five degrees teaching. The baby's in-
ability to get up, stay put, come, go away, or talk is compared to
five characteristics of the Tathāgatha, or Buddha, described in the
Mahāparinirvāna Sutra.[11] Similar to the infant, according to the
sutra, the Buddha does not raise the thought of any dharma; does
not abide in any dharma; does not have a body capable of actions
such as coming; does not go anywhere because already in nirvāṇa;
and finally has not actually said anything, despite all his lifelong
teaching.

For such baby talk as "Baba wawa," Dongshan asks, "is anything said or not?" But likewise, even with all the Buddha's eloquence and skillful efforts to speak appropriately to the range of his different students, none of the sutras can fully approach the ultimate meaning of the highest universal reality. As alluded to in many of Dongshan's stories, no description or account can touch the real meaning, which is not in the words that are not yet right, although the "Jewel Mirror Samādhi" has also claimed that this meaning is not beyond words. The tension about how to convey this, and how to use language beyond "defiled" literary forms, is developed further with this "baba wawa," and through the course of the "Jewel Mirror Samādhi."

However, quite apart from its teaching about the limitations of speech or discourse, as well as about non-abiding and so forth, this analogue between the Buddha and an infant is included here because it is one of a series of instances of fives, which speak to the fivefold nature of the relationship between inclined and upright, or particular and universal, and introduces the teaching of the five degrees.

———

In the illumination hexagram, inclined and upright interact,
Piled up they become three, the permutations make five,
Like the taste of the five-flavored herb, like the five-pronged vajra.

The cascade of fives is enhanced here with further examples. The first example, which deserves extended comment, is a particular hexagram from the Chinese classic, the *Yi Jing*, or *Book of Changes* (in the older Wade-Giles transliteration, the *I Ching*). The roots of this text date back to the beginning of the third millennium B.C.E., according to legend, although its primary form was probably constructed a little before 1000 B.C.E., certainly before Confucius (551–479 B.C.E.), who along with his successors added to the many layers of commentary now included in the text. The reference to the *Yi Jing* in the "Jewel Mirror Samādhi" may be largely due to this particular six-lined hexagram involving another example of five in its composition. As a classic Chinese text, the *Yi Jing* would have been familiar to most Chinese people, its use as a divination tool familiar even to nonliterate folks, more familiar even than lines from Shakespeare would be in English.

Before discussing this complex *Yi Jing* citation, two other brief examples of fives follow it: First, the five-flavored herb is a traditional Chinese herb, in one source identified with the hyssop plant, in another with the *zhi* plant that grows in the mountains of Southern China.[12] Supposedly, it combines the traditional five flavors, pungent, sweet, bitter, sour, and salty, which correspond with the five elements in traditional Chinese medicine: earth, wood, fire, metal, and water.

The second example of fives, the five-pronged *vajra* (*dorje* in Tibetan), is a ritual implement used in Vajrayāna, also known as tantric or esoteric Buddhism. This is the predominant form of Tibetan Buddhism, but it was significant in East Asia, foundational to much of Japanese Buddhism, and sufficiently present in Tang and Song Chinese Buddhism that this reference would have been familiar there. The vajra is a short scepter (five to seven inches long) with usually five prongs, one central and four around it, extending out on either end. Sometimes it would have only one or three prongs, or other variations. The vajra is figuratively a diamond thunderbolt, representing the adamantine, indestructible, and impenetrable power of the ultimate teaching and reality.[13] The five prongs represent the five elements in Buddhist cosmology: earth, water, fire, air, and space. But there are a great many sets of fives in Buddhism that are indicated by this vajra, including in Vajrayāna especially five buddhas associated with the center and the four directions in mandalas. The middle prong also represents the ultimate, and the four around it signify the phenomenal world encompassing and taking refuge in the central ultimate. Another part of the intricate, complex symbolism of the vajra is that the five prongs appear the same on both ends of the vajra, showing the

nonduality of the two polarities of duality and nonduality. All of
the many groups of five evoked in the vajra symbolism further the
fiveness in the interfolding of the double fire illumination hexagram of the Yi Jing.[14] These highlight the naturalness of the five
degrees, in which ultimate and particular, or upright and inclined,
interact and integrate.

The Yi Jing began as a divination tool supposedly based on the
lines on tortoise shells. Later, tossed yarrow stalks or coins were
used for divination purposes, but this classic work's philosophical
and cosmological depths go far beyond fortune telling. The Yi Jing
is based on combinations of six solid yang and broken yin lines
arranged into six-line hexagrams. Each of the six lines might be
stable or changing, to produce many possible new hexagrams after
the initial one, resulting in a total of sixty-four possible separate
hexagrams. Yang represents the active or creative principle, yin the
receptive. Each hexagram provides a basic reading, a judgment, and
an image, each with layers of commentary, along with commentary for each line, especially relevant when the lines are changing.
The image is derived at least in part from the combination in each
hexagram of two three-lined trigrams. The eight possible trigrams,
with combinations of solid and broken lines, are identified with
natural elements: sky, lake, thunder, fire, earth, mountain, water,
and wind (also called wood). Combining the eight trigrams with
each other yields the sixty-four hexagrams. The resulting image for
a hexagram is the first, or lower or inner, trigram below the upper
or outer trigram. So, for example, earth trigram (three open lines)
below the fire trigram (solid lines below and above an open line in
the middle) yields the hexagram for Advance or Progress, with light
emerging over the earth. The primary layers of commentary in the
classic Yi Jing were composed by Confucian thinkers, but other
Chinese religious and philosophic movements, especially Daoism,
looked to it as an important reference and added commentaries.[15]

The Illumination hexagram, number 30 of the sixty-four hexagrams of the Yi Jing, is composed of the fire trigram both below and
above. It is ostensibly mentioned in the "Jewel Mirror Samādhi"

because "piled up [its trigrams] become three, the permutations make five." This refers to an elaborate process for working with the trigrams of a particular hexagram that has been interpreted in a variety of ways for this hexagram. But this process applied to the Illumination, or double-fire, hexagram yields five combinations. This apparently is the main reason it is referenced in the poem. A series of five trigrams and hexagrams, culminating with the Illumination hexagram, along with five associated circular diagrams, were derived to indicate the five degrees. As indicated in the following diagram of the hexagrams, these five are first, the wind trigram, when doubled becoming the hexagram Gentle or Penetrating. Second is the lake trigram, when doubled becoming the hexagram Joyous. Third is the Predominance of the Great hexagram, which is wind below the lake. Fourth is the Inner Truth hexagram, which is lake below the wind. And fifth is the culminating double-fire "Illumination, or Clinging, hexagram, which was thereby considered the most harmonious and stable hexagram, completely balancing the dialectical polarity of inclined and upright, or apparent and real.[16]

This interpretation began with Dongshan's disciple Caoshan but was much amplified by later Caodong scholars, especially Jiyin Huihung (12th cent.; Jpn.: Jakuon Ekō).[17] In ongoing later analyses about the five degrees within Chinese Caodong and Japanese Sōtō, as well as in Neo-Confucianism, the *Yi Jing* played a prominent part.

The fiveness of the combining lines in the double-fire Illumination hexagram cited in the "Jewel Mirror Samādhi" is part of the series of fives that introduce the five degrees, in which inclined and upright interact. The characters translated literally in the previous lines as inclined and upright might also be rendered as apparent and real or partial and true. They signify the particular and universal, or the phenomenal and ultimate, or the relative and absolute, respectively. Dongshan and Chan discourse generally also refers to them with the metaphors of vassal and lord, or guest and host. The five degrees, which will be discussed more in the next chapter, can be designated as (1) the apparent within the real; (2) the real within

57. 巽 Xun Gentle, Penetrating	61. 中孚 Zhong fu Inner truth
58. 兌 Dui Joyous	30. 離 Li Clinging
28. 大過 Da guo Preponderance of the Great	

Five Hexagrams.

the apparent; (3) emerging from within the real; (4) moving in the midst of both (real and apparent); and (5) arriving completely in both.

A useful, original analysis of the relevance of the illumination *Li* hexagram based on traditional *Yi Jing* thought has been suggested by scholar Brook Ziporyn, who points out that this hexagram functions as a mirror.[18] Both top and bottom fire trigrams are identical, yang-yin-yang. But in *Yi Jing* theory the top trigram bears the opposite valence, yin-yang-yin, so that in this hexagram these two trigrams are both the same and different, like form and reflection beholding each other. Thus Ziporyn sees this particular hexagram functioning as a mandala representing the complex dynamic between universal and particular, or sameness and difference, also at play in the whole five-degree pattern. The Illumination hexagram text itself also seems relevant for the "Jewel Mirror Samādhi." Illumination is a common image for spiritual awakening or elevation, and this hexagram is called Fire, Illumination, or Clinging. As it is composed of the two fire trigrams, it echoes the line "Turning away and touching are both wrong, for it is like a massive fire." A line that follows a bit further says, "Within causes and conditions, time and season, it is serene and illuminating." But also worth considering, in terms of the clinging aspect, is the line "In darkest night it is perfectly clear; in the light of dawn it is hidden." Clinging is cited for this hexagram inasmuch as fire clings to its fuel, that which burns. Also in the fire trigram, the open or dark lines cling to the bright active lines around them. The traditional Confucian commentary states, "What is dark clings to what is light and enhances the brightness of the latter. A luminous thing giving out light must have within itself something that perseveres; otherwise it will burn itself out."[19] Such perseverance, and sources of nourishment, becomes a major theme in the last section of the "Jewel Mirror Samādhi."

The Fire hexagram also states in its primary judgment that raising a cow is fortunate. This represents the importance of cultivating gentle flexibility and compliance as a balance to active brightness. One may readily see the whole direction of the *Yi Jing* as the balancing of energies, certainly the emphasis in Daoist commentaries on this classic text. The *Yi Jing* greatly predates Laozi, the legendary sage and author of the classic *Dao De Jing* (*The Way and Its Power*), often considered the founder of Daoism. But one might see the *Yi Jing* as a vastly older product of the Daoist thread in Chinese culture that emphasizes natural harmony and balance. Later Daoism used the *Yi Jing* as a metaphor and instruction manual for Daoist alchemical meditation processes involving balancing meditative energies in the body to develop awareness and health. An eighteenth-century Daoist commentary on the Illumination or Fire hexagram speaks of the cow as representing receptivity and says, "If people can nurture illumination with flexible receptivity, turning the light of consciousness around to shine inward, shutting out deviation and preserving truthfulness, first illumining inside, then illumining outside, then inside and outside will both be illumined, open awareness will be clear; . . . naturally illumining the qualities of enlightenment and resting in the highest good."[20] Such Daoist commentaries on the *Yi Jing* serve as cryptic alchemical meditation instructions.[21]

This Daoist commentary on the Illumination hexagram cited in the "Jewel Mirror Samādhi" about "turning the light of consciousness around to shine inward" closely recalls a number of meditation instructions from Dongshan's Caodong lineage. Dong-shan's eighth-century predecessor Shitou, in the "Sōanka" ("Song of the Grass Hut") says, "Turn around the light to shine within, then just return. The vast inconceivable source [like the massive fire] can't be faced or turned away from."²² In the twelfth century, Hongzhi said, for example, "Take the backward step and directly reach the middle of the circle from where light issues forth."²³ And in thirteenth-century Japan, in his early writing of "Fukanzazengi" Dōgen said, "Learn to take the backward step that turns the light and shines it inward. Body and mind of themselves will drop away, and your original face will manifest."²⁴ The closeness of the Dao-ist meditative commentary on the *Yi Jing* hexagram mentioned in the "Jewel Mirror Samādhi" with these Caodong/Sōtō meditation instructions reveals a meditative context for the hexagram's use in the poem.

Returning to the fivefold permutations of the Illumination hexagram, the five degrees are introduced in the "Jewel Mirror Samādhi" only incompletely, if not cryptically. They will be discussed further in the next chapter, but they do play a role in the "Jewel Mirror Samādhi" itself. I have not seen this noted in any five degrees commentary, but the five degrees might be located in the poem's text via the only five lines in which the character for *upright* or *real, shō* in Sino-Japanese, appears. This character, which also means "true," has been translated here variously according to context, but we have already seen the first four occasions, and the fifth is in the next line, so its only five occurrences are in the first half of the poem.

The first line, corresponding with "the apparent within the real," is "In darkest night it is *perfectly* [or truly] clear." The darkness of night is correlated with the ultimate reality beyond all distinctions, as discussed with the imagery of dark and light in Shitou's "The Harmony of Sameness and Difference." Within the ultimate, particulars emerge and can stand forth.

The second line, with the character *shō*, corresponding with the second degree, of "the real within the apparent," is "You are not it, but in *truth* it is you." This adds to the context of this crucial line, that within the phenomenal reality of the constructed self remains the deeper truth that is the ultimate person of interconnected totality.

The third line, corresponding with the third degree, of "emerging from within the real," is "In the end it says nothing, for the words are not yet *right* [or true]." An infant emerged from the womb is fully immersed in the nondiscriminating wholeness of ultimate reality, like one emerging from deep experience of communion with the reality of suchness, as in heightened meditative awareness. But in both cases there are not yet the words or expression to convey this and help others onto the path of realization.

The fourth line of the "Jewel Mirror Samādhi," in which this character for *real* appears, is the one we are discussing: "In the illumination hexagram, inclined and *upright* [or true] interact," corresponding to the fourth degree of moving in the midst of both. We have seen how this hexagram has been employed to show the fivefold interacting of inclined, partial, or relative with the other side of the upright, true, or absolute. The *Yi Jing* serves as an imperfect image of this, with the receptive yin and creative yang interacting as limited analogues of partial and true.

Finally, the fifth line, in which the character for *true* or *real* appears in the "Jewel Mirror Samādhi," representing the fifth degree of arriving completely in both, is the very next line: "Wondrously embraced within the *real* [or true], drumming and singing begin together." Here is no longer simply mutual interaction, but complete integration of particular and universal arising together.

In the complex theories and commentaries about the five degrees, various other descriptions have been suggested as to how they appear in the "Jewel Mirror Samādhi."

—

Wondrously embraced within the real, drumming and singing
  begin together.
Penetrate the source and travel the pathways; embrace the
  territory and treasure the roads.

Something is wondrously, mysteriously, subtly, exquisitely, beau-
tifully embraced within the real, within the ultimate perfect upright truth. When that happens, arising together, there emerges a
pair that can be translated as drumming and singing. This refers to
instant, unmediated inquiry and response, or literally hitting and
yelling back. Again, suchness responds to sincere inquiry, without
any mediation through analysis or deliberation. In such an em-
bracing situation, no separation comes between call and response,
between the universal ineffable reality and conditioned phenomena as its manifest expression in this present situation.

This integration is amplified in the follow-up line. In "penetrate
the source and travel the pathways," "penetrate" and "travel" are
the same verb. Along with those meanngs, this Chinese character also means "to connect," "to transmit," "to circulate," and here
especially "to commune"—with the source, or essence, and the
pathways, journey, or progression. A deep intimacy with a whole
process of practice is conveyed here, both of exploring the source
and inner reaches of suchness, and of ranging into the frontiers of
creative expression. In the second half of the line, the same verb
rendered here as "embrace" or "treasure" is again repeated, the same
verb as in the previous, "Wondrously embraced within the real."
It might be read also as "cherish" and literally includes the meaning of clasping something close to one's breast. This imagery
celebrates the dear, precious treasure of the whole affair of this
drumming and singing and instant, unmediated call and response,
and the whole fivefold interaction involved.

———

You would do well to respect this; do not neglect it.

This line is perhaps the most challenging to translate in the whole poem, or at least the line with the most vivid contrary interpretations. The first two characters together form a compound that means "respectful" or "reverent," so that the first half of this line might be read literally as "respectfulness is fortunate or auspicious." Here this implies respecting suchness itself, and the whole process of its unfolding previously described, which is certainly most worthy of respect. The second half of the sentence, "do not neglect it," might also be read more strongly as not to stubbornly or obstinately violate, disobey, or transgress it.

However, the first half of this line has been translated very differently. The first character by itself also can mean "to miss," "to make a mistake," or "to be wrong." So this line has been translated, for example as "If you miss it, that's a good sign. Don't neglect it"[25] and "To be wrong is auspicious; do not oppose it."[26] Those meanings, while understandable readings for the line itself, do not fit so well into the context of the entire song of the "Jewel Mirror Samādhi." But perhaps they might serve as warnings not to hold too strongly to any one of the five degrees. And it might miss the point or be mistaken to adhere to some particular understanding or interpretation of the fivefold interactivities of the apparent and the real as orthodox or certifiably correct.

Indeed, mutual respectfulness is a central key to helpful, constructive practice and to ethical expression of meditative awareness amid everyday activity. But practically speaking, it is also necessary to be willing to make mistakes, to blunder through trial and error for the sake of wider awareness and more fully helping relieve suffering. Only through making mistakes can we learn and open our capacity to be aware, responsive, and respectful.

—

*Natural and wondrous, it is not a matter of delusion or
    enlightenment.*
*Within causes and conditions, time and season, it is serene and
    illuminating.*
*So minute it enters where there is no gap, so vast it transcends
    dimension.*
A hairsbreadth's deviation, and you are out of tune.

The "natural" of "natural and wondrous" means literally "heavenly
and genuine," referring to the Dharma of suchness as a quality
flowing from the nature of reality. This is subtle and wondrous beyond the duality of delusion or enlightenment. The actuality and
practice of suchness does not involve some preference for enlightenment or delusion; practice and awakening are not about achieving some special, glamorous experience of enlightenment and do
not require destroying all delusion.

The strong emphasis running through the history of the Cao-
dong/Sōtō lineage has been the integration of experience of the
ultimate with its expression in the phenomenal realm. Going back
a few generations before Dongshan, Shitou said in his "Sandōkai"
("Harmony of Difference and Sameness"), "Merging with sameness is still not enlightenment."[27] In another story about Shitou
mentioned in chapter 7, when asked about the essential meaning
of Buddhadharma, Shitou replied, "Not to attain, not to know."[28]
Later, Dōgen often cautioned against grasping for enlightenment
and trying to evade the delusions of the phenomenal world.

The poem goes on to say that it is exactly within the phenomenal causes and conditions of particular times and seasons that
suchness is serenely illuminating. This happens not in some exotic transcendent realm. But it is far beyond our usual perceptual
senses, transcending our conventional view of the dimensions of
size and space, limited by our ordinary imagination. It is extremely
minute, entering where we see no gap, and vast beyond our usual

sense of dimensionality. Such practice involves shifting perspectives beyond our highly limited human perceptions of reality. Dongshan first came to his teacher Yunyan when inquiring about how to hear nonsentient beings expounding the Dharma. Later, Dongshan would talk of the bird's path that humans are unable to see. This wondrously subtle suchness and the integration of its ultimate reality with phenomena abide beyond our ability to grasp or know.

Dōgen speaks of this often. In his "Genjōkōan" essay, he talks about being out in a boat where it seems that the shore is moving, not the boat. When in the middle of the ocean, it seems circular, as the specific details of the wide shoreline are out of view. He discusses how water looks different to diverse kinds of beings, obviously quite unalike to fish and to humans.[29] Similarly, we all know the limits of human perceptions of simple sound and smell senses as compared to dogs, for example. In his essay "Bendōwa," Dōgen proclaims that all entities and practitioners imperceptibly assist each other to actualize the present awakening. However, this guidance cannot be perceived by humans, because "[that] which is associated with perceptions cannot be the standard of enlightenment [and cannot be reached by] deluded human sentiment."[30] In his "Mountains and Waters Sutra," Dōgen cites a line from the Caodong teacher Furong Daokai: "The green mountains are constantly walking; a stone woman gives birth at night." Although this defies our usual sense of logic, Dōgen comments extensively on how the mountains walking are related to our own walking, and that we must know one to truly know the other. In the black night of ultimate, universal reality, even a barren, stone woman becomes fertile.[31]

These perspectives may recall the strange, mysterious worldview of the Mahāyāna sutras that are the background of Zen. In many of these sutras bodhisattvas and buddhas suddenly appear from different buddha fields from vastly distant times or spaces in order to hear Śākyamuni Buddha teach. For example, among plentiful other amazing visions, the Flower Ornament or Avataṃsaka Sūtra describes how numerous buddhas and bodhisattvas perform awakening activity in every single atom throughout all worlds in the cosmos.[32] In the Lotus Sutra a mummified buddha from a vastly ancient buddha field arrives in his stupa and floats in midair to listen *whenever* the Lotus Sutra is taught, and later hordes of ancient venerable bodhisattvas spring forth from the open space under the earth, ready to assist whenever they are needed to maintain the teaching.[33] And in the sutra that bears his name, the bodhisattva layman Vimalakirti picks up a whole universe and holds it in his hand, without disturbing beings therein, showing those in his universe who would be inspired and enter the path by seeing it, and then returns it to its former place.[34] What do such descriptions imply about the actuality of our realm of practice?

This multidimensional reality is highlighted in my favorite American Buddhist movie, *Men in Black*.[35] The film includes a great many Dharma aspects, including especially revealing radical innovations on our conventional view of the reality of our world. It further dramatizes skillful training of successors, renunciation, not clinging to self identity, locating alternate sources of media information, tolerance of ambiguities, appropriately compassionate response to a range of highly diverse beings, generosity toward the ignorant, and vivid demonstrations of the deeper realities of size and space beyond our limited human perspectives. Without revealing major plot elements, at one point a pug says scornfully, "You humans, when you gonna learn that size doesn't matter? Just cause something's important doesn't mean it's not very, very small."

This is not merely some ancient esoteric Eastern conceit, or Hollywood fantasy, but resonates with viewpoints in modern physics. The various strands of theoretical modern physics including quantum mechanics, string theory, and supersymmetry are speculative and certainly not fully intelligible to me. Some string theory approaches conceive of eleven or more dimensions of reality. Leonard Susskind, called the father of string theory, says, "Space can be filled with a wide variety of invisible influences that have all sorts of effects on ordinary matter."[36] Physicist and science writer

Brian Greene says, "Our universe has many more dimensions than meet the eye—dimensions that are tightly curled into the folded fabric of the cosmos."[37] In a recent book, Greene describes how all modern physics theories lead to the probable reality of a highly dynamic cosmos with multiple or parallel universes related to our own sphere of awareness.[38] Many modern physicists theorize that we do not see various other dimensions besides the familiar three in our own reality simply because they are extraordinarily small.[39]

In such a context of multiple, often hidden dimensions, what might it mean to experience a hairsbreadth deviation, or to be out of tune? Several lines further along, the "Jewel Mirror Samādhi" suggests a useful standard for attunement and natural accord. But given a multidimensional reality, perhaps nondeviation from this attunement would be a matter of not grasping onto any one particular view or perspective on the nature of the reality of suchness, but remaining open to seeing freshly and accepting new information, or even accepting the possibility of multiple realities. This supports the view of suchness as not absolute or static but as dynamically shifting in accord with the conditions of the phenomenal world, or perhaps of multiple phenomenal realms, the view going back to Chinese Huayan and emphasized in Japanese Tendai, discussed in chapter 9.

Practically, not deviating from attunement to the serene illumination of the present time and season may be a matter of delicate balancing between different aspects of reality, and not being too high strung or too loose. Within the shifting of causes and conditions, attentively returning to balance with suchness over and over again remains vital to our practice.

—

Now there are sudden and gradual, in which teachings and
approaches arise.
When teachings and approaches are distinguished, each has its
standard.
Whether teachings and approaches are mastered or not, reality
constantly flows.

The approaches of sudden or gradual awakening in Chan history
go back to the dispute depicted in a partisan manner in the *Platform Sutra of the Sixth Patriarch.*[40] This text, composed by disciples of Huineng, who has been recognized in subsequent Chan/
Zen history as the Sixth Ancestor, contains teachings attributed
to him but also an apocryphal, polemical account of a dispute
between Huineng and another disciple of the Fifth Ancestor,
Shenxiu (605?–706; Jpn.: Jinshū). Huineng founded what became
known as the Southern school, which promoted sudden awakening, whereas Shenxiu, who was much more popular in their time,
led the Northern school, which supported gradual teaching. In the
Platform Sutra Huineng speaks of sudden teaching via immediate
insight, just seeing into the nature of mind.[41] Gradual teaching was
described as the slow cultivation of character development from
meditative practices and sutra study over many years or even lifetimes. Later in the Song period, sudden awakening was seen by
some in terms of a sudden dramatic experience of awakening impelled by koan introspection meditation.

At various times Zen teachers have spoken in terms of integration of sudden and gradual. A prominent example is of the great
Korean master Chinul (1158–1210), who, as a direct result of studying the Platform Sutra, though also via the influence of writings
from Guifeng Zongmi (780–841; Jpn.: Keihō Shūmitsu), a master of both Chan and Huayan, developed a teaching of "sudden
awakening and gradual cultivation."[42] Chinul saw that even after
sudden awakening, perfection of skill in means and refinement

of wisdom were necessary to support bodhisattva compassion and ease the sufferings of all beings, the entire purpose of practice.[43] Chinul also suggests that sudden awakening is only the result of lifetimes of cultivation and that this cultivation must in turn have been inspired by an initial awakening.[44]

Dongshan's understanding of sudden awakening, as expressed in his stories and view of suchness, is not about some sudden dramatic experience of awakening as a later result from practice, but precedes these experiences much more immediately. As in the viewpoint of starting at the top of the mountain expressed in chapter 8, the fundamental reality of suchness is present from the very beginning, and practice or cultivation is not a matter of achieving something, but a matter of the necessity to realize and express what is already immediately present. This is indeed one interpretation of Huineng's sudden approach. Such a sudden perspective persists throughout the Caodong/Sōtō lineage—for example, in Hongzhi's statement "The field of boundless emptiness is what exists from the very beginning. You must purify, cure, grind down, or brush away all the tendencies you have fabricated into apparent habits. Then you can reside in the clear circle of brightness."[45] The problem, and the need for subtle teaching, is the habit of conditioned patterns of thinking and attachment. A dramatic experience of realization will not change a lifetime of psychological issues and habits overnight. But, according to Hongzhi, and the Dongshan legacy, these attachments are illusory fabrications that may indeed be seen through and put aside.

In these lines from the "Jewel Mirror Samādhi," all the approaches to sudden and gradual are simply acknowledged. But nevertheless, apart from being a matter of arduous study or mastery, "reality constantly flows." Right within practice, reality as such precedes any approach to its practice and any particular techniques of accomplishment, and is ever available to our awareness.

—

Outside still and inside trembling, like tethered colts or cowering
   rats,
The ancient sages grieved for them, and offered them the dharma.

The first line strongly suggests the practical reality of upright sitting meditation. One sits still and silent, hopefully relaxed but aware, bound to the form of cross-legged or other upright sitting postures. But within, whether from physical pain in the knees or elsewhere, or more seriously from the inner turmoil of emotional or spiritual pain, one may tremble or cower, seeking to escape from suffering and dissatisfaction. Stillness provides the opportunity to observe the inner trembling, to face the reality of such an unsettled world that we often try to squirm away from. It is not enough to present a merely external pose of stillness. True calm abiding must reach all the way inside in the face of both the inner and the outer worldly turmoil.

The ancient sages, all the ancestral teachers in the Chan lineages and the great teaching masters whose dialogues and commentaries are studied, as well as the ancient buddhas in the sutras, were all motivated exactly by their concern for suffering beings. And the "Jewel Mirror Samādhi" states it strongly. They were sad, and grieved about the woes of the world, and the distress of particular beings.

—

Led by their inverted views, they take black for white.
When inverted thinking stops, the affirming mind naturally
   accords.

Suffering beings have inverted, topsy-turvy views of reality. Personal resistance to the realities of life and death creates anxiety and enhances suffering due to erroneous perceptions or expectations.

Not seeing clearly, we may wish to be anywhere but where we are, and thus we fail to see the wholeness of what is. Inverted views of reality may also reflect attachment to self and clinging to our cherished views of the world and of our constructed self.

From a modern perspective we might note that suffering is not solely a matter of individual distorted perceptions about suchness or reality. Communal, societal systems of injustice and oppression are certainly responsible for a great deal of the world's misery. These, too, derive from communal or worldly topsy-turvy thinking based on greed, hatred, and delusions, not seeing the possibilities of societal kindness and cooperation that can be nurtured in the accord of affirming mind. Communal inverted views are often promoted subtly by corrupted media and educational systems, which then need to be discerned and transformed.

When we are willing to be present and upright in the situation of where we are, this inverted thinking based on avoidance can cease, and affirming mind arises. This does not mean passivity, as natural accord may include affirming our helpful, wholesome responses to reality when we see more clearly. The word *affirm* here also means "to consent," "to permit," "to accept," and also "willingness," or "to undertake" something. An affirming mind opens to learning or accepting new information or teachings. We cannot control reality, but we can speak the truth of what we see and be open to see more fully as we look further at the shifting reality. The affirming mind presents an appealing image for the awareness expressed by the "Jewel Mirror Samādhi," which leads to natural accord or attunement. The character for *accord* further means "to acknowledge," "to commit," and even "to forgive." "The affirming mind naturally accords" is a rich phrase for the positive stance encouraged in this poem.

—

If you want to follow in the ancient tracks, please observe the sages
    of the past.
One on the verge of realizing the Buddha Way contemplated a tree
    for ten kalpas,
Like a battle-scarred tiger, like a horse with shanks gone gray.

Following the examples of the ancient ones, the sages of the past,
is a time-honored, prevalent emphasis throughout East Asian culture, and might be seen as a legacy of Confucianism and ancestor
veneration. In Chan and Zen it is especially important, seen even
in this verse attributed to the eighth-century Caodong founder
Dongshan, fairly early in Chan history. Most of the literature of
Zen, down to the present, consists of dialogues or paradigmatic
stories about the classic masters (often enshrined in the traditional
koan collections), or of their sermons. Additional layers upon layers of commentary have appeared throughout the generations, including this book.

The one who spent ten kalpas on the verge of realizing the Buddha Way, or of attaining full buddhahood, is from a story in chapter 7 of the Lotus Sutra.[46] According to the story in the sutra, a vast
number of inconceivably long kalpas or eons ago, a buddha named
Mahābhijñājñānabhibhū (Excellent in Great Penetrating Wisdom
Tathagata) sat under the bodhi tree right at the point of attaining
supreme awakening, but the full Dharma of the buddhas did not
appear to him for ten kalpas. Throughout this interval, heavenly
flowers rained down around him and heavenly beings performed
divine music for him. Finally, he did become a full buddha, and the
sutra goes on to detail how his sixteen sons and billions of heavenly
kings then requested this buddha to teach, and finally he taught
the enduring Lotus Sutra for eight thousand eons. The sixteen sons
all became buddhas, the youngest eventually becoming Śākyamuni
Buddha.

The ancient buddha who just sat under the tree for ten long ages
is compared in the "Jewel Mirror Samādhi" to a battle-scarred tiger

or an old gray warhorse. Dongshan here is suggesting active bodhi-sattva work, not quite attaining full buddhahood but remaining in the world to help liberate beings and not pass away into full nirvāṇa himself. Rather than completing personal fulfillment, helping beings is the point of practice. There are many historical and ongoing examples of venerable Zen monks who disdain any accomplishment but enjoy a humble life of engagement with peo-ple in the world.

The image of the buddha waiting for ten kalpas is also the sub-ject of case 9 of the *Gateless Barrier* koan collection.[47] Unlike the interpretation mentioned above, some commentators on this case see this buddha's time under the tree as involving attachment to quiescent practice that he had to overcome before attaining bud-dhahood. But in the context of this poem and Dongshan's teach-ing, this "sage of the past" is being lauded for stopping short of full attainment.

I note that there are a variety of other readings that have been given for the line about the tiger and horse, as the characters de-scribing them are somewhat archaic and uncertain. The tiger has been read as lame, with tattered ears, or leaving part of its prey, which rather than weariness or a weathered veteran, might alter-natively suggest the power of not needing to consume all of its kill, though I find this interpretation less likely. The horse has been read, for example, as hobbled, shoeless, or with a white left hind leg, an unclear reference that might indicate either a venerable or vulnerable situation.

—

Because some are common, jeweled tables and ornate robes;
Because some are wide-eyed, cats and white oxen.

Here Dongshan points to skillful means for presenting the jewel mirror and the teaching of suchness for the sake of helping the variety of beings based on their particular dispositions. Those who are common, lowly, or modest in their awareness and spiritual development are impressed by jeweled tables, pedestals, or altars and by ornate, brocade robes. This is another reference to the Lotus Sutra and the parable of the prodigal son previously discussed in chapter 6. When the wandering, destitute son happens upon the estate of his now very wealthy father, all he can see is his father's jeweled footstool and richly decorated robes, and the frightened son initially flees.[48] Thereafter, he can only realize his rightful legacy after years of menial labor. However, here in the "Jewel Mirror Samādhi," teachers of suchness employ the jeweled tables and ornate robes to impress and attract those of lesser capacity or class background. But perhaps such displays may also appeal to those who appreciate aesthetic demonstrations of the richness of suchness.

The "wide-eyed" in the following line could be read as those capable of wonder. The phrase might also be taken as "because there exists" the wondrous, the startlingly different, the astonishing, or the strange and eccentric. So for those capable of wonder, or because of the wondrous or startlingly different aspect of suchness, the Buddha ancestors offer the simple cat and white oxen, or cat and cow.[49]

A couple of traditional Zen stories are alluded to here. The white ox recalls the ten ox-herding pictures, which also appear in a set of six pictures. In various renditions, these depict stages of training that include both pictures and verses beginning with the practitioner searching for the ox; then proceeding through various steps such as glimpsing traces of the ox; seeing the ox; then catching and taming the ox; to the ox forgotten; and eventually returning to the marketplace with bliss-bestowing hands, helping new seekers.[50] In some versions of the pictures, the ox progresses from all black to mixed to pure white, echoing the cart of the white ox representing the great One Vehicle that saves all beings in the Lotus Sutra.

More relevant to the "Jewel Mirror Samādhi" line is the story about Nanquan in the *Book of Serenity*, case 69. In that story Nanquan, an early teacher of Dongshan, as described in the beginning of chapter 2, tells the assembly, "The buddhas of past present and future do not know it is: cats and cows know it is."[51] The same characters for cats and cows appear in this line of the "Jewel Mirror Samādhi" as in Nanquan's statement. This story and the involved commentary about Yunyan in the *Book of Serenity* case are discussed in chapter 3 in the section "Yunyan's Failure with Nanquan."

Cats and cows are not burdened by excessive discrimination, discursive cognition, or self-consciousness. Therefore, unlike humans, they are immediately aware of just this suchness, and in some ways know what it is before them. Cows are peaceful and contented. Cats have a composed presence and often a sensitive, alert awareness of their surroundings. Buddhas, on the other hand, while free of self-clinging still are capable of reflection and discrimination. This might be one reason they would not fully and simply know "it is." But we might also hear Nanquan praising not knowing in this utterance. We may recall the various questions about whether Yunyan knew "it is" or not, and wonder again. Buddhas know that they cannot completely know the inconceivable, ultimate reality. In his added sayings to *Book of Serenity*, case 69, after "The buddhas of past, present and future do not know it is," Wansong adds, "Just because they know it is." After "cats and cows know it is," he adds, "Just because they don't know it is."

Cats and cows are simple everyday creatures, perhaps soothing those who are astonished or startled by the rich suchness of reality, or helping alleviate one-sided attachments to ultimate reality. But also, for the wide-eyed who wonder about suchness, how to know it and how to express it, these cats and cows may help sustain and enrich the question of what it is.

———

With his archer's skill Yi hit the mark at a hundred paces,
But when arrows meet head-on, how could it be a matter of skill?

Yi was a mythological Chinese archer from around 2300 B.C.E. who at the request of the great legendary Emperor Yao was said to have shot nine of ten suns from the sky to save the crops from being scorched. Yi is here seemingly conflated with another legendary archer named Yang, from a first-century B.C.E. historical chronicle, who could hit a willow leaf at a hundred paces.⁵² In any event, this line refers to a legendary, extremely skillful archer.

Two arrows meeting head-on refers to another legendary Chinese story from the Liezi, a Daoist classic said to date back to the fifth century B.C.E., though not compiled until the fourth century C.E. A famed archer named Feiwei had an ambitious student Jichang, who decided to kill his teacher so he could become the greatest archer in the world.⁵³ But when he fired an arrow at his teacher, Feiwei immediately knew and fired an arrow back. The arrow points met in midair, and Jichang realized his folly and selfishness.

The image of arrows meeting head-on is also used in Shitou's "Harmony of Difference and Sameness," the previously mentioned predecessor to the "Jewel Mirror Samādhi."⁵⁴ This image represents a total engagement and integration with suchness, or with phenomena fully meeting phenomena, such that it goes beyond even the remarkable worldly skill of a legendary archer. In the "Harmony of Difference and Sameness" this event is compared with box and lid fitting together. This matching relates to the theme of teacher and student totally meeting, as well as a perfectly appropriate statement of reality, or a complete accord with the affirming mind.

———

The wooden man starts to sing; the stone woman gets up dancing.
It is not reached by feelings or consciousness, how could it involve
deliberation?

The provocative image "The wooden man starts to sing; the stone woman gets up dancing" sounds ludicrous, like a tin man wishing for a heart. How could an inert wooden man sing? How can a stone woman dance? We may recall Dongshan's early questions about nonsentient beings expressing the Dharma. This vision reverberates with various traditional Zen references to vitality arising from the utter stillness of upright meditative sitting. Sustained, settling practice allows access to deep sources of creative energy and revival of spirit that can support awakened, beneficial activity in the world. Many classic images exemplify this.

One version of this revitalization imagery arises in conjunction with East Asian seasonal poetic references. Spring renewal from winter coldness serves as a useful metaphor for this spiritual dynamic. Among a cascade of other nature similes for liberated activity, Hongzhi talks about spring arising in everything, saying, "People of the Way journey through the world responding to conditions, carefree and without restraint. Like clouds finally raining, like moonlight following the current, like orchids growing in the shade, like spring arising in everything, they act without [attachment to] mind, they respond with certainty."[55] Dōgen said at an annual winter Enlightenment Day commemoration, "The plum blossom opens afresh on the same branch as last year."[56] The natural elements spring forth in song and dance from the apparently withered, wintry landscape.

A monk once asked Xiangyan Zhixian (d. 898; Jpn.: Kyōgen Chikan), "What is the Way?" Xiangyan replied, "A dragon sings in a withered tree," another stirring representation of vitality emerging from decay. Xiangyan was a successor of Guishan, who first directed Dongshan to his teacher Yunyan, as related in chapter 1. When the monk told Xiangyan he did not understand the dragon singing in a withered tree, Xiangyan said simply, "There is an eyeball in a skull."[57] Later a monk asked Shishuang, successor of Yunyan's brother Daowu, "What is a dragon singing in a withered tree?" and Shishuang responded that it still holds joy. When asked about the eyeball in the skull, Shishuang said that consciousness remained.

Another monk asked Dongshan's successor Caoshan about the dragon singing in a withered tree, and Caoshan said, "The blood vein does not get cut off," referring to the ongoing succession of the intimately transmitted Dharma of suchness. The monk asked about the eyeball in the skull, and Caoshan said, "It doesn't dry up." When the monk asked if anyone had heard the dragon, Caoshan said that there was nobody in the whole world who had not heard it. The monk asked what kind of song it was, and Caoshan said he didn't know, but all who hear it lose themselves. From whence comes the joyful consciousness that allows the blood vein to keep flowing? These playful variations on the dragon's song loosen up the field for the stone woman to lose herself in dance.

One source of the wooden man image might be the Perfection of Wisdom Sutra analogy of a bodhisattva as a wooden puppet, lacking discrimination, free of passions, performing the Buddha work without hesitation.[58] Nevertheless, the wooden man in the "Jewel Mirror Samādhi" manages to bring forth a song, unlike the unfortunate wooden Indian in Hank Williams's classic song "Kaw-Liga" who "never let it [his love] show" to the Indian maid over by the antiques store. The stone woman who gets up dancing when hearing the wooden man's song is a highly pregnant image, echoed in Furong Daokai's twelfth-century scene of the stone woman giving birth at night, in the darkness beyond distinctions. This stone woman, a conventional image for a barren woman, is cited above, along with the green mountains constantly walking, in relation to the shifting perspectives inspired by the "Jewel Mirror Samādhi" line "So minute it enters where there is no gap, so vast it transcends dimension." Serene stillness is pregnant, and can shine. And these images remained pregnant in the Dongshan lineage. In Hongzhi's verse for the first of the five degrees, the partial within the true, he envisions a prequel to the wooden man's singing: "At midnight the wooden boy pounds on the moon's door. In darkness the jade woman is startled from her sleep."[59] These are appearances of phenomenal rousings within the ultimate of midnight.

A great many more references to this memorable image of wooden man and stone woman filter through the records of the Dongshan lineage. But they also appear prominently in the Rinzai

Zen collections of the capping phrases used in the koan curricu-lums. For example, Victor Sōgen Hori's valuable volume *Zen Sand* includes, among others, the sublime "The stone woman dances the dance of long life, / The wooden man sings songs of great peace." Also, "Putting on his shoes, the wooden man went away at mid-night / Wearing her bonnet, the stone woman returned at dawn" reflects interaction going into the ultimate and returning to the phenomenal. And "The wondrous activity is totally enacted in the world, / The wooden man walks calmly through the fire" is an image of complete integration and awakening.[60]

The "Jewel Mirror Samādhi" asks, "It is not reached by feelings or consciousness, how could it involve deliberation?" Illumination cannot be arrived at via mere sentiment or emotions and is not produced through conscious manipulations any more than it can be a matter of skill or expertise, like that of an adept marksman. Dongshan emphasizes the inner, alchemical nature of this reality of suchness. The singing of dragons and the dancing of compassion emerge in their own organic process from the sustained, faithful engagement and assimilation of the ultimate with the phenomena in just this situation. Dōgen quotes Hongzhi saying, in part to cele-brate the end of a summer practice period, "Directly attain the way of lord and minister in cooperation, and the spirit energy of parent and child in harmony. Up in the lapis lazuli palace, the jade woman rolls her head; in front of the bright moon hall, the stone man rubs his hands." Dōgen adds, "We simply need to remind ourselves again and again about all the generations of effort." And after a pause, "There will be no end of counting."[61] The closing section of the "Jewel Mirror Samādhi" turns to how to sustain the song and dance of the wooden men and stone women.

———

Ministers serve their lords, children obey their parents;
Not obeying is not filial, failure to serve is no help.
With practice hidden, function secretly, like a fool, like an idiot;
Just to do this continuously is called the master among masters.

The first two lines of this section are likely the most anachronistic in the whole poem in reflecting the feudal culture when this was written, as well as Confucian values that are foreign to modern Western practitioners. The second half of the line is actually that children, or it might be translated as just "sons," obey or submit to their "fathers" specifically, reflecting the totally patriarchal culture of China, and actually most premodern cultures. Of course, discrimination against women is still rampant in our time and society, but at least in current American Buddhism awareness of this history and these issues and efforts at redressing inequalities sanction a translation of "parents." But the reference to ministers or vassals serving their lords is a clear relic of feudal society, which lasted much longer in East Asia than in Europe.

The mention of obedience and filial piety, a Confucian value central to traditional Chinese culture, requires the most reinterpretation to the context of modern Western practitioners. While respect for elders is a value for some in our culture, it is not a universally held value. Modern Western developmental psychology in our shifting, nontraditional society also recognizes the need for rebellion or at least to establish individual identity, or "leaving home," as part of reaching adulthood. But even in the West, Zen provides a context to promote respect if not veneration for the ancestors in the tradition through all the inspiring old stories in the teachings.

The character for *obey* in the original could also be read as "following" one's responsibilities, and a modern sense of the significance of these lines might generally include to be dutiful and harmonize or be responsible in bodhisattva service to those in need. In the context of the "Jewel Mirror Samādhi," the import of these two lines relates to the use of lord and vassal as metaphors for host and guest, which were common Chan means of designating the absolute and relative, or universal and particular, whose relationship is the context of the five degrees. Ministers serving lords or guests caring for hosts represent the particular or phenomenal at the service of ultimate truth. The interaction of host and guest is often used as an image for the relationship of teachers and students, but often simultaneously for the interweaving of universal and particular, and the unfolding of the five degrees.

The inspiration to keep one's practice secret or hidden is commonly expressed in bodhisattva lore and scriptures. Aside from great archetypal, venerated bodhisattva figures like Mañjuśri exemplifying wisdom or the compassionate Avalokiteśvara, generally bodhisattvas are seen as working anonymously in the world in order to benefit and awaken all beings in all kinds of modes. Teachers are encouraged to intimately convey and transmit the practice of suchness humbly, without gaining any reward or recognition. At the end of his long verse "The Guidepost for Silent Illumination," Hongzhi says about the Dongshan legacy, "Our school's affair hits the mark straight and true. Transmit it to all directions without desiring to gain credit."[62]

Many stories of great masters, both historically and mythically, depict them as foolish and even appearing dull or stupid, though nevertheless providing great benefit. There are many noteworthy historical examples in the Buddhist tradition. At the great Nālanda monastery in India, Śāntideva (685?–763?) was considered stupid and lazy by his fellow monks, who compelled him to give a public talk, hoping to have him expelled. But Śāntideva presented a great discourse on the bodhisattva path and practices, *The Bodhicaryā-vatāra*, and then disappeared into the sky. This remains a classic text in Tibetan Buddhism and an extensively studied model in Western Buddhism.[63] In China the Chan monk Budai (10th cent.; Jpn.: Hotei) was a foolish, ragged vagabond who wandered the streets but was later accepted as an incarnation of the bodhisattva

Maitreya. In the familiar guise of the fat, jolly, laughing Buddha, his images are now simply designated Milofo (Maitreya Buddha) in all Chinese temples.[64] In Japan the Sōtō monk and poet Ryōkan was celebrated as a "great fool," the Dharma name he took himself, due to his forgetfulness, his often silly play with children, and his carefree mendicant lifestyle. But he was also a fully trained master, a skilled meditator, and a learned student of Dharma, whose calligraphy was treasured during his own life, and whose widely beloved poetry endures today.[65] Many more examples of fools with great hidden practice could be cited.

Dongshan's long verse ends, "Just to do this continuously is called the master among masters." The last phrase also could be read as "the host within the host." The five degrees are not exclusive to the Dongshan lineage, as they are also studied in the Linji/ Rinzai lineage and were commented on extensively, for example, by the Japanese master Hakuin Ekaku (1686–1769), founder of the modern Rinzai school.[66] Linji himself wrote about the four guests and hosts, culminating with the host within the host, in which the limited sense of self is transcended.[67] Hongzhi's verse comments on Linji's "The Four Guests and Hosts," for the host within the host include "Without disturbing the golden sun, ten thousand virtues are perfected. The palace moss, without design, contains the moon."[68] At this culmination of the process in which "It actually is me," all virtues are perfected without disturbing the natural order of light and dark, sun and moon. Beyond any design, manipulation, or desire, the very moss growing on the palace walls reflects the fullness of the moon.

The encouragement to persist and do this continuously in effect repeats Yunyan's exhortation to Dongshan to "preserve it well" or "be most thoroughgoing." Most important is the sustaining of the practice of the Dharma of suchness. This ongoing awareness is the ultimate integration of the universal and phenomenal and the complete fulfillment and realization of suchness. This practice is endless. The effort is simply to foster and nourish it in all beings.

CHAPTER THIRTEEN

The Five Degrees

Context and Background of the Five Degrees

The five degrees teachings and all the related commentaries are worthy of several lengthy books. In this work focused on Dongshan's practice teachings, this chapter offers a brief overview, emphasizing teachings attributed to Dongshan himself. From the previous chapters it is apparent that Dongshan's teaching about suchness and the art and challenges of conveying its practice can be presented and discussed without recourse to the five degrees. The five degrees teaching appears almost as an afterthought near the end of Dongshan's *Recorded Sayings* and plays no part in his section of the *Jingde Transmission of the Lamp*. While the five degrees do appear indirectly and cryptically in the "Jewel Mirror Samādhi," there is certainly much more to that teaching poem. The role of the five degrees in the "Jewel Mirror Samādhi" is discussed in detail in chapter 12. The many stories in this book are a very small portion of the numerous stories concerning Dongshan in the *Recorded Sayings* and *Transmission of the Lamp* that do not concern the five degrees. The stories I have selected for comment inform the issues of suchness and its teaching and include all the stories about Dongshan chosen by Hongzhi to feature in his collection that became the *Book of Serenity*. However, there appears toward the end of the *Recorded Sayings* two sets of verses attributed to Dongshan concerning the five degrees. So this teaching indeed plays some part in the Dongshan legacy and has been the focus of much of the commentary about Dongshan.

Following Alfonso Verdu, whose treatment of these teachings is by far the most thorough in English, I have called them the five "degrees" (Ch.: *wuwei*; Jpn.: *go i*), although they have often been designated the five "ranks" in English.[1] In Dongshan's usage and perspective, these five are aspects of the dialectical nature of reality and its practice, not primarily stages or hierarchical developments. As "degrees," they might only be seen in their first reading or comprehension as gradual degrees of accomplishment, but thereafter are clearly more like the 360 degrees of a circle, or of a compass, each an equal phase or aspect of the fullness of reality. Rather than stages of development, the five signify ontological interrelationships of the two fundamental aspects of upright and inclined, or of the ultimate or universal reality with the particular or phenomenal reality. Verdu comments, "The Five Degrees represent an attempt to visualize explicitly the five perspective moments that are implicitly identical for the enlightened mind."[2] William Powell, translator of the *Recorded Sayings*, suggests "positions" or "modes," as more neutral, appropriate alternatives to the more hierarchical rendition of "rank," since they "do not have any clearly ascending order."[3] Interestingly, modern Chinese translators of these five have called them "relations" or "positions," as in "Five Relations between Particularity and Universality" or "Five Positions of Prince and Minister."[4]

A significant portion of Chinese Caodong scholarship after Dongshan, as well as some in Japanese Sōtō history, has addressed technical aspects of the five degrees formula. But many teachers in the Sōtō lineage, including especially Dōgen, downplay the five degrees system. However, one of the three Japanese Sōtō Zen transmission documents, attributed to Dōgen himself, consists of diagrams and teachings that interpret and express the heart of the five degrees teachings. The formal five degrees system arguably became more important for the Linji lineage than it was in Caodong. Later in Japan the five degrees, in this context perhaps more appropriately called the five ranks, became significant in Rinzai Zen. This role was thanks to the comments by the formative Rinzai master Hakuin, who adopted the five ranks into the modern Rinzai koan curriculum.[5]

In order to fully consider the five degrees and the aspects of the interrelationship of particulars and universal that they describe, we must consider the background of East Asian Mahāyāna Buddhist philosophy. Especially important as a foundation to this teaching is the Huayan formulation of the fourfold *dharmadhātu* that serves as a direct precursor to the five degrees.

The Fourfold Dharmadhātu

The importance of Chinese Huayan Buddhist philosophy as a background for Dongshan has been mentioned in relation to Buddha nature theory and nonsentient beings expounding the Dharma, and in terms of interconnectedness as a context for seeing nonself. Huayan was also important to Shitou and his "Harmony of Difference and Sameness," which was a precursor to the "Song of the Jewel Mirror Samādhi." But the Huayan fourfold dharmadhātu is even more directly a forerunner to the five degrees teaching.

The fourfold dharmadhātu, or four realms of reality, begins with the realm of phenomenal events, or particulars, *shi* in Chinese. Second is the realm of principle, *li* in Chinese, which corresponds with universality or ultimate reality. Third is the unobstructed interfusion of these first two, the particulars and the universal, analogous to the way form and emptiness are expressions of each other in early Mahāyāna thought. Emptiness does not exist outside of forms, and forms are themselves empty. In the same way (although they are not exactly equivalent terms), particulars are expressions of the universal, and the universal actually exists only in its particular expressions. The fourth realm of reality, or dharmadhātu, is the mutual unimpeded nonobstruction of particulars with other particulars. Each event freely and totally supports every other phenomenal expression, a viewpoint with subtle and helpful implications, and a basis for understanding interconnectedness and dependent co-arising teachings.

The Huayan founders developed this fourfold dharmadhātu into an intricate, profound philosophical teaching, including ten aspects each of the third and fourth dharmadhātus. Huayan patriarch Chengguan (738–839; Jpn.: Chōkan) is usually credited with the full fourfold dharmadhātu teaching, although the earlier Huayan founder Dushun (557–640; Jpn.: Tojun) provided a background for much of it with his writings. An important later Huayan patriarch, Guifeng Zongmi, was also a Chan master who helped bridge the two traditions. Zongmi emphasized the third dharmadhātu, of the interaction of universal and particular, more than the fourth, of particulars with each other, which had been more emphasized in earlier Huayan.[6] The five degrees presented by Dongshan are a direct development of these fourfold dharmadhātu teachings, but describe a fivefold interaction of the particulars and the universal, the first two of the dharmadhātus.

Dongshan's Verses on the Five Degrees

Immediately before the "Jewel Mirror Samādhi" in the *Recorded Sayings* text, Dongshan presents two sets of verses on the five degrees, which are relationships between the real, true, or upright (Ch.: *zheng;* Jpn.: *shō*) on the one hand, and the partial, particular, phenomenal, or inclined (Ch.: *pian;* Jpn.: *hen*), on the other. In the *Recorded Sayings* the five relationships or degrees are (1) phenomena within the real, (2) the real within phenomena, (3) coming from within the real, (4) moving within both, and (5) arriving within both. Verdu reads the two sides as equality and diversity, and they have also been rendered as host and guest, lord and vassal, or prince and minister. The sheer proliferation and variety of terms for these two polarities help make this teaching confusing at times. But awareness of the interactive relationship between the universal and phenomenal aspects of reality helps balance and inform actual ongoing practice. However, focus on this interrelationship as a theoretical philosophical system can become merely an intellectual distraction. In Dongshan's *Recorded Sayings*, the fivefold interaction is notably not presented as an abstract, formal, or didactic teaching, but instead is suggested via two separate sets of five short verses, without any comment.[7] Rather than philosophical categories, Dongshan portrays the five degrees via poetic images. Despite all the mention of the five degrees or ranks in the references to Dongshan, these poems are the only teachings explicitly about the five degrees that are directly attributed to Dongshan. They are included here in full.

Phenomena within the Real
At the outset of the dead of night, before moonlight,
Do not be surprised to meet without recognizing
A glimmer faintly familiar from olden days.

In the first verse, within the darkened ultimate sameness of universal reality beyond all distinctions, Dongshan depicts the faint remnants of particular phenomenal potentialities. The last line might be interpreted as glancing at an old friend or a shadow of oneself not quite recognized, but which looms in the darkness.

The Real within Phenomena
An old woman waking late at dawn stands before an ancient mirror,
Clearly seeing her face, but nothing else genuine.
Don't turn away from your visage, reaching for reflections.

The second verse features the realm of phenomena including old age and partial images. Yet something wondrous of true reality still lurks there, clearly glimpsed amid the hazy shadows and distracting reflections.

The first two verses feature the ultimate and then the particular, respectively. But within each, as complements, lie the particular, and then the ultimate reality.

Coming from within the Real
Amid nothingness there is a path apart from the dusts.
If you can simply avoid the current emperor's taboo name
You will surpass the eloquence of orators of past dynasties.

The third verse depicts the emergence from serene, silent experience of the ultimate reality of emptiness or equality, beyond discriminations. One is arising from such an occurrence without hot and cold or any grasses for ten thousand miles, but with no means to express or share it. Dongshan suggests that the eloquence to share what is meaningful results from not speaking excessively. The taboo against speaking the emperor's personal name (mentioned in chapter 10) is used as an image for not saying too much, especially about the ephemeral ultimate reality. This certainly fits Dongshan's praise for his teacher Yunyan not explaining everything.

Moving within Both
Two swords crossed in a duel that need not be avoided,
Skillfully wielded, like a lotus amid flames,
Naturally have vigor to ascend the heavens.

"Moving within Both" indicates active engagement with both the real and the phenomenal, which, however, are still seen as separate sides, like two swords crossed in conflict. Yet they are handled skillfully, with the determination and vitality to energetically fulfill the bodhisattva way and liberate beings.

Arriving within Both
Falling into neither being nor nonbeing, who dares
     harmonize?
People deeply wish to escape the stream of the ordinary,
And yet after all return to sit in the warm coals and ashes.

In "Arriving within Both," the particulars and the ultimate are not at all separate, without settling into one aspect or the other. Beyond merely harmonizing two differing sides, their integration is fully realized. Though feeling the wish to be free of the mundane karmic stream, one naturally returns to just sit in the warm coals or ashes of life and death.[8]

Verses on Five Degrees of Accomplishment

Right after these five verses, and just before the "Jewel Mirror Samādhi" in the *Recorded Sayings*, Dongshan offers verses on the five degrees described in terms of categories of accomplishment. These poems closely parallel the previous five degrees, but do somewhat depict these five degrees as stages of practice development, at least until the final verse. These five poems themselves are introduced in the text with a monk asking Dongshan about each of them by the names: "looking upon"; "serving"; "accomplishing"; "accomplishing mutually"; and "accomplishment of accomplishment."[9] Dongshan responds to the monk with somewhat enigmatic questions for the first three.

When asked, "What is 'looking upon'?" Dongshan responds, "When eating, what is it?"

Asked about "serving," Dongshan inquires, "When ignoring, what is it?"

Asked about "accomplishing," Dongshan replies, "When throwing down a mattock, what is it?"

When asked about "accomplishing mutually," Dongshan says more plainly, "Not attaining things."

Asked finally about "accomplishment of accomplishment," Dongshan says, "Nothing shared."

Dongshan's verses that correspond with this version of the five degrees follow thereafter in the *Recorded Sayings*, although without repeating the names, which are inserted below.

Looking Upon

The sage kings from the outset took as their model Emperor
  Yao,
And governed the people with ceremony, their dragon waists
  bent respectfully.
Passing through the crowded markets and streets,
Benevolent rule was celebrated and culture flourished.

Emperor Yao was a great legendary leader, said to have ruled from
2357 to 2255 B.C.E. before passing over his own son as incompe-
tent and naming Shun, a worthy commoner, as his successor. In
the first verse, of "Looking Upon," such ancient models of wisdom
and compassion foster benevolence of lords to vassals. More generally, this example encourages turning from worldly concerns and
inspires for all a conversion and deepening intention of mindful
commitment toward spiritual practice.

Serving

For whom do you bathe and apply makeup and adornments?
The cuckoo's call urges all wanderers home.
Countless flowers have all fallen, yet the cry continues
Among jagged peaks, in deep wooded thickets.

The second verse, of "Serving," indicates mindfully engaging and
carrying out the practice. The subtle but pervasive personal call,
attributed to the cuckoo, has led to preparations and efforts to
offer assistance in the world. Wayfarers return home to the aspiration for compassion and benefiting all beings. This call echoes
deep throughout the ragged landscapes of the heart, and people
faithfully respond as best they can.

Accomplishing

Flowers blossom on a withered tree, in a spring beyond the
  kalpas,
Riding backward on a jade elephant, chasing the *chilin*.

Now hidden beyond the myriad lofty peaks,
The moon is clear and breeze pure at the approach of sunrise.

"Accomplishing" indicates the wondrous immersion in nondiscrimination, hidden within the lofty peaks, now hazy rather than jagged. Life emerges from the gaunt in a time beyond ages. A *chilin* (Jpn.: *kirin*) is a fabulous, mythical animal representing sages or eminent people, and sometimes described as a Chinese unicorn, as it has a single, fleshy horn. With a dragonlike head it has a deer body, horse hooves, ox tail, and multicolored fur. The chilin is a Daoist image for the goal of harmony fulfilled. The jade elephant represents purity, eminence, and knowledge. Riding backward indicates acceptant surrender to the process of the Way, but also going counter to the worldly stream of fame and gain. Just before the sunrise breaks, the noble great heart attuned to the ultimate has been sighted, but still not fully integrated.

Accomplishing Mutually
Ordinary beings and buddhas do not inhibit each other.
Mountains are naturally high, waters naturally deep.
What the myriad distinctions and numerous differences show
   is that
Where the partridges call out, hundreds of flowers bloom
   afresh.

"Accomplishing Mutually" expresses return to caring interaction with ordinary beings, appreciating the partridge's song and the opening flowers. Buddhas and deluded sentient beings do not interfere with or hinder each other. Each has its place. As contrasted with the fourth verse in the previous set of five verses, in which swords are crossed in a duel, ultimate and particular are not dialectically interacting in opposition and resolution here. Rather, the different facets are more cooperatively sharing in mutual expression. This subtle difference may have had implications for Caoshan and later viewpoints in five degrees theories.

The last two lines of this verse evoke springtime and the emergence of vitality. Later on, the tenth-century Linji master Fengxue Yanzhao (896–973; Jpn.: Fuketsu Enshō) was asked how to go beyond speech and silence as the dichotomy of differentiation and equality. Fengxue responded, "I always remember Jiangnan in springtime, the partridges calling and the hundred flowers fragrant." This question and response is cited as case 24 in the *Gateless Barrier* koan collection.[10]

Accomplishment of Accomplishment
The head sprouting horns is no longer bearable.
The mind desiring buddhahood is a cause for shame.
In the endless empty kalpa nobody has ever known
Why to journey south and seek the fifty-three [bodhisattva guides].

For the head sprouting horns, see chapter 3, the section "Yunyan's Failure with Nanquan," where Nanquan talks about horns growing on the head as an image for becoming less or other than human, but, also, for fully expressing reality without speaking. Finally, in the verse "Accomplishment of Accomplishment" the universal interpenetrating connectedness celebrated in stories of buddhas and great bodhisattvas is nothing special; there is no need to be other than commonplace humans, practicing the Way. The fifty-three refers to the wondrous bodhisattva teachers the pilgrim Sudhana visited as he traveled south in the Gandhavyūha Sutra, which is the last chapter of the Avataṃsaka Sūtra. In this fifth verse even such accomplishments are forsaken, with no special attainment desired or sought. A reasonable alternative reading of the last two lines as separate sentences is offered by Verdu. In that case the last line indeed recommends taking the pilgrimage to the fifty-three bodhisattvas, which culminates with Sudhana's entry into the inconceivably vast tower of Maitreya Bodhisattva with the adornments of Vairocana Buddha. The tower of Maitreya contains infinite other inconceivably vast towers, and indeed all phenomena, mutually interpenetrating and interacting with each other with total noninterference, illustrating the fourth dharma-dhātu, representing the ultimate accomplishment as complete mutual interconnectedness.[11]

Caoshan and the Five Degrees after Dongshan

Dongshan's two sets of verses and the allusions to fivefold interaction between inclined and upright in the "Jewel Mirror Samādhi" are the only references to the five degrees directly attributed to Dongshan. It was Dongshan's disciple Caoshan who promoted, expanded, and somewhat systematized the five degrees teachings.

Caoshan offered two versions of the five degrees, "The Five De-grees of Lord and Vassal" and the "Manifestation of the Secret of the Five Degrees." He also commented on Dongshan's verses defin-ing the aspect of the upright as identical with the realm of empti-ness and the inclined as identical with the realm of form. Caoshan furthermore identified the upright or real with the lord and the in-clined or apparent with the vassal. For Caoshan the inclined within the upright (or apparent within the real) represented a more one-sided rejection of the universal, directing oneself toward the par-ticular, while the opposite was a full rejection of the particular and entry into the universal. He designated the synthesis of both as the "Mysterious Void" or "True Principle." This rendition seems to simplify the five-part process back to the three-part dialectic of Shitou's original harmonizing of difference and sameness. At the very least, Caoshan's versions of the five degrees complicate the meaning of the third and fourth degrees of Dongshan.[12] Caoshan's versions set the stage for varied interpretations of the third and fourth degrees in later five degrees theories.

Caoshan's "Five Degrees of Lord and Vassal" start with "The lord looks at his vassal," which can be read as "Equality becomes diversity."[13] The second degree is "The vassal turns to his lord," or "Diversity resolves into equality." The third is "The lord alone," or "Abiding in equality." The fourth is "The vassal alone," or "Abiding in diversity." The fifth is "The lord and vassal meet on the road," or "The merging together of equality and diversity." This first version of Caoshan's five degrees might be interpreted as dispensing with Dongshan's third and fourth degrees, emerging from the ultimate and the two together, and simply restating Dongshan's first two degrees in two variant ways. Alternatively, Caoshan's first two degrees here might perhaps be interpreted as variations on Dongshan's third and fourth degrees. At any rate, Caoshan is shifting the terms somewhat.

Caoshan's use of lord and vassal to personalize equality and diversity, also known by such abstractions as real and apparent, universal and particular, upright and inclined, and so forth, recalls the ministers and lords of the "Jewel Mirror Samādhi" and the use of host and guest terminology. Personalizing these abstract terms may have in part been appealing to Confucian patrons of Zen and been familiar in terms of the hierarchical aspects of monastic positions. But also this personalizing reflects the role of teacher and student in the study of these five degrees, and of the Dharma of suchness generally.

Caoshan's second main description of the five degrees in terms of the manifestation of the five degrees, or secret meaning of the five degrees, is much closer in structure to Dongshan's original five verses. The descriptions Caoshan offered for them emphasize the elusive, ineffable quality of each.[14]

Dongshan used *Yi Jing* hexagrams as illustrations for the five degrees. Caoshan instead employed circular black-and-white symbols appropriated from Zongmi, the Huayan and Chan teacher whose dialectic was a precursor for the five degrees.[15] Zongmi analyzed the Yogācāra *ālayavijñāna* theory of consciousness as identical with the dharmadhātu in terms of ten stages of origination and ten corresponding stages of reversion of awareness and realization. Zongmi presented this process in terms of a fivefold structure that in some ways anticipated the Caodong five degrees, and Zongmi then provided elaborate black-and-white circle diagrams for all of these ten stages of origination and reversion.[16]

Dongshan Symbols	Caoshan Symbols				
☷ (trigram)	(circle)	The real comprising the seeming	Shift	Host	Prince
☳ (trigram)	(circle)	The seeming comprising the real	Submission	Guest	Minister
hexagram	(circle)	Resurgence of the real	Achievement	Host coming to light	Prince looking at minister
hexagram	(circle)	The seeming uniting with the real	Collective achievement	Guest returning to host	Minister returning to prince
hexagram	(circle)	Integration of the real and the seeming	Absolute achievement	Host in host	Prince and minister in harmony

Five Positions.

Dongshan's contemporary Yangshan was also noted for his use of such black-and-white circle symbols and may have helped inspire Caoshan's use of circles.

Caoshan's use of circle symbols to depict the five degrees featured mixtures of black elements, which indicate the darkness and absence of distinctions in the ultimate or the real, and of white for the light of day that allows discrimination of particulars in the phenomenal realm, the apparent or the seeming. The chart above of the five positions or degrees shows how Caoshan's circle diagrams align with the *Yi Jing* trigrams or hexagrams, discussed in relation to Dongshan's "Jewel Mirror Samādhi" in the previous chapter.[17] Following the circle diagrams are descriptions of Dongshan's verses for the five degrees and five degrees of accomplishment. The last two columns are later versions of the five based on Caoshan in terms of host and guest and prince and minister, a variation of Caoshan's lord and vassal.

Caoshan wrote a great deal more about the five degrees and used circle symbols in a variety of ways. He seems to have enjoyed abstrusely playing with the five degrees, including changing the order of the first four. Here are two of his many other additional descriptions. For coming from within the absolute, usually the third degree, Caoshan says, "The whole body revealed, unique; the root source of all things, in it there is neither praise nor blame." For the final degree, of arrival within both at once, he depicts a state beyond either phenomena or ultimate:

> As the ear does not enter sound, and sound does not block up the ear, the moment you turn therein, there have never been any names fixed in the world. . . . This is not mind or objects, not phenomena or principle; it has always been beyond name or description. Naturally real, forgetting essence and appearance, this is called simultaneous realization of both relative and absolute.[18]

Later Caodong Five Degrees Study

Interest in the five degrees faded after Caoshan and his immediate disciples. His later successors are little known, and his lineage did not survive more than a few generations. But Caodong study of the five degrees was revived in the eleventh century, along with revival of the Caodong lineage generally, thanks to Touzi Yiqing. Touzi is officially listed in the Sōtō lineage as successor of Dayang Qingxuan, although they never met. Dayang survived all of his disciples, but he conveyed transmission confirmation to Fushan Fayuan (991–1067; Jpn.: Fusan Hōen), a Linji lineage successor also in full Dharma accord with Dayang. Fushan did not take on the Caodong lineage himself, but transmitted it to his student Touzi, who had previously studied Huayan philosophy, as well as the five degrees teachings. Touzi's disciple Furong Daokai was a renowned teacher who established strong standards for the Caodong monastic community and had dozens of successors.

Hongzhi Zhengjue (1091–1157), two generations after Furong Daokai, was one of the most noted Song Chan masters, who initiated the *Book of Serenity* koan collection and also articulated the Caodong meditation praxis of serene illumination. Hongzhi wrote a set of five verses commenting wittily on Dongshan's five degrees verses:[19]

The Partial within the True
The blue sky clears and the River of Stars' cool flood dries up.
At midnight the wooden boy pounds on the moon's door.
In darkness the jade woman is startled from her sleep.

The True within the Partial
Ocean and clouds rendezvous at the top of the spirit
    mountain.
The old woman returns, hair hanging down like white silk,
And shyly faces the mirror coldly reflecting her image.

Coming from within the True
In moonlit night the huge sea monster sheds its scales.
Its great back rubs the heavens, and it scatters clouds with its
    wing feathers.
Soaring here and there along the bird's path—difficult to
    classify.

Coming from within Both Together
Meeting face to face we need not shun each other's names.
In the changing wind, no injury to the profound meaning.
In the light, a road to the natural differences.

Arriving within Both Together
The Big Dipper slants across the sky before dawn.
In dewy cold the crane begins to waken from its dreams.
As it flies out of the old nest, the pine tree up in the clouds
    topples.

Hongzhi plays with images from Dongshan. In his "Partial within the True" the ultimate real is set not in the dead of night invoked by Dongshan, but with the drying up of the flood of the River of Stars, an East Asian poetic name for our Milky Way. Instead of Dongshan's faintly familiar glimmer of phenomena, Hongzhi playfully borrows the wooden man singing and stone woman dancing from the "Jewel Mirror Samādhi" and has a wooden boy pounding on the moon to startle a jade woman.

In Hongzhi's second-degree verse he seems to have the true or real overwhelm the partial or phenomenal, as Dongshan's old woman returns with hair hanging down. But as she shyly faces the cold ancient mirror, the very ocean and clouds gather atop the spirit mountain.

Hongzhi's third-degree verse for the "Coming from within the True" evokes the third of Dongshan's second set of verses of accomplishment. In that verse Dongshan describes riding backward on a jade elephant and chasing a fabulous, composite chilin creature. Hongzhi outdoes the latter with a huge sea monster that sheds its scales, rubs heaven with its back, and scatters the clouds with its wing feathers. And yet Hongzhi incisively evokes the power of the third degree, emerging from within the ultimate, through Dongshan's image of soaring along the bird's path. Indeed, this is "difficult to classify."

Hongzhi's fourth-degree verse may reflect the later confusion between the third and fourth degrees, as it comments on Dongshan's original verse for the third degree. Indeed, instead of Dongshan's fourth "Moving within Both," Hongzhi calls it "Coming from within Both Together." Hongzhi says, "We need not shun each other's names," reflecting Dongshan saying to simply avoid the taboo name. Whereas Dongshan says, "Amid nothingness there is a path apart from the dusts," Hongzhi states, "In the light, a road to the natural differences." Here Hongzhi embraces a return to phenomena and the particular from the objectless realm. Hongzhi's final verse, on "Arriving within Both Together," seems to stand alone, exultant and apart from any of Dongshan's verses. Whereas Dongshan's final verse ends with returning to the everyday to sit in the warm coals and ashes, Hongzhi portrays an elegant, long-lived crane waking from its dreams. It flies up from its cold nest in the clouds. Suddenly, the old pine tree just topples over. Does the whole scene vanish? Or has something brand new appeared?

Major Caodong interpreters of the complex five degrees theories after Caoshan were Hongzhi's rough contemporary Jiyin Huihong (12th cent.; Jpn.: Jakuon Ekō), and later Yongjue Yuanxian (1578–1657; Jpn.: Eikaku Genkan).[20] Huihong's analysis established a primary interpretation of the five degrees, depending strongly on the "Jewel Mirror Samādhi" and *Yi Jing* trigrams and hexagrams, as well as Dongshan's verses. To somewhat oversimplify, Huihong saw the third and fourth degrees as significantly differing but presenting a developmental tension. Yuanxian later strongly criticized Huihong's interpretations. Yuanxian described the third and fourth degrees as similar and complementary, building on one another, but also sometimes the third as pivotal and the fourth as contrasting with the fifth. Yuanxian's analysis emphasizes Caoshan's circular symbols, as well as the *Yi Jing* hexagrams.

Later developments of five degrees thought in China included study within Neo-Confucianism, with a range of use of *Yi Jing* hexagrams, including some from prominent Neo-Confucianist philosopher Zhou Dunyi (1017–73).[21] These Neo-Confucian speculations, combined with theories of Yuanxian and also Huihong, were included in later eighteenth-century syncretic Japanese Sōtō doctrinal studies of the five degrees.[22] However, a problem with the Neo-Confucian approaches arises with the inaccuracy and inadequacies of the Chinese yin and yang as used to represent the apparent and real, or phenomenal and universal polarity of Dongshan's Buddhist five degrees. Using charts with hexagrams as well as circle symbols, Verdu discusses in detail how the Neo-Confucian versions of five degrees based on yin and yang, as well as on the Neo-Confucian "Great Ultimate" ideal fail to match Mahāyāna principles and, in Verdu's opinion, thereby compromise Yuanxian's approaches.[23] Verdu offers further five degrees interpretations from a Japanese Sōtō esoteric text, *Chūteki-himitsusho*, based on various sets of five buddhas, five seed syllables, five wisdoms, and other related fives from the Japanese Vajrayāna Shingon teaching.[24] Verdu finds these interpretations more helpful in developing a five degrees dialectic congruent with Huayan and true bodhisattva ideals.

The purpose of Dongshan's teaching and the five degrees is to support awakening practice. Detailed discussion of all the theoretical and philosophical implications of the dialectical development of the five degrees is far beyond the scope of this book. However, given the forty years since Verdu's groundbreaking study, new studies by contemporary Buddhist scholars of the rich philosophical potential of the five degrees are overdue.

Dōgen's indirect allusions to the five degrees will be discussed below. Dōgen strongly discouraged study of the five degrees as a systematic teaching tool. But later in Japanese Sōtō the five degrees became a focus of study through the influence of Gasan Jōseki (1276–1366), previously mentioned near the end of chapter 3 in connection with his teacher Keizan's two moons.[25] Gasan followed Jiyin Huihong's interpretations to emphasize realization of the Dharma in the phenomenal world. Gasan's successors were influential in spreading the Sōtō school, and also continued study of five degrees dialectics in Japan to the extent that study of Dōgen's writings were eclipsed for centuries.[26] Even during the revival of Dōgen studies in the seventeenth and eighteenth centuries, a leading Sōtō scholar, Shigetsu E'in (1689–1764) from the Gasan lineage, was acclaimed for his studies of the five degrees.[27]

Linji and Hakuin Use of the Five Degrees

The five degrees teaching was incorporated into the Linji school in China by Fenyang Shanzhao (947–1024; Jpn.: Funyō Zenshō), who also developed the *gongan* or koan as a Linji teaching tool. Fenyang had studied in the Caodong lineage before receiving Linji transmission. He wrote his own set of verses for the five degrees, but with his own slightly revised arrangement, featuring coming from within the real (the third degree for Dongshan) as his first degree.[28] All surviving Linji lineages descend from Fenyang.

The five degrees were further absorbed into Linji teaching by Yuanwu, who quoted Dongshan's verses on the five degrees and commented on them in the *Blue Cliff Record* case 43 about Dongshan's place beyond hot or cold, discussed in chapter 5. The five degrees were later included in Linji koan systems through this reference to them by Yuanwu. While Dōgen sharply criticized discussion of the story of hot and cold in terms of the five degrees, as discussed in chapter 5, we can see Yuanwu's commentary as his effort to apply the five degrees teaching to specific Zen stories.

The dynamic Japanese master Hakuin Ekaku (1686–1769) is the teacher from whom descends all of modern Japanese Rinzai Zen. Hakuin initiated the modern Rinzai koan curriculum and incorporated the five degrees as one of the highest portions of that curriculum. He considered Caoshan's interpretation of the five degrees the most profound doctrine in Zen.[29] Hakuin wrote an extensive commentary on Dongshan's primary five verses, which begins by bemoaning the lack of appreciation by his contemporary practitioners for the five degrees teaching, and declares how precious it is.[30] Yet, like Dōgen earlier, he strongly criticizes all of the intellectual theorizing around it: "Never have I seen anything to equal the perversion of the Five Ranks, the carping criticism, the tortuous explanations, the adding of branch to branch, the piling up of entanglement upon entanglement."[31] Hakuin values the "reciprocal interpenetration" of the apparent and the real and treasures the process involved.

Yet unlike the primary viewpoint of Dongshan and certainly of Dōgen, Hakuin clearly sees the five as "ranks" one must pass though and attain in sequence. He says, "My only fear is that a little gain will suffice you. How priceless is the merit gained through step-by-step practice of the Five Ranks of the Apparent and the Real! By this practice you not only attain the Four Wisdoms, but you personally prove that the Three Bodies are also wholly embraced within your own body."[32] For Hakuin the first rank, of the apparent within the real, is where the practitioner experiences the "Great Death" and enters into emptiness. But he stresses the need to go beyond immersion in emptiness. In the second rank, of the real within the apparent, he quotes Dōgen's teaching from "Genjōkōan" (mentioned in chapter 2), "To carry the self forward and experience myriad things is delusion. That myriad things come forth and experience the self is awakening."[33] At each rank Hakuin emphasizes the need to vigorously push beyond that to the next rank as a stage of progress in practice, culminating with the fifth, which he calls "Unity Attained."

Hakuin clearly sees these five not merely as ontological positions of interpenetration of the dialectic between universal and particular. Instead, he pushes to the extreme the implications of Dongshan's second set of verses of the five as a process of accomplishment. While Hakuin's approach of attainment certainly counters Dongshan's emphasis on the stageless bird's path and engaging the present suchness, one cannot help but appreciate and admire the spirit of Hakuin's character and determination. Undoubtedly, his practice approach has been helpful to many practitioners.

In terms of modern Rinzai koan practice, Victor Sōgen Hori comments that at the stage when the five ranks are used in the curriculum, they do not really introduce anything new to the monks.[34] Rather, the five ranks require them to systematize the koans they have already passed using Dongshan's fivefold classifications. Hori very astutely notes that among all the many terms already mentioned for what I have often called universal and particular, he prefers not to use "real" and "apparent," to avoid the implication that the "real" or ultimate is more real than the "apparent" or phenomenal reality. The point is that the five degrees is exactly about the interaction and integration of these two aspects of reality. Hori prefers "straight" and "crooked," versions of the terms "upright" and "inclined" that I have employed.

Binary Thinking and Biological Pentamerism

It is very difficult for us not to think of and see the world in terms of dualities and dichotomies. We have designed our world in binary terms, from computers to common decision making, in terms of merely two options, one from column A and one from column B. This dualistic thinking stems at least in part from the biological fact of our nature as bilateral and binary beings, with front and back, left and right, male and female. And yet what the "Jewel Mirror Samādhi" attempts to do in introducing the five degrees teaching is to present aspects of a fivefold, pentamerous reality, such as the five-flavored herb or the five-pronged vajra.

Any alternative to our dualistic mode of thinking must be difficult for us to imagine and may seem totally alien. We may find it inconceivable to conceptualize beyond two distinctions. However, animals need not be solely binary. On our very own planet we have echinoderms, with five-point radial symmetry rather than binary symmetry. Modern examples are starfish, sea urchins, sand dollars, sea cucumbers, and crinoids.[35]

But echinoderms included a much greater variety of forms during the Cambrian period, from about 540 million to 488 million years ago. This period ended with one of the earth's primary mass extinctions of species, such as the one we are currently witnessing. In one of his books on the processes of evolution, paleontologist and popular science writer Stephen Jay Gould notes that often in evolution early highly prevalent and diverse species such as the echinoderms later become a small minority. He states, "All modern echinoderms occupy the restricted realm of five-part symmetry.

Yet none of these ancient groups shows any signs of anatomical insufficiency, or any hint of elimination by competition from surviving designs."[36] In Gould's view, there is no inherent reason the great variety of early echinoderms with fivefold radial symmetry could not have evolved and developed much further on this planet.

It is difficult to generalize from echinoderms about the potential awareness of creatures with fivefold radial symmetry. Echinoderms' main sense awareness is tactile, although also sensing some variance in light and the chemical nature of the surrounding water. They have a central nerve ring, and some have had ganglia. Interestingly, early echinoderms were one of the closest relatives among primitive invertebrates to chordates, from whom vertebrates evolved. However, they are incapable of living in fresh water or on land and in various other ways do not have the prerequisites for evolving intelligence as we commonly understand it.

Thus, it may remain in the realm of science fiction to imagine intelligent beings with fivefold radial symmetry. But if pentamerous animals were to somehow evolve and develop some form of intelligent awareness, they would likely think in a very different—fivefold—manner, not only in terms of binary distinctions. Seeing the five degrees as simultaneous possibilities and not yet another system of stages or hierarchies may involve something like a fivefold, or five-flavored, awareness.

An expanded view of intelligence and awareness may be further informed by current scientific research and speculation about plant "intelligence," as described in Michael Pollan's article mentioned in chapter 1. A variety of plants clearly demonstrate the capacity for intelligent behavior in the sense of adapting to changing circumstances and communicating at some distance with other members of its species.[37] Plants have further revealed a kind of intelligence, with the ability to adapt to solve problems.[38] Because plant response and adaptation occur at a much slower time scale than human activity, we do not commonly recognize their functioning. Without a brain or nerve center, plants respond with awareness to environmental indications via what has been described as a "network" form of intelligence.[39] Based on these examples from echinoderms and plants, we might envision Dongshan's five degrees construct as simply an illuminating medium for expressing awakened awareness beyond our customary, limited opinions about consciousness or intelligence.

Dōgen's Implicit Commentaries on the Five Degrees

As already discussed in chapter 5 in the section "Dōgen's Comments," while lavishly praising Dongshan, Dōgen strongly criticized the five degrees or five ranks as a systematic teaching, as well as anyone analyzing and discussing Dongshan's teaching in terms of that formulation. Dōgen says plainly, "Do not mistakenly say that Dongshan's buddha-dharma is the five ranks of oneness and differentiation."[40] However, without ever mentioning the five degrees, at times Dōgen himself uses a fivefold structure in his teachings that might be seen as implicitly a reflection of the five degrees.

Perhaps Dōgen's most famous essay is "Genjōkōan" ("Actualizing the Fundamental Point"), written in 1233, now considered part of one of his massive master works, Shōbōgenzō (True Dharma Eye Treasury). Certainly, it is not at all necessary to analyze it in these terms, but the very first paragraph of "Genjōkōan" might be seen as a description of the five degrees.

Thomas Cleary, in his introduction to "Genjōkōan," the title of which he provocatively but insightfully translates as "The Issue at Hand," claims that the essay

contains a number of key points stated in a most concise fashion. The very first paragraph contains a complete outline of Zen, in a covert presentation of the so-called "five ranks" (go i) device of the original Chinese Sōtō Zen school. The scheme of the five ranks—relative within absolute, absolute within relative, coming from within the absolute, arriving in the relative, and simultaneous attainment in both relative and absolute—is not overtly used in Dōgen's work, perhaps because of the confusion surrounding it, but its structures are to be found throughout *Shōbōgenzō*.[41]

"Genjōkōan" has been ably translated and commented on in a number of works in English. Its first paragraph has often been subtly interpreted without any recourse to the five degrees. That paragraph is presented here, divided into the five parts that may be seen as corresponding with the five degrees:

1. As all things are buddha-dharma, there is delusion and realization, practice, and birth and death, and there are buddhas and sentient beings.
2. As the myriad things are without an abiding self, there is no delusion, no realization, no buddha, no sentient being, no birth and death.
3. The buddha way is, basically, leaping clear of the many and the one;
4. thus there are birth and death, delusion and realization, sentient beings and buddhas.
5. Yet in attachment blossoms fall, and in aversion weeds spread.[42]

The first line reflects the range of phenomena appearing within the ultimate truth of Buddha Dharma. In the second line emptiness is apparent within all phenomenal elements. In the third section appears the leaping clear or emergence from the whole dichotomy of difference and sameness. But in the fourth section, part of the same sentence as the third, the various dichotomies are both present and mutually engaged. Finally, in the fifth section, attachment and aversion and the simple everyday reality of life and death are fully accepted without any sense of distinction or disdain.

While that paragraph can be seen as reflecting the five degrees, many traditional and modern commentaries insightfully discuss it with no reference at all to the five degrees. This includes a recently published translation with commentaries on "Genjōkōan" by eminent nineteenth-century master Nishiari Bokusan and prominent twentieth-century masters Shunryū Suzuki and Kosho Uchiyama.[43]

Dōgen's other massive masterwork, *Eihei Kōroku*, consists for the most part of very short sermons, or Dharma hall discourses, addressed to his monks in his last ten years of teaching at Eiheiji monastery. One talk from 1248, number 266 out of the total of 531, might be seen as a subtle expression of the five degrees. Here is this Dharma hall discourse in its entirety:

> Sometimes I, Eihei, enter the ultimate state and offer profound discussion, simply wishing for you all to be steadily intimate in your mind field. Sometimes, within the gates and gardens of the monastery, I offer my own style of practical instruction, simply wishing you all to disport and play freely with spiritual penetration. Sometimes I spring quickly leaving no trace, simply wishing you all to drop off body and mind. Sometimes I enter the samādhi of self-fulfillment, simply wishing you all to trust what your hands can hold.
>
> Suppose someone suddenly came forth and asked this mountain monk, "What would go beyond these [kinds of teaching]?"
>
> I would simply say to him: Scrubbed clean by the dawn wind, the night mist clears. Dimly seen, the blue mountains form a single line.[44]

Dōgen might likely deny that this has anything to do with the five degrees. Elsewhere I have discussed this same Dharma hall discourse at some length as a template for five aspects of how Dōgen sees the practice of zazen.[45] Perhaps Dōgen was not thinking at all of the five degrees teaching as he spoke.

Nevertheless, the five degrees structure is apparent, and moreover Dōgen illuminates the practice significance of each of the five here. "Sometimes I enter the ultimate state and offer profound discussion, simply wishing for you all to be steadily intimate in your mind field" expresses the phenomenal within the real. The point of this degree in practice, according to Dōgen, is within the background of ultimate mind to become intimate with our own particular habits of thinking and sense of identity. Within the wider realm of awareness we each can sit steadily here in the present situation.

The second degree, of the real within the phenomenal, is expressed fully with "Sometimes within the gates and gardens of the monastery, I offer my own style of practical instruction, simply wishing you all to disport and play freely with spiritual penetration." Here Dōgen provides practical instructions for taking care of the particulars of the phenomenal world, even within the gates of the monastery. Yet the function of this degree is to freely penetrate and playfully express the ultimate, right within such simple everyday circumstances.

Dōgen activates emerging from the ultimate real when he says, "Sometimes I spring quickly leaving no trace, simply wishing you all to drop off body and mind." Coming from within immersion in the real is startling, sudden, and evokes a magnificent jade elephant and a mythical beast in Dongshan's second set of verses, a huge feathered sea monster in Hongzhi's third verse. The point of such dramatic and exultant experience is in arising from it, thereby just letting go, or dropping off body and mind, as Dōgen is fond of saying.

Moving within both sides of the particular and the universal, or upright and inclined, is expressed when, "Sometimes I enter the samādhi of self-fulfillment." This samādhi or concentrated awareness of self-fulfillment, self-enjoyment, or self-realization involves settling and attention to face the totality of our self, sometimes called non-self. The meaning of this position is Dōgen's "simply wishing you all to trust what your hands can hold." This degree allows the practice of active, dynamic acceptance of one's situation, trusting one's own capacity. By engaging our karmic potential, we can learn to face our limitations and use our abilities with flexibility.

236 | THE FIVEFOLD SUCHNESS

After being asked what might go beyond these four teachings, Dōgen offers the final degree, of arriving within both together: "Scrubbed clean by the dawn wind, the night mist clears. Dimly seen, the blue mountains form a single line." Freshened by the dawn wind, in the hazy morning, the universal equality and the particular distinctions arriving in the breeze appear simultaneously, blowing in the wind. Each of the many blue mountains of diverse difficulties and challenges, together with the greater wholeness, form but a single line on the horizon.

The Five Degrees and the Practice of Suchness

Many people find it difficult to sustain focus on the mere details of everyday existence without a sense of something that goes beyond, of the wholeness and meaningfulness of interconnectedness. Yet obsessive focus on the ultimate or universal that is not applied personally and practically remains sterile and artificial. The five degrees offer a structure for realizing how the vision of wholeness and the universal that may emerge as the backdrop of meditative practice can interact organically with the particularities of our everyday activities and relationships. Acting helpfully in response to the difficulties of the phenomenal world and deepening communion with the ultimate, or "higher power," are mutually supportive and actually not at all separate. Awareness of how these patterns appear and interact can foster balance in our practice. Thus, these five degrees are relevant and encouraging for contemporary spiritual practice.

Each of the five degrees in itself presents a lively, dynamic expression of wholeness and the practice life of suchness. The phenomenal within the real engages the call to turn the light within and proceed against the grain of worldly gain, to drop into the deep heart of spiritual practice. The real within the phenomenal presents radical acceptance and communion with the ancient timeless awakened ones, singing the haunting melody of the wondrous, ever-present nirvāṇa. Coming from within the real celebrates the startling emergence from unfathomable joyfulness, in which the three bodies of Buddha and more do not fall into any categories, but smile with intimacy in the face of all suffering. Moving within both real and phenomenal is the open round circle of the sky expressing all pure buddha fields, the land itself mysteriously empty and beneficent. Arriving within both together, naked and exposed, the indomitable person of great peace with beating red heart tenderly transforms all without a speck of separation.

Aside from and beyond all five of these vibrant positions, the teachings embedded in the stories about Dongshan provide a rich legacy that has been sustained in lively practice traditions. Dongshan's subtle teachings about engagement with suchness remain vital today for Zen people and are available for all those who wish to find meaning amid the challenges of modern lives. We meet this teaching through moving in many dimensions and directions.

We meet suchness vertically through engagement with teachers and the teaching traditions represented by sutras and koans, but also in many other handed-down enlivening cultural traditions. We meet suchness and its benefits horizontally through willingness to engage open-heartedly with our friends and neighbors, all fellow beings, to support mutual benefit and creative, sustainable livelihoods and communities. This liberative work sometimes requires going against the grain of our society and culture to realize something deeper than conventional prejudices. We may be asked to go beyond our comfort zones, to where it is very hot or cold. But it is possible to open up reality and return to the source of our present awareness, to see or hear just this. Then we may heed the call to return to help out within the conventional realities that have caused distress for our brother and sister beings. Awakened heart-mind and the transformation of conditioned circumstances may seamlessly accord, responding to beings as appropriate to the present capacities. Please take good care of this gift, and enjoy your practice of suchness.

Notes

ABBREVIATIONS: Throughout the notes, *Taishō* will refer to Taka-kusu Junjirō, ed., *Taishō Shinshū Daizōkyō* (Tokyo: Taishō Issaikyō Kankokai, 1924–33).

INTRODUCTION

1. See the discussion later in this introduction about the origins of the Cao-dong lineage.

2. See, for example, the studies of John McRae, *Seeing through Zen* (Berke-ley: University of California Press, 2003); Griffith Foulk, various articles including "Controversies Concerning the 'Separate Transmission'" in Peter Gregory and Daniel Getz, Jr., *Buddhism in the Sung* (Honolulu: University of Hawai'i Press, 1999), 220–94; Albert Welter, *The Linji Lu and the Creation of Chan Orthodoxy: The Development of Chan's Records of Sayings Literature* (New York: Oxford University Press, 2008); and Morten Schlütter, *How Zen Became Zen: The Dispute over Enlightenment and the Formation of Chan Buddhism in Song-Dynasty China* (Honolulu: University of Hawai'i Press, 2008).

3. The most prominent of the surviving lamp transmission texts is *Jingde Chuandenglu* (Jpn.: Keitoku Dentōroku), compiled by Daoyuan in 1004. It is one of the main sources for stories about Dongshan, along with his *Recorded Sayings* and the koan collections. For a translation of most of the section on Dongshan, see Chang Chung-yuan, trans., *Original Teachings of Ch'an Buddhism* (New York: Vintage Books, 1969), 58–70. The original *Jingde Chuandenglu* is in *Taishō*, 2076: 51.321b–323b. For a translation of the Indian lineage in the *Jingde Chuandenglu*, and some of the early Chinese lineage including a few generations after the Sixth Ancestor but not the precursors of Dongshan's lineage, see Sohaku Ogata, trans., *The Transmission of the Lamp: Early Masters* (Durango, Colo.: Longwood Academic, 1986).

4. See John Blofeld, trans., *The Zen Teaching of Huang Po: On the Transmission of Mind* (New York: Grove Press, 1958); and Urs App, trans. *Master Yunmen:*

From the Record of the Chan Master "Gate of the Clouds" (New York: Kodansha International, 1994).

5. See William Powell, *The Record of Tung-shan* (Honolulu: University of Hawai'i Press, 1986), 3–4. The *Recorded Sayings* of Dongshan, in Chinese, *Ruizhou Dongshan Liangjie Chanshi Yulu*, or *Dongshan Yulu* for short, can be found in *Taishō*, T1986: 47.519b–526c. In these notes I will provide original Chinese references from the *Taishō* for Dongshan's *Recorded Sayings* and for his section of the *Jingde Transmission of the Lamp*—see note 3 above—but only citations from English translations for other works.

6. For the *Blue Cliff Record* (Ch.: Biyanlu; Jpn.: Hekiganroku), see Thomas Cleary and J. C. Cleary, trans., *The Blue Cliff Record* (Boston: Shambhala; 3-volume edition, 1977; 1-volume edition, 2005, cited unless otherwise specified). For the *Book of Serenity* (Ch.: Congronglu; Jpn.: Shōyōroku), see Thomas Cleary, trans., *The Book of Serenity* (Boston: Shambhala, 2005). A number of reasonable translations of the *Gateless Barrier* (Ch.: Wumenguan; Jpn.: Mumonkan) have been published, but I will generally cite Zenkei Shibayama, *The Gateless Barrier: Zen Comments on the Mumonkan* (Boston: Shambhala, 2000).

7. Not much material is available in English for Wansong Xingxiu (1166–1246), except that he was commentator and compiler of the *Book of Serenity* and another koan collection initiated by Hongzhi. He was Dharma heir of Xueyan Man (d. 1206; Jpn.: Seggan Man), who was five generations after Furong Daokai. The historical record is unclear, but Xueyan was connected to Furong's disciple Jingyin Zijue (n.d.; Jpn.: Jōin Jikaku). Among Wansong's disciples were Yelu Chucai (1190–1244), a layman who persuaded Wansong to write the *Book of Serenity*, and who was an important advisor to Genghis Khan and his successor. Yelu influenced the Mongol rule toward Buddhism and moderate social policies. Wansong spent most of his teaching career near modern Beijing spreading Caodong teaching among the Khan rulers and court. Another Wansong disciple, Linquan Conglun (n.d.; Jpn.: Rinsen Jūrin), wrote two koan collections, the *Empty Valley*, based on cases and comments by Touzi Yiqing, and the *Vacant Hall*, based on cases and comments by Danxia Zichun. Wansong's disciple Xueting Fuyu (1203–75; Jpn.: Settei Fukuyū) was abbot at the Shaolin Monastery, which he established as a center for martial arts and the Caodong lineage; his lineage still continues.

8. See Schlütter, *How Zen Became Zen*, 157–58, for a detailed discussion of the textual history of the Baojing Sanmei, and of textual sources for Dongshan's teaching.

9. See, for examples in English, Chang, *Original Teachings*, 41–57; John Wu, *The Golden Age of Zen* (Taipei, Taiwan: United Publishing Center, 1975), 171–90; and Alfonso Verdu, *Dialectical Aspects in Buddhist Thought: Studies in Sino-Japanese Mahāyāna Idealism* (Lawrence: University of Kansas, Center

for East Asian Studies, 1974), 115–87. A recent book in this vein, which appeared too late to be appropriately evaluated or cited in this work, is Ross Bolleter, *Dongshan's Five Ranks: Keys to Enlightenment* (Somerville, Mass.: Wisdom Publications, 2014).

10. Wu, *The Golden Age of Zen*, 177.

11. *Shōbōgenzō*, "Shunjū" ("Spring and Autumn") in Kazuaki Tanahashi, trans. and ed., *Treasury of the True Dharma Eye: Zen Master Dōgen's Shōbōgenzō* (Boston: Shambhala, 2010), 633.

12. Powell, *The Record of Tung-shan*, 63; *Taishō* 1986: 47.525c.

13. For later Song dynasty questions about the early figures in this developing lineage, see Schlütter, *How Zen Became Zen*, 140, 173.

14. See Taigen Dan Leighton with Yi Wu, trans. *Cultivating the Empty Field: The Silent Illumination of Zen Master Hongzhi* (Boston: Tuttle, 2000), 71–75; also, Shunryu Suzuki, *Branching Streams Flow in the Darkness: Zen Talks on the Sandokai*, edited by Mel Weitsman and Michael Wenger (Berkeley: University of California Press, 1999).

15. In this official lineage one obvious anomaly is that Touzi Yiqing (1032–1118) is listed as a successor to Dayang Qingxuan, who died in 1027. Dayang outlived all his disciples, but he conveyed the transmission confirmation to Fushan Fayuan (991–1067), a Linji lineage successor in Dharma accord with Dayang. Fushan was unwilling to take on responsibility for the Caodong lineage himself but transmitted it to his student Touzi Yiqing. For Touzi see also chapter 13, the section "Later Caodong Five-Degrees Study."

16. See Sangharakshita, *The Eternal Legacy: An Introduction to the Canonical Literature of Buddhism* (London: Tharpa, 1985), 218–20, which includes relevant citations from the Lankāvatāra Sūtra.

17. Thomas Kasulis, *Zen Action Zen Person* (Honolulu: University of Hawaii Press, 1981), 85–86. Italics by Kasulis.

18. Cleary, *Book of Serenity*, 207; Powell, *The Record of Tung-shan*, 28–29; *Taishō* 1986: 47.520b.

19. For a brilliant, highly illuminating, academic presentation of Dōgen's panoramic approach to koans, see Steven Heine, *Dōgen and the Kōan Tradition: A Tale of Two Shōbōgenzō Texts* (Albany: State University of New York Press, 1994).

20. Takashi James Kodera, *Dogen's Formative Years in China: An Historical Study and Annotated Translation of the Hōkyō-ki* (Boulder, Colo: Prajña Press, 1980), 54–55.

CHAPTER ONE · *Nonsentient Beings Expounding Dharma*

1. Powell, *Record of Tung-shan*, 23; *Taishō* 1986: 47.519b. The Heart Sutra is a foundational, popular short version of the Perfection of Wisdom, or

prajñāpāramitā, group of sutras, with many translations available. For an illuminating traditional commentary see Kūkai's "The Secret Key to the Heart Sutra" in Yoshito Hakeda, *Kūkai: Major Works* (New York: Columbia University Press, 1972), 262–75. For a provocative, highly insightful modern historical analysis, see Jan Nattier, "The *Heart Sūtra*: A Chinese Apocryphal Text?" in *Journal of the International Association of Buddhist Studies* 15, no. 2 (1992): 153–224.

2. Powell, *Record of Tung-shan*, 23–25; *Taishō* 1986: 47.519b–c. The whole story discussed in this chapter and the next appears in Chang, *Original Teachings*, 58–61; *Jingde Transmission of the Lamp* in *Taishō* 2076: 51.321b–321c. See also Yi Wu, *The Mind of Chinese Ch'an (Zen): The Ch'an School Masters and Their Kung-ans* (San Francisco: Great Learning, 1989), 99–101.

3. Powell, *Record of Tung-shan*, 24–25; *Taishō* 1986: 47.519b–c.

4. Ibid. Such interlinked caves with communities of hermits were not uncommon through Chinese Buddhist history, and numbers of such cliff grottoes can still be seen, some with magnificent Buddhist images. Among these are the famed Dunhuang caves in Western China, where important texts from the Tang period were found in the early twentieth century.

5. For Zhanran, see Linda Penkower, "T'ien-t'ai during the T'ang Dynasty: Chan-jan and the Sinification of Buddhism" (PhD diss., Columbia University, 1993); and Robert Sharf, "How to Think with Chan Gong'an," in *Thinking with Cases: Specialist Knowledge in Chinese Cultural History*, ed. Charlotte Furth, Judith Zeitlin, and Ping-chen Hsiung, 213–14 (Honolulu: University of Hawaii Press, 2007).

6. Robert Sharf, *Coming to Terms with Chinese Buddhism: A Reading of the Treasure Store Treatise* (Honolulu: University of Hawai'i Press, 2002), 247.

7. Sharf, "How to Think," 212. This article by Sharf includes a valuable survey of the history of this issue in China. See also the stimulating discussion in Robert Sharf, "Is Nirvāna the Same as Insentience? Chinese Struggles with an Indian Buddhist Ideal" in *India in the Chinese Imagination: Buddhism and the Formation of Medieval Chinese Culture*, ed. John Kieschnick and Meir Shahas (Philadelphia: University of Pennsylvania Press, 2013).

8. For the Avataṃsaka Sūtra itself, see Thomas Cleary, *The Flower Ornament Scripture* (Boston: Shambhala, 1984–93). For commentaries on the Huayan school philosophy, see Thomas Cleary, *Entry into the Inconceivable: An Introduction to Hua-yen Buddhism* (Honolulu: University of Hawai'i Press, 1983); and Peter Gregory, *Tsung-mi and the Sinification of Buddhism* (Honolulu: University of Hawai'i Press, 2002). For the Lotus Sutra, see Gene Reeves, *The Lotus Sutra* (Boston: Wisdom, 2008).

9. See Jacqueline Stone, *Original Enlightenment and the Transformation of Medieval Japanese Buddhism* (Honolulu: University of Hawaii Press, 1999), 9, 14, 170; and Penkower, "T'ien-t'ai during the T'ang Dynasty," 371, 404, 430n68.

10. Robert Sharf, "On the Buddha-nature of Insentient Things: How to Think about a Ch'an Kung-an," section II of online, preliminary version of portions of the already cited essay, "How to Think," second to last paragraph, http://kr.buddhism.org/zen/koan/Robert_Sharf-e.htm.

11. Sharf, "How to Think," 222.

12. One of the major sources for this teaching was the Mahāparinirvāna Sutra. See Mark Blum, *The Nirvana Sutra* (Berkeley: Numata Center for Buddhist Translation and Research, 2013). Another canonical source is "The True Lion's Roar of Queen Śrīmālā" in Garma C. C. Chang, ed., *A Treasury of Mahāyāna Sūtras: Selections from the Mahāratnakūta Sūtra* (University Park: Pennsylvania State University Press, 1983), 363–86. See also the helpful discussion of issues involved in this teaching in Sallie King, *Buddha Nature* (Albany: State University of New York Press, 1991).

13. Lambert Schmithausen, *Plants in Early Buddhism and the Far Eastern Idea of the Buddha-Nature of Grasses and Trees* (Lumbini, Nepal: Lumbini International Research Institute, 2009).

14. See the fascinating article by Michael Pollan, "The Intelligent Plant," *New Yorker*, December 23 & 30, 2013, 92–105.

15. Sharf, "How to Think," 216.

16. Sharf, "Is Nirvāna the Same as Insentience?"

17. Sharf, "How to Think," 220.

18. See Albert Welter, "Zen Syncretism: An Examination of Dōgen's Zen Thought in Light of Yongming Yanshou's Chan Teachings in the *Zongjing Lu*," in *Dōgen Textual and Historical Studies*, ed. Steven Heine, 188–91 (New York: Oxford University Press, 2012).

19. See Tanahashi, *Treasury of the True Dharma Eye*, 548–57.

20. See Shohaku Okumura and Taigen Dan Leighton, trans. *The Wholehearted Way: A Translation of Eihei Dōgen's Bendōwa with Commentary by Kōshō Uchiyama Roshi* (Boston: Tuttle, 1997), 22–23.

21. Powell, *Record of Tung-shan*, 25; *Taishō* 1986: 47.519c.

22. Powell, *Record of Tung-shan*, 26; *Taishō* 1986: 47.519c–520a.

23. Powell, *Record of Tung-shan*, 26; *Taishō* 1986: 47.520a.

24. For another rendition see Chang, *Original Teachings*, 58–59; *Jingde Transmission of the Lamp* in *Taishō* 2076: 51.321b–321c. A version of the whole story from the Wudeng Huiyuan, a thirteenth-century compilation of five lamp transmission texts, can be found in Cleary and Cleary, *Blue Cliff Record*, 612–14. For Dōgen's version with his commentary, see Taigen Dan Leighton and Shohaku Okumura, trans. *Dōgen's Extensive Record: A Translation of Eihei Kōroku* (Boston: Wisdom, 2004), 405–7, 570–71.

25. Tanahashi, *Treasury of the True Dharma Eye*, 552.

26. Ibid., 553.

27. For current research on dhārani, see, for example, Paul Copp, "Anointing

Phrases and Narrative Power: A Tang Buddhist Poetics of Incantation," *History of Religions* 52, no. 2 (2012); and Paul Copp, *The Body Incantatory: Spells and the Ritual Imagination in Medieval Chinese Buddhism* (New York: Columbia University Press, 2013).

28. See Hirakawa Akira, *A History of Indian Buddhism: From Śākyamuni to Early Mahāyāna* (Honolulu: University of Hawaii Press, 1990), 300–1.

29. See Cleary, *Book of Serenity*, 229.

30. For Avalokiteśvara and the bodhisattva of compassion's diverse iconography, see Taigen Dan Leighton, *Faces of Compassion: Classic Bodhisattva Archetypes and Their Modern Expression*, rev. ed. (Boston: Wisdom, 2012), 167–209.

31. Cleary, *Book of Serenity*, 229–30.

32. Wallace Fowlie, trans., *Rimbaud: Complete Works, Selected Letters* (Chicago: University of Chicago Press, 1966), 193. It has recently been suggested that some modes of what has been called synesthesia might be better defined as "ideasthesia," in which sensory elements are mingled not with other sensory inputs, but rather with semantic elements of meaning. See http://en.wikipedia.org/wiki/Ideasthesia, which cites combinations of letters and colors, akin to Rimbaud's example. However, Rimbaud seems to correlate colors with the sounds of the letters, rather than their semantic context. He does pose a modern analogue to Dongshan, presenting a quality of awareness beyond the conventional limits of conceptualization.

33. Leighton and Okumura, *Dōgen's Extensive Record*, 202.

34. See Chang, *Original Teachings*, 65; *Jingde Transmission of the Lamp* in *Taishō* 2076: 51.322c; or Powell, *Record of Tung-shan*, 52; *Taishō* 1986: 47.524b.

35. Leighton and Okumura, *Dōgen's Extensive Record*, 569.

36. Ibid., 405–7.

CHAPTER TWO · *Depicting This Reality*

1. Powell, *Record of Tung-shan*, 23; *Taishō* 1986: 47.519a; see also Chang, *Original Teachings*, 58; *Jingde Transmission of the Lamp, Taishō* 2076: 51.321b.

2. This story can be found in Powell, *Record of Tung-shan*, 27–28; *Taishō* 1986: 47.520a; Chang, *Original Teachings*, 59–60; *Jingde Transmission of the Lamp, Taishō* 2076: 51.321b–321c; and in the commentary to case 49 in Cleary, *Book of Serenity*, 206–7. It should be noted that the phrase "describe your reality," this reality, or "genuine image" might also be read as someone asking whether Dongshan received Yunyan's "portrait" (Jpn.: *chinzō*), which later in Chan history was bestowed as an insignia of Dharma transmission. That this word is used here is evidence of the later provenance of this story in the *Recorded Sayings*. But in context the story indicates something deeper, the actual Dharma, or teaching of reality, presented by Yunyan.

3. Powell, *Record of Tung-shan*, 27; *Taishō* 1986: 47.520a.
4. Cleary, *Book of Serenity*, 206.
5. See, for example, the Satipaṭṭhāna Sutta, Bhikku Ñāṇamoli and Bhikku Bodhi, trans., *The Middle Length Discourses of the Buddha: A Translation of the Majjhima Nikāya* (Boston: Wisdom, 1995), 145–55. For a modern treatment see Mark Epstein, *Thoughts without a Thinker* (New York: HarperCollins, 1995), 109–28.
6. For the Huayan Fourfold Dharmadhātu see Cleary, *Entry into the Inconceivable*, 24–42, 147–69; and Garma C. C. Chang, *The Buddhist Teaching of Totality: The Philosophy of Hwa Yen Buddhism* (University Park: Pennsylvania State University Press, 1971), 18–21, 136–70.
7. Fowlie, *Rimbaud*, 302–5.
8. For a full discussion of the complexity of this idea of manas in Yogācāra, see Dan Lusthaus, *Buddhist Phenomenology: A Philosophical Investigation of Yogācāra Buddhism and the Ch'eng Wei-shih lun* (London: RoutledgeCurzon, 2002), including pp. 57, 145–46, 171–73, 310–11. For a good introduction to Yogācāra, see Tagawa Shun'ei, *Living Yogācāra* (Boston: Wisdom, 2009). See also Reb Anderson, *The Third Turning of the Wheel: Wisdom of the Samdhinirmocana Sutra* (Berkeley: Rodmell Press, 2012); and Red Pine, trans. and commentary, *The Lankavatara Sutra* (Berkeley: Counterpoint, 2012).
9. Fowlie, *Rimbaud*, 302–3.
10. For *I'm Not There*, see www.imdb.com/title/tt0368794/. For one Zen-influenced view of Dylan's career, see Steven Heine, *Bargainin' for Salvation: Bob Dylan, a Zen Master?* (New York: Continuum, 2009), 92–94. In this book, Heine uses a Zen dialectic approach to analyze the shifting phases of Dylan's career in terms of the shifting interplay of dualistic phases of certainty and moralistic conviction with, on the other hand, nondualistic periods of intense questioning. Heine sees the Haynes movie's approach of a circle of multiple characters as insufficient and claims that the works of the last fifteen years or so are Dylan's Middle Way synthesis between the previous personae.
11. See Greil Marcus, *Invisible Republic: Bob Dylan's Basement Tapes* (New York: Henry Holt, 1997), 198–204. The song "I'm Not There" was never officially released by Dylan, until the 2014 *Basement Tapes: The Bootleg Series Vol. 11*. It is also available, with Dylan singing, as the last song on the 2007 CD from the movie *I'm Not There*.
12. Ibid., 200.
13. Tanahashi, *Treasury of the True Dharma Eye*, 29. This has also been translated as "Acting on and witnessing myriad things with the burden of oneself is 'delusion.' Acting on and witnessing oneself in the advent of myriad things is enlightenment." Thomas Cleary, trans., *Shōbōgenzō: Zen Essays by Dōgen* (Honolulu: University of Hawaii Press, 1986), 32. Another translation offers

"Conveying oneself toward all things to carry out practice-enlightenment is delusion. All things coming and carrying out practice-enlightenment through the self is realization." Shohaku Okumura, *Realizing Genjōkōan: The Key to Dōgen's Shōbōgenzō* (Boston: Wisdom, 2010), 1.

14. See Robert Morrell, *Early Kamakura Buddhism: A Minority Report* (Berkeley: Asian Humanities Press, 1987), 57. This helpful list of four mistaken approaches to practice, along with merely accepting things as they are, includes to rely on performance of works, to rely on cessation of mental operations, and to rely on elimination of the passions. This list is contained in the Perfect Enlightenment Sutra, an important text in Chinese Buddhism, and was commented on by the important Chan and Huayan master Guifeng Zongmi (780-841; Jpn.: Keihō Shūmitsu).

15. See Powell, *Record of Tung-shan*, 27–28; *Taishō* 1986: 47.520a; and Chang, *Original Teachings*, 60; *Taishō* 2076: 51.321c, for translations as "him."

16. Powell, *Record of Tung-shan*, 27; *Taishō* 1986: 47.520a.

17. Cleary, *Book of Serenity*, 206; see also Chang, *Original Teachings*, 60–61; *Jingde Transmission of the Lamp*, *Taishō* 2076: 51.321c; Powell, *Record of Tung-shan*, 28; *Taishō* 1986: 47.520a–b. Powell translates the final comment as "If he knew reality, why did he go to the trouble of answering that way?"

18. Cleary, *Book of Serenity*, 207; see also Chang, *Original Teachings*, 61–62; *Jingde Transmission of the Lamp*, *Taishō* 2076: 51.321c; Powell, *Record of Tung-shan*, 28–29; *Taishō* 1986: 47.520b.

19. Ibid.

20. Based on Cleary, *Book of Serenity*, 208, except that I have changed Cleary's more abstract, philosophical rendition of "absolute and relative" to "upright and inclined" and his "jade machine" to "jade works." See also *Taishō* 2001: 48.23a.

21. Shunryu Suzuki, *Not Always So: Practicing the True Spirit of Zen*, ed. Edward Espe Brown (New York: HarperCollins, 2002), 78. This talk appears as from February 23, 1971, in "Suzuki Roshi Lecture Transcripts," courtesy of David Chadwick and San Francisco Zen Center.

22. Suzuki, *Not Always So*, 108–9.

23. Tenshin Reb Anderson, *Warm Smiles from Cold Mountains* (San Francisco: San Francisco Zen Center, 1995), 87.

CHAPTER THREE · *Yunyan's Journey to Suchness*

1. Powell, *Record of Tung-shan*, 63; *Taishō* 1986: 47.525c.

2. Powell, *Record of Tung-shan*, 3.

3. Thomas Cleary, trans., *Sayings and Doings of Pai-chang: Ch'an Master of Great Wisdom* (Los Angeles: Center Publications, 1978), 26.

4. See Cleary, *Book of Serenity*, case 8, 32–36; and Shibayama, *Gateless Barrier*,

case 2, 32–41. For a full discussion of a range of implications of this story, see Steven Heine, *Shifting Shape, Shaping Text: Philosophy and Folklore in the Fox Kōan* (Honolulu: University of Hawai'i Press, 1999).

5. Albert Welter, *Monks, Rulers, and Literati: The Political Ascendancy of Chan Buddhism* (New York: Oxford University Press, 2006), 84–85. Welter questions the biological link between Daowu and Yunyan, calling them "alleged brothers."

6. Francis Cook, trans., *The Record of Transmitting the Light: Zen Master Keizan's Denkoroku* (Somerville, Mass.: Wisdom, 2003), 188–89. See also Andrew Ferguson, *Zen's Chinese Heritage* (Somerville, Mass.: Wisdom, 2000), 142–43.

7. Cook, *Record of Transmitting the Light*, 188. See also Ferguson, *Zen's Chinese Heritage*, 142–43. Dōgen includes this story in his koan collection in volume 9 of *Eihei Kōroku* as case 20; see Leighton and Okumura, *Dōgen's Extensive Record*, 549–50.

8. Cleary, *Book of Serenity*, 292.

9. Ibid., 291.

10. See ibid., case 9, 37–41; Cleary and Cleary, *Blue Cliff Record*, case 63, 406–8; and Shibayama, *Gateless Barrier*, case 14, 107–13. Dōgen suggests that in Nanquan's place he would have accepted the monks' silence and released the cat; see Leighton and Okumura, *Dōgen's Extensive Record*, 588–589nn158–60.

11. Also in the commentary to case 69, see Cleary, *Book of Serenity*, 291.

12. Ibid., 291–93.

13. This story is also included by Dōgen, with his verse comment, as case 61 in his koan collection in volume 9 of his Eihei Kōroku; see Leighton and Okumura, *Dōgen's Extensive Record*, 577–78.

14. Cleary, *Book of Serenity*, 291.

15. Shohaku Okumura, unpublished translation, *Shōbōgenzō* "Kannon" by Dōgen, 1242.

16. Cleary, *Book of Serenity*, case 21, 91–94.

17. When I was *shuso*, or head monk, at Tassajara monastery in California in the spring 1990 practice period, I chose this story as the case for the shuso ceremony at the end of the practice period, when all the students and returning former head monks publicly question the current head monk as the culmination of that training. Such questioning can be fierce. Indeed, Dongshan once questioned a head monk so insistently that the head monk passed away the next day, and Dongshan became known as "one who questions head monks to death." See Powell, *Record of Tung-shan*, 33–34; *Taishō* 1986: 47.521a.

18. Cleary, *Book of Serenity*, 93, 91.

19. Ibid., 94.

20. Ibid., 92.

21. Ibid., 544. In case 83 of Dōgen's *Mana Shōbōgenzō* collection of three

hundred koan cases without comment, Dōgen does attribute the same dialogue to Daowu with Yunyan. This collection without comments is not to be confused with the more noted *Shōbōgenzō*, which has extended essays by Dōgen. See Kazuaki Tanahashi and John Daido Loori, trans., with commentary by John Daido Loori, *The True Dharma Eye: Zen Master Dōgen's Three Hundred Koans* (Boston: Shambhala, 2005), 110; or Gudo Wafu Nishijima, *Master Dogen's Shinji Shobogenzo* (Essex, UK: Windbell, 2003), 111.

22. Cleary, *Book of Serenity*, 164.

23. Ibid., 165. Li Bo, one of the classic Tang poets, was famed not only for his wonderful poetry, but also as a Daoist mystic who loved wine and the moon. He was an Imperial court favorite who also spent years in exile; according to legend, he drowned when drunkenly reaching over the side of a boat to embrace the reflection of the moon. See, for example, J. P. Seaton and James Cryer, trans., *Bright Moon, Perching Bird: Poems by Li Po and Tu Fu* (Middletown, Conn.: Wesleyan University Press, 1987).

24. Cleary, *Book of Serenity*, 164–65.

25. Tanahashi, *Treasury of the True Dharma Eye*, 454.

26. Leighton and Okumura, *Dōgen's Extensive Record*, 308–9.

27. Ibid., 462–64.

28. Thomas Cleary, *Timeless Spring: A Soto Zen Anthology* (Tokyo: Weatherhill, 1980), 138–39.

29. For Keizan and Gasan, see William Bodiford, *Sōtō Zen in Medieval Japan* (Honolulu: University of Hawaii Press, 1993), 81–107; and Bernard Faure, *Visions of Power: Imagining Medieval Japanese Buddhism* (Princeton, N.J.: Princeton University Press, 1996).

30. See Dōgen's *Shōbōgenzō* essay, "One Bright Pearl" ("Ikka no Myōju"), in Tanahashi, *Treasury of the True Dharma Eye*, 34–38.

CHAPTER FOUR · *No Grass for Ten Thousand Miles*

1. Cleary, *Book of Serenity*, 382–84. See also Powell, *Record of Tung-shan*, 48; *Taishō* 1986: 47.523b–c. Ten thousand "miles" is in Chinese ten thousand *li*, which literally amounts to a bit less than twenty-five thousand miles, but the number ten thousand is commonly used in Buddhism and Chinese to signify any very large number.

2. From the song "Big Yellow Taxi," in Joni Mitchell's album *Ladies of the Canyon*, 1970.

3. Powell, *Record of Tung-shan*, 48; *Taishō* 1986: 47.523b–c; Cleary, *Book of Serenity*, case 68, p. 287.

4. Cleary, *Book of Serenity*, 383.

5. Powell, *Record of Tung-shan*, 44; *Taishō* 1986: 47.522c.

6. Cleary, *Book of Serenity*, 383.

7. See Ruth Fuller Sasaki, Yoshitaka Iriya, and Dana Fraser, trans., *The Recorded Sayings of Layman P'ang: A Ninth-Century Zen Classic* (New York: Weatherhill, 1971), 75.

8. Leighton and Okumura, *Dōgen's Extensive Record*, 542.

9. Ibid., 263.

10. Ibid., 480.

11. For "The Harmony of Difference and Sameness" and "The Song of the Grass Hut," see Leighton, *Cultivating the Empty Field*, 72–75. See also Ben Connelly, *Inside the Grass Hut: Living Shitou's Classic Zen Poem* (Somerville, Mass.: Wisdom, 2014).

12. Leighton and Okumura, *Dōgen's Extensive Record*, 88–89, 193–94; Cleary and Cleary, *Blue Cliff Record*, case 87, 478–79.

13. Cleary, *Book of Serenity*, 17–18.

CHAPTER FIVE · *Beyond Heat or Cold*

1. Powell, *Record of Tung-shan*, 49; *Taishō* 1986: 47.523c; Cleary and Cleary, *Blue Cliff Record*, 258–63.

2. Anderson, *Third Turning of the Wheel*, 24.

3. For comparison of Dongshan and the Caodong tradition with Linji and his tradition, see Schlütter, *How Zen Became Zen*, 157–58.

4. Jack London, *To Build a Fire and Other Favorite Stories* (Mineola, N.Y.: Dover, 2008), 1–14. See also www.jacklondons.net/buildafire.html.

5. Ibid., 2.

6. Ibid., 12.

7. Ibid., 14.

8. Reeves, *Lotus Sutra*, 354–55.

9. See James Benn, "The *Lotus Sutra* and Self-Immolation," in *Readings of the Lotus Sutra*, ed. Stephen Teiser and Jacqueline Stone (New York: Columbia University Press, 2009), 107–31; and James Benn, *Burning for the Buddha: Self-Immolation in Chinese Buddhism* (Honolulu: University of Hawai'i Press, 2007).

10. Chan Khong, *Learning True Love: How I Learned & Practiced Social Change in Vietnam* (Berkeley: Parallax Press, 1993), 38–40.

11. Ibid., 96–106.

12. See Jeffrey Bartholet, "Aflame: A Wave of Self-Immolations Sweeps Tibet," *New Yorker*, July 18 & 15, 2013, 45; Asia News, "China Arrests 600 Tibetans after Self-Immolations," Reader Supported News (RSN), May 31, 2012, http://readersupportednews.org/news-section2/329-126/11701-china-arrests-600-tibetans-after-yesterdays-self-immolations; Christopher Bodeen, "Two Dozen Tibetans Have Set Themselves on Fire This Month," Reader Supported News (RSN), November 29, 2012, http://readersupportednews.org/news-section2/328-121/14782-focus-two-dozen-tibetans-have-set-them

selves-on-fire-this-month; Michael Biggs, "Ultimate Sacrifice: What's the Difference between Self-Immolators and Suicide Bombers?" Foreign Policy, December 3, 2012, www.foreignpolicy.com/articles/2012/12/03/ultimate _sacrifice#.UL3lR02oZ_w.email; "Lhamo Tseten, Tibetan Farmer, Self-Immolates in China," World Post, October 26, 2012, www.huffingtonpost .com/2012/10/26/lhamo-tseten_n_2022548.html.

13. "Understanding the Self-Immolations: A Timeline," Tibet Press Watch, Winter 2012, www.savetibet.org/tibet-press-watch-winter-2012.

14. Bartholet, "Aflame," 45–49.

15. James Hansen, "Game Over for the Climate," New York Times, May 9, 2012.

16. "Climate Parents: For Kids' Future, Mark Hertsgaard Urges Families to Take On Global Warming," Democracy Now, July 20, 2012, www.democracynow. org/2012/7/20/climate_parents_for_kids_future_mark#transcript [video].

17. See Bill McKibben, Eaarth: Making a Life on a Tough New Planet (New York: St. Martin's Griffin, 2011).

18. Ibid., 10.

19. Ibid., 45.

20. Chang, Treasury of Mahāyāna Sūtras, 270, 265.

21. Cleary and Cleary, Blue Cliff Record, 260.

22. Ibid., 261–63. See also Powell, Record of Tung-shan, 49; Taishō 1986: 47.523c.

23. Tanahashi, Treasury of the True Dharma Eye, 631–37.

24. Ibid., 631–32.

25. Ibid., 636.

26. Ibid., 632–33.

27. Ibid., 633.

28. Ibid., 634.

29. Ibid., 634–35.

30. Ibid., 635.

31. Ibid., in "Dragon Song" ("Ryūjin"), the essay that chronologically immediately preceded "Spring and Autumn" ("Shunju"), 627–30.

32. Leighton and Okumura, Dōgen's Extensive Record, 223.

33. Tanahashi, Treasury of the True Dharma Eye, 636.

34. Leighton and Okumura, Dōgen's Extensive Record, 587–88.

35. "Suzuki Roshi Lecture Transcripts," courtesy of David Chadwick and San Francisco Zen Center, from July 26, 1969, at Tassajara and August 19, 1969, at Sōkōji.

CHAPTER SIX · The White Rabbit

1. Powell, Record of Tung-shan, 32–36; Taishō 1986: 47.520c–521b.

2. Powell, Record of Tung-shan, 35; Taishō 1986: 47.521b; Cleary, Book of Serenity, 237–40.

3. Cleary, *Book of Serenity*, 237.
4. Ibid., 237–38.
5. Reeves, *Lotus Sutra*, 142–46.
6. Ibid., 225.
7. Powell, *Record of Tung-shan*, 35; *Taishō* 1986: 47.520a. This statement in the *Recorded Sayings* is also quoted by Wansong in his commentary to case 93 of the *Book of Serenity*; see Cleary, *Book of Serenity*, 400.
8. Cleary, *Book of Serenity*, 238.
9. Reeves, *Lotus Sutra*, 215–17.
10. Ibid., 251–53.
11. Cleary, *Book of Serenity*, 238.
12. Ibid., 239.
13. Ibid., case 37, p. 165. This is Hongzhi's verse about seeing the moon through ivy, discussed in chapter 3.
14. See "Man in the Moon," Wikipedia, http://en.wikipedia.org/wiki/Man_in_the_Moon.
15. Lewis Carroll, *Alice's Adventures in Wonderland & Through the Looking-Glass*, with *Alice's Adventures*, originally published in 1865 (New York: New American Library, 1960), 17–18.
16. Reeves, *Lotus Sutra*, 279–90.

CHAPTER SEVEN · *The Bird's Path*

1. See Powell, *Record of Tung-shan*, 55; *Taishō* 1986: 47.524c; and also Chang, *Original Teachings*, 67; *Jingde Transmission of the Lamp* in *Taishō* 2076: 51.322c.
2. See Powell, *Record of Tung-shan*, 85n156. The alternative source for "without a thread on your feet" is the Zutang Ji (The Collection from the Patriarch Hall), a lamp transmission text completed in 952 with a section on Dongshan. Powell cites that version of the story to translate the line as "without hemp sandals on one's feet." For a slightly different interpretation of this story, see Lu K'uan Yü [Charles Luk], *Ch'an and Zen Teaching*, Series 2 (London: Rider, 1961), 141–42 and 142n1.
3. For a good survey of issues involved in Buddhist paths, see Robert Buswell, Jr., and Robert Gimello, eds., *Paths to Liberation: The Mārga and Its Transformations in Buddhist Thought* (Honolulu: University of Hawaii Press, 1992).
4. See Robert Thurman, trans., *The Holy Teaching of Vimalakīrti: A Mahāyāna Scripture* (University Park: Pennsylvania State University Press, 1976), 153; or Walpola Rahula, *What the Buddha Taught* (New York: Grove Press, 2d edition, 1974), 45–50.
5. There are many useful translations of the classic *Dao De Jing*, by the great Daoist founder Laozi from around the sixth century B.C.E. For example, see Thomas Cleary, *The Essential Tao* (San Francisco: HarperSanFrancisco,

1991); Guy Leekley, *Tao Te Ching: A New Version for All Seekers* (Woodlands, TX: Anusara, 2004); Yi Wu, *The Book of Lao Tzu (The Tao Te Ching)* (San Francisco: Great Learning, 1989); Man-jan Cheng, *Lao-tzu: "My Words Are Very Easy to Understand,"* trans. Tam Gibbs (Richmond, Calif.: North Atlantic Books, 1981); and the early version: Arthur Waley, *The Way and Its Power: A Study of the Tao Te Ching and Its Place in Chinese Thought* (New York: Grove Press, 1958).

6. See Philip Yampolsky, *The Platform Sutra of the Sixth Patriarch* (New York: Columbia University Press, 1967), 110. Yampolsky indicates where this story first appears in the Song dynasty in the introduction to his translation of a Tang dynasty edition of the Platform Sutra from the Dunhuang caves. For the *Gateless Barrier* version of the story, see Shibayama, *Gateless Barrier*, 166–67.

7. Anderson, *Third Turning of the Wheel*, 142.

8. See Powell, *Record of Tung-shan*, 85n155.

9. Gil Fronsdal, trans., *The Dhammapada* (Boston: Shambhala, 2005), 25. See also John Ross Carter and Mahinda Palihawadana, trans., *The Dhammapada* (New York: Oxford University Press, 1987), 28, 175–77.

10. Edward Conze, trans., *The Perfect Wisdom in Eight Thousand Lines & Its Verse Summary* (Bolinas, Calif.: Four Seasons Foundation, 1973), 25.

11. Edward Conze, trans., *The Large Sutra on Perfect Wisdom* (Berkeley: University of California Press, 1975), 118.

12. Cleary, *Flower Ornament Scripture*, 702. The Daśabhumika Sūtra, though considered one of the earliest Mahāyāna sutras, was later incorporated as chapter 26 into the much larger Avataṃsaka Sūtra.

13. Powell, *Record of Tung-shan*, 44; Taishō 1986: 47.522c.

14. Powell, *Record of Tung-shan*, 67; Taishō 1986: 47.526b.

15. Cleary and Cleary, *Blue Cliff Record*, 634–35; or in the 3-volume edition, vol. 2, 463–64.

16. See Peter Berthold, *Bird Migration: A General Survey*, 2nd ed. (New York: Oxford University Press, 2001); Hugh Dingle, *Migration: The Biology of Life on the Move* (New York: Oxford University Press, 1996); Scott Weidensaul, *Living on the Wind: Across the Hemisphere with Migratory Birds* (Vancouver: Douglas & McIntyre, 1999); and "Bird Migration," Wikipedia, http://en.wikipedia.org/wiki/Bird_migration.

17. Okumura, *Realizing Genjōkōan*, 4; for commentary on this passage see pp. 157–79. Among other good translations are "Genjōkōan" in Tanahashi, *Treasury of the True Dharma Eye*, 29–33; Cleary, *Shōbōgenzō: Zen Essays*, 32–35; and Norman Waddell and Masao Abe, trans., *The Heart of Dōgen's Shōbōgenzō* (Albany: State University of New York Press, 2002), 40–45. See also Nishiari Bokusan et al., trans. and commentaries, *Dogen's Genjo Koan: Three Commentaries* (Berkeley: Counterpoint, 2011).

18. Tanahashi, *Treasury of the True Dharma Eye*, 340.
19. Bob Dylan, "Ballad in Plain D," from the album *Another Side of Bob Dylan*, bobdylan.com/us/songs © 1964 by Warner Bros. Inc., renewed 1992 by Special Rider Music.
20. Taigen Dan Leighton and Shohaku Okumura, trans., *Dōgen's Pure Standards for the Zen Community: A Translation of Eihei Shingi* (Albany: State University of New York Press, 1996), 139–47.
21. All quotations in this section are from Gary Snyder, *The Practice of the Wild* (Berkeley: Counterpoint, 1990), 154–65.
22. Leighton and Okumura, *Dōgen's Extensive Record*, 93.

CHAPTER EIGHT · *On the Mountaintop*

1. Cleary, *Timeless Spring*, 45. See also Powell, *Record of Tung-shan*, 49; *Taishō* 1986: 47.523c; Chang, *Original Teachings*, 62–63; *Jingde Transmission of the Lamp* in *Taishō* 2076: 51.322a; Lu, *Ch'an and Zen Teaching*, 144–45; Ferguson, *Zen's Chinese Heritage*, 185. The Powell translation indicates that at the end of the dialogue, Dongshan disapproved of the monk. Although I can understand Powell's interpretation as "I've been suspicious," from my reading of the original in context, I read it as only *formerly* having "questioned" or "doubted" this monk. This positive reading is given by Cleary, Ferguson, and Lu cited above, while the Chang version from the *Jingde Transmission of the Lamp* omits that final line.
2. Cleary, *Book of Serenity*, 140–41.
3. Powell, *Record of Tung-shan*, 39; *Taishō* 1986: 47.521c. For a different reading of this story see Ferguson, *Zen's Chinese Heritage*, 211.
4. For all quotations in this section, see J. Krishnamurti, "Truth is a Pathless Land," Bernie's Home Page, http://bernie.cncfamily.com/k_pathless.htm.
5. Paul Williams, *Mahāyāna Buddhism: The Doctrinal Foundations* (London: Routledge, 1989), 198–99; see also 197–204, 267, 275. See also Sangharakshita, *The Eternal Legacy*, 164, 173, 188–89, 225, 229, 244. Sangharakshita translates *bodhicitta* as "Will to Enlightenment."
6. Randy Newman, "It's Lonely at the Top," from the album *Sail Away*, 1972.
7. Kazuaki Tanahashi, *Sky Above, Great Wind: The Life and Poetry of Zen Master Ryokan* (Boston: Shambhala, 2012), 151.
8. Reb Anderson, *Being Upright: Zen Meditation and the Bodhisattva Precepts* (Berkeley: Rodmell Press, 2001), xv–xvi.
9. See Anderson, *Third Turning of the Wheel*, 182.
10. From the *Compendium of the Five Lamps (Wudeng Huiyuan)*, 1252, cited in App, *Master Yunmen*, 111–12.
11. From the single "There Is a Mountain," released in 1967. See Donovan Leitch, *The Autobiography of Donovan: The Hurdy Gurdy Man* (New York: St.

Martin's Press, 2005), 180–81. Donovan's album *Sutras*, 1996, contains songs with explicit references to Buddhist texts, including "Nirvana," with all lyrics from the Heart Sutra. His song "The Way" quotes from the *Dao De Jing*.

12. Cleary, *Shōbōgenzō*, 89–90. See also Tanahashi, *Treasury of the True Dharma Eye*, 155; and Carl Bielefeldt's translation with introduction for the Sōtō Zen Text Project, http://scbs.stanford.edu/sztp3/translations/shobogenzo/translations/sansuikyo/sansuikyo.translation.html.

13. Tanahashi, *Treasury of the True Dharma Eye*, 162. See Cleary, *Shōbōgenzō*, 97.

14. Cleary, *Shōbōgenzō*, 99. See also Tanahashi, *Treasury of the True Dharma Eye*, 164.

CHAPTER NINE · *A Person of Suchness*

1. See Schlütter, *How Zen Became Zen*, 93–94.

2. Cleary, *Shōbōgenzō*, 47.

3. Leighton and Okumura, *Dōgen's Extensive Record*, 533.

4. See Cleary, *Shōbōgenzō*, 49–50; Tanahashi, *Treasury of the True Dharma Eye*, 324–25; Hee-Jin Kim, *Flowers of Emptiness: Selections from Dōgen's Shōbōgenzō* (Lewiston, N.Y.: Edwin Mellen Press, 1985), 201–2; and Nishijima, *Master Dogen's Shobogenzo*, Book 2, 119–20.

5. Tanahashi, *Treasury of the True Dharma Eye*, 324.

6. Cleary, *Shōbōgenzō*, 49.

7. Ibid.

8. Author's rendition. See Cleary, *Shōbōgenzō*, 54–55; Tanahashi, *Treasury of the True Dharma Eye*, 330–31.

9. Kasulis, *Zen Action Zen Person*, 85–86.

10. Leon Hurvitz, *Scripture of the Lotus Blossom of the Fine Dharma*, rev. ed. (New York: Columbia University Press, 2009), 22–23.

11. Reeves, *Lotus Sutra*, 76.

12. Young-ho Kim, *Tao-Sheng's Commentary on the Lotus Sutra* (Albany: State University of New York Press, 1990), 198n14.

13. Reeves, *Lotus Sutra*, 425n2. See also Hurvitz, *Scripture of the Lotus Blossom*, 317–18.

14. Stephen Teiser and Jacqueline Stone, "Interpreting the *Lotus Sūtra*" in *Readings of the Lotus Sūtra*, ed. Stephen Teiser and Jacqueline Stone (New York: Columbia University Press, 2009), 36.

15. Jacqueline Stone, *Original Enlightenment and the Transformation of Medieval Japanese Buddhism* (Honolulu: University of Hawai'i Press, 1999), 7.

16. Ibid., 13–14.

17. Ibid., 14.

18. Ibid., 191–96.

19. Ibid., 192.

20. Ibid., 193.
21. See "Is Silent Illumination Quietistic?" in Leighton, *Cultivating the Empty Field*, 13–16.
22. Leighton and Okumura, *Dōgen's Extensive Record*, Dharma hall discourse 38, p. 105.
23. Ibid. Dharma hall discourse 21, p. 92; Powell, *Record of Tung-shan*, 52; *Taishō* 1986: 47.524a.
24. Leighton and Okumura, *Dōgen's Extensive Record*, Dharma hall discourse 21, p. 92. Italics in original indicate compiler's description rather than Dōgen's words.
25. See chapter 13; and Leighton, *Cultivating the Empty Field*, 8–12.

CHAPTER TEN · *Always Close*

1. Cleary, *Book of Serenity*, 422–24; Powell, *Record of Tung-shan*, 56; *Taishō* 1986: 47.524c–525a; Chang, *Original Teachings*, 68; Lu, *Ch'an and Zen Teaching*, 146; *Taishō* 2076: 51.323a15–16.
2. For dating of Dongshan's *Recorded Sayings*, see Powell, *Record of Tung-shan*, 3–4. The lamp transmission reading accords with Dongshan remaining presently concerned about this. Interestingly, Chang renders Dongshan's response as "I often think about it," and Lu offers, "I am always keen about this." See citations in the previous note.
3. Powell, *Record of Tung-shan*, 86n162.
4. See Williams, *Mahāyāna Buddhism*, 168–79, 123; or Donald Mitchell, *Buddhism: Introducing the Buddhist Experience*, 2nd ed. (New York: Oxford University Press, 2008), 131–32.
5. Isshū Miura and Ruth Fuller Sasaki, *Zen Dust: The History of the Koan and Koan Study in Rinzai (Lin-Chi) Zen* (New York: Harcourt, Brace & World, 1966), 286–87.
6. Cleary, *Book of Serenity*, 422; Powell, *Record of Tung-shan*, 41–42; *Taishō* 1986: 47.522b.
7. Powell, *Record of Tung-shan*, 37; *Taishō* 1986: 47.521c; Leighton and Okumura, *Dōgen's Pure Standards*, 35, 174–75.
8. Cleary, *Book of Serenity*, 422–23.
9. Ibid., 422.
10. Ibid., 423.
11. Bob Dylan, "All I Really Want to Do" in the album *Another Side of Bob Dylan*, www.bobdylan.com/songs © 1964 by Warner Bros. Inc.. renewed 1992 by Special Rider Music.
12. Cleary, *Book of Serenity*, 423; *Taishō* 2001: 48.27b.
13. Leighton and Okumura, *Dōgen's Extensive Record*, 229.
14. Ibid., 428.

CHAPTER ELEVEN · *Caring for the One Not Ill*

1. Powell, *Record of Tung-shan*, 67–68; *Taishō* 1986: 47.526b; Chang, *Original Teachings*, 69–70; Lu, *Ch'an and Zen Teaching*, 155–57; *Taishō* 2076: 51.323a29–323b20; Cleary, *Book of Serenity*, 402–7. See also Ferguson, *Zen's Chinese Heritage*, 186–87.

2. Powell, *Record of Tung-shan*, 68; *Taishō* 1986: 47.526b.

3. Ibid.; Chang, *Original Teachings*, 70; Lu, *Ch'an and Zen Teaching*, 157; *Taishō* 2076: 51.323b20.

4. Chang, *Original Teachings*, 69; Lu, *Ch'an and Zen Teaching*, 155–56; *Taishō* 2076: 51.323a29–323b04. Powell, *Record of Tung-shan*, 67; *Taishō* 1986: 47.526b.

5. Powell, *Record of Tung-shan*, 67; *Taishō* 1986: 47.526b; Chang, *Original Teachings*, 69; Lu, *Ch'an and Zen Teaching*, 156; *Taishō* 2076: 51.323b05–323b07.

6. See Cleary, *Book of Serenity*, 402; Powell, *Record of Tung-shan*, 67; *Taishō* 1986: 47.526b; Chang, *Original Teachings*, 69–70; Lu, *Ch'an and Zen Teaching*, 156; *Taishō* 2076: 51.323b08–323b11.

7. Cheng Chien Bhikshu (Mario Poceski), *Sun-Face Buddha: The Teaching of Ma-Tsu and the Hung-chou School of Ch'an* (Berkeley: Asian Humanities Press, 1992), 135–-36; Ogata, *Transmission of the Lamp Early Masters*, 270–71.

8. Cleary, *Book of Serenity*, 402–3.

9. Ibid., 403. See also Powell, *Record of Tung-shan*, 67; *Taishō* 1986: 47.526b; and Lu, *Ch'an and Zen Teaching*, 156. The *Taishō* version of the *Transmission of the Lamp* selection on Dongshan has a slightly different ending, without the gātha.

10. Victor Sōgen Hori, *Zen Sand: The Book of Capping Phrases for Kōan Practice* (Honolulu: University of Hawai'i Press, 2003), 684.

11. This verse reportedly appears in the *Chanyuan Qinggui* monastic code, published in 1103, and was imported to Japan by the Obaku school of Zen. However, it does not actually appear in that text, and I could not locate it in various other likely sources. See Yifa, *The Origins of Buddhist Monastic Codes in China: An Annotated Translation and Study of the Chanyuan Qinggui* (Honolulu: University of Hawai'i Press, 2009).

12. Cleary, *Book of Serenity*, 404–5.

13. Leighton, *Cultivating the Empty Field*, 73. See also Connelly, *Inside the Grass Hut*.

14. Cleary, *Book of Serenity*, 167–70.

CHAPTER TWELVE · *The Jewel Mirror Samādhi*

1. As a resource for the chapters both on the "Jewel Mirror Samādhi" and on the five degrees, I have appreciated the unpublished "Jewel Mirror Samadhi Translation Study" by Charlie Pokorny, 2008, with its exhaustive notes on

available English materials on both, including many more details than can be addressed in these brief chapters.

2. *Taishō* 1986: 47.525c–526a; Powell, *Record of Tung-shan*, 63–65.
3. Schlütter, *How Zen Became Zen*, 158, which includes discussion about the source and age of the "Jewel Mirror Samadhi."
4. *Taishō* 1986: 47.525c–526a. This translation is the author's adaptation close to the version (initially translated by Taigen Dan Leighton, Shohaku Okumura, Carl Bielefeldt, and Griffith Foulk and reviewed in conference) in Sōtō Zen Text Project, *Soto School Scriptures for Daily Services and Practice* (Tokyo: Sōtōshū Shūmucho, 2001), 33–37; Roman letter transliterations of the Japanese, pp. 110–13. For other renditions, see Powell, *Record of Tung-shan*, 63–65; Cleary, *Timeless Spring*, 39–45; Thomas Cleary, *The Five Houses of Zen* (Boston: Shambhala, 1997), 72–75; Kazuaki Tanahashi and Tensho David Schneider, eds., *Essential Zen*, trans. Tom Cabarga, Philip Whalen, and Kazuaki Tanahashi (San Francisco: HarperSanFrancisco, 1994), 63–66; Sheng-yen, *The Poetry of Enlightenment: Poems by Ancient Ch'an Masters* (Elmhurst, N.Y.: Dharma Drum Publications, 1987), 75–78; and Lu, *Ch'an and Zen Teaching*, 149–54.
5. Cleary, *Book of Serenity*, 342.
6. Leighton, *Cultivating the Empty Field*, 74–75; and Suzuki, *Branching Streams*.
7. See Ogata, *Transmission of the Lamp*, 29; Cleary and Cleary, *Blue Cliff Record*, case 13, 88–93; and for Keizan's version see Cook, *Record of Transmitting the Light*, 93–95, or Thomas Cleary, trans., *Transmission of Light: Zen in the Art of Enlightenment* (San Francisco: North Point Press, 1990), 67–69.
8. Cleary and Cleary, *Blue Cliff Record*, 88.
9. See Dōgen's "Gyōbutsu Īgi" ("The Awesome Presence of Active Buddhas") in Tanahashi, *Treasury of the True Dharma Eye*, 270.
10. Author's translation. See Cleary, *Shōbōgenzō*, 72; and Tanahashi, *Treasury of the True Dharma Eye*, 464. In this passage Dōgen uses the same Chinese character as in the "Jewel Mirror Samādhi" for "turning away" but a different phrase "aiming toward," rather than touching or grasping, and a different character than in the "Jewel Mirror Samādhi" for "wrong."
11. *Taishō* 12.728–729; see Powell, *Record of Tung-shan*, 87–88, 88n180, who says they are in chapter 20 of the sutra. The comparison is in chapter 27 of the Mahāparinirvāna Sutra, according to a draft translation by Eric Greene in the unpublished "Jewel Mirror Samadhi Translation Study" by Charlie Pokorny, in which these five aspects of "Baby Practice" are described as akin to that of the tathāgatha.
12. Chan Master Sheng Yen, *The Infinite Mirror: Commentaries on Two Chan Classics* (Boston: Shambhala, 2006), 110; and Verdu, *Dialectical Aspects*, 182n54.

13. Dale Saunders, *Mudrā: A Study of Symbolic Gestures in Japanese Buddhist Sculpture* (Princeton, N.J.: Princeton University Press, 1960), 184–86, 189–90.

14. For many examples of fives in Buddhism, see William Edward Soothill and Lewis Hodous, *A Dictionary of Chinese Buddhist Terms* (Delhi, India: Motilal Banarsidass, 1937, reprinted 1987), 112–30.

15. An early classic English translation is Richard Wilhelm and Cary Baynes, trans., *The I Ching or Book of Changes*, 3rd ed. (Princeton, N.J.: Princeton University Press, 1950, 1967). Useful translations of the *Yi Jing* with Daoist and Buddhist commentaries are Thomas Cleary, trans., *The Taoist I Ching* (Boston: Shambhala, 1986), and Chih-hsu Ou-i, *The Buddhist I Ching*, trans. Thomas Cleary (Boston: Shambhala, 1987). The former is based on a late-eighteenth-century commentary from the Complete Reality Daoist school and correlates the *Yi Jing* with alchemical Daoist meditation processes. Zhixu Ouyi (Chih-hsu Ou-I in Wade-Giles transliteration) was an early-seventeenth-century Buddhist thinker who drew on many sources to produce a unique full Buddhist commentary, although Dongshan as well as other East Asian Buddhists sometimes referred to the *Yi Jing*.

16. See Lu, *Ch'an and Zen Teaching*, 151; and Verdu, *Dialectical Aspects*, 130–39. See Verdu for a discussion of later studies in China and Japan of the five degrees, as well as the roots of this theory in Indian Yogacara and Chinese Huayan. See Verdu, *Dialectical Aspects*, 229–38. The hexagram chart is from Charlie Pokorny's "Jewel Mirror Samadhi Translation Study."

17. Verdu, *Dialectical Aspects*, 132–33.

18. Brook Ziporyn, "The Use of the Li Hexagram in Chan Buddhism and Its This-Worldly Implications," in *Shengyanyanjiu*, vol. 3 (May 2012) 83–124.

19. Wilhelm and Baynes, *I Ching*, 119.

20. Cleary, *Taoist I Ching*, 127.

21. See Chang Po-Tuan, *The Inner Teachings of Taoism*, trans. Thomas Cleary, commentary by Liu I-ming (Boston: Shambhala, 1986), which uses *Yi Jing* trigrams and hexagrams and circular diagrams like many later five degrees commentaries.

22. Leighton, *Cultivating the Empty Field*, 72–73.

23. Ibid., 40.

24. Leighton and Okumura, *Dōgen's Extensive Record*, 533.

25. Tanahashi and Schneider, *Essential Zen*, 64.

26. Sheng-yen, *Poetry of Enlightenment*, 76.

27. Leighton, *Cultivating the Empty Field*, 74–75; and Suzuki, *Branching Streams*.

28. Leighton and Okumura, *Dōgen's Extensive Record*, 93.

29. Tanahashi, *Treasury of the True Dharma Eye*, 29–33; Cleary, *Shōbōgenzō*, 29–35.

30. Okumura and Leighton, *Wholehearted Way*, 22–23.

31. Cleary, *Shōbōgenzō*, 87–99; and Tanahashi, *Treasury of the True Dharma Eye*, 154–64.

32. Cleary, *Flower Ornament Scripture*, 176–79.

33. Reeves, *Lotus Sutra*, 235–46, 279–90.

34. Thurman, *Holy Teaching of Vimalakīrti*, 93–95.

35. *Men in Black*, 1997, was directed by Barry Sonnenfeld and starred Tommy Lee Jones, Will Smith, and Linda Fiorentino; see www.imdb.com/title/tt0119654/.

36. Leonard Susskind, *Cosmic Landscape: String Theory and the Illusion of Intelligent Design* (New York: Little, Brown, 2006), 94. For my comments on how contemporary physics relates to Dōgen's expansive viewpoints on time and space, see Taigen Dan Leighton, *Visions of Awakening Space and Time: Dōgen and the Lotus Sutra* (New York: Oxford University Press, 2007), 118–21.

37. Brian Greene, *The Elegant Universe: Superstrings, Hidden Dimensions, and the Quest for the Ultimate Theory* (New York: Vintage Books, 2003), 6.

38. Brian Greene, *The Hidden Reality: Parallel Universes and the Deep Laws of the Cosmos* (New York: Vintage Books, 2011).

39. Ibid., 97–102.

40. For a translation of the earliest extant version from the Tang dynasty, unearthed from the Dunhuang caves in the twentieth century, see Yampolsky, *The Platform Sutra of the Sixth Patriarch*, which includes extensive helpful modern academic commentary. For a translation of the traditional rendition studied in most of Zen, based on a 1291 compilation of previous texts, see Thomas Cleary, *The Sutra of Hui-neng, Grand Master of Zen* (Boston: Shambhala, 1998).

41. Varying but overlapping presentations are in Yampolsky, *Platform Sutra*, 116, 162–70; and Cleary, *Sutra of Hui-neng*, 60–67.

42. Robert Buswell, Jr., *Tracing Back the Radiance: Chinul's Way of Zen* (Honolulu: University of Hawaii Press, 1991), 57–62, 101; Mitchell, *Buddhism*, 257–59.

43. Buswell, *Tracing Back the Radiance*, 58–59.

44. Ibid., 101.

45. Leighton, *Cultivating the Empty Field*, 30.

46. See Reeves, *Lotus Sutra*, 179–97.

47. See Shibayama, *Gateless Barrier*, 77–81.

48. Reeves, *Lotus Sutra*, 142–46.

49. The old characters used in the original for "cat" have also been rendered as the badger-like *tanuki*, as "otter," and even as "slave."

50. D. T. Suzuki, *Manual of Zen Buddhism* (New York: Grove Weidenfeld, 1960), 127–44.

51. Cleary, *Book of Serenity*, 290–94.

52. The story of Yang is from the *Shi Ji* (*Record of History*) by Sima Qian (145–86 B.C.E.). See Powell, *Record of Tung-shan*, 89nn188–189; and Leighton and Okumura, *Dōgen's Extensive Record*, 555.

53. Powell, *Record of Tung-shan*, 89n190. See also Eva Wong, trans., *Lieh-Tzu: A Taoist Guide to Practical Living* (Boston: Shambhala, 2001).

54. Leighton, *Cultivating the Empty Field*, 74–75; and Suzuki, *Branching Streams*.

55. Leighton, *Cultivating the Empty Field*, 53.

56. Leighton and Okumura, *Dōgen's Extensive Record*, 223.

57. See Chang, *Original Teachings*, 77–78; Lu, *Ch'an and Zen Teaching*, 178–79. Dōgen discusses this story in *Shōbōgenzō* "Ryūgin" ("Dragon Song"). See Tanahashi, *Treasury of the True Dharma Eye*, 627–30; or Nishijima, *Master Dogen's Shobogenzo*, Book 3, 227–30.

58. Conze, *Perfect Wisdom in Eight Thousand Lines*, 258.

59. Leighton, *Cultivating the Empty Field*, 62.

60. Hori, *Zen Sand*, 541 [14.381], 579 [14.630], 583 [14.656].

61. Leighton and Okumura, *Dōgen's Extensive Record*, 307–8.

62. Leighton, *Cultivating the Empty Field*, 68.

63. See Śāntideva, *A Guide to the Bodhisattva Way of Life*, trans. Vesna A. Wallace and B. Alan Wallace (Ithaca, N.Y.: Snow Lion, 1997); Śāntideva, *The Bodhicaryāvatāra*, trans. Kate Crosby and Andrew Skilton (New York: Oxford University Press, 1995); Shantideva, *A Guide to the Bodhisattva's Way of Life*, trans. Stephen Batchelor (Dharamsala, India: Library of Tibetan Works and Archives, 1979).

64. For Budai (Hotei), see Leighton, *Faces of Compassion*, 258–60.

65. For Ryōkan see Ryūichi Abe and Peter Haskel, trans. with essays, *Great Fool: Zen Master Ryōkan—Poems, Letters, and Other Writings* (Honolulu: University of Hawai'i Press, 1996).

66. For Hakuin's commentary on the five degrees, see Isshū Miura and Ruth Fuller Sasaki, *The Zen Koan: Its History and Use in Rinzai Zen* (New York: Harcourt, Brace & World, 1965), 62-72.

67. See Chang, *Original Teachings*, 95–97.

68. Leighton, *Cultivating the Empty Field*, 63.

CHAPTER THIRTEEN · *The Five Degrees*

1. Alfonso Verdu's brilliant 1974 book, *Dialectical Aspects in Buddhist Thought: Studies in Sino-Japanese Mahāyāna Idealism*, remains by far the most thorough source in English for the five degrees. He includes roots in related Buddhist philosophies such as Indian Yogacara and Chinese Huayan, as well as discussions of the later, complex five degrees scholarship traditions. Unfortunately, this book is very difficult to locate and much in need of republication.

2. Verdu, *Dialectical Aspects*, 117.
3. Powell, *Record of Tung-shan*, 86n169. However, Powell does use the term "Five Ranks" in his translation of the text.
4. For "Five Relations between Particularity and Universality" see Chang, *Original Teachings*, 46. For "Five Positions of Prince and Minister" see Lu, *Ch'an and Zen Teaching*, 135; and Wu, *Golden Age of Zen*, 177.
5. See Miura and Sasaki, *Zen Koan*, 62–72; and Miura and Sasaki, *Zen Dust*, 310, 315, 318, 321–23, 381.
6. For good discussions of the fourfold dharmadhātu see Chang, *Buddhist Teaching of Totality*, 136–70; Cleary, *Entry into the Inconceivable*, 24–42, for a summary, and Dushun and Chengguan, 43–124, for primary source essays. See Chang, *Original Teachings*, 41–43, 53, for a clear comparison of the fourfold dharmadhātu and the five degrees. For further discussion and the role of Zongmi, see Gregory, *Tsung-mi and the Sinification of Buddhism*, 67–68, 164–65, 177.
7. The poems here are my versions from the Chinese, with reference to Powell, *Record of Tung-shan*, 61–62; *Taishō* 1986: 47.525c; Cleary and Cleary, *Blue Cliff Record*, case 43, 261–63; and Verdu, *Dialectical Aspects*, 121–28. See also Lu, *Ch'an and Zen Teaching*, 135–36; Wu, *Golden Age of Zen*, 179–87; Miura and Sasaki, *Zen Koan*, 67–72; and Heinrich Dumoulin, *Zen Buddhism: A History*, vol. 1, *India and China* (New York: Macmillan, 1988), 225–26.
8. Some commentators see the last line as a failure, a fall back into worldliness from ultimate truth. But such a view reflects understanding these verses as describing a ladder of attainment to the transcendent, rather than five degrees or aspects of the fivefold interaction of the ultimate with the everyday. For example, see Verdu, *Dialectical Aspects*, 128.
9. *Taishō* 1986: 47.525c; Powell, *Record of Tung-shan*, 61–63; Verdu, *Dialectical Aspects*, 140–55; Wu, *Golden Age of Zen*, 183–87; Lu, *Ch'an and Zen Teaching*, 137–38. The renderings of the verses are again the author's from the Chinese, with reference to the versions of Powell, Verdu, and Wu.
10. See Shibayama, *Gateless Barrier*, 175–81; Thomas Cleary, *No Barrier: Unlocking the Zen Koan* (New York: Bantam, 1993) 116–19; and Robert Aitken, *The Gateless Barrier: The Wu-men Kuan (Mumonkan)* (San Francisco: North Point Press, 1990), 155–59. See also Leighton and Okumura, *Dōgen's Extensive Record*, 125.
11. Verdu, *Dialectical Aspects*, 148–50. For the Gandhavyūha Sutra see Cleary, *Flower Ornament Sutra*, 1135–518; and for Maitreya's tower, ibid., 1452–502.
12. See Verdu, *Dialectical Aspects*, 157–58, which I have used as the basis for this description of Caoshan's approach, altering some of the terminology.
13. These five degrees of lord and vassal are described in Verdu, *Dialectical Aspects*, 156–68.
14. Ibid., 169–77.

15. Ibid., 119.

16. Ibid., 77–106.

17. The Five Positions chart is from Charlie Pokorny's "Jewel Mirror Samādhi Translation Study." A version of this diagram, and another related one, can be found in Lu, *Ch'an and Zen Teaching*, 151.

18. Cleary, *Timeless Spring*, 51–52.

19. Leighton, *Cultivating the Empty Field*, 62.

20. Verdu, *Dialectical Aspects*, 131–39, 193–94.

21. Ibid., 195–211.

22. Ibid., 192–93, includes a list of these later Japanese Sōtō five degrees texts.

23. Ibid., 191–213.

24. Ibid., 216–28.

25. Keizan also provided Gasan with a set of circle diagrams as varied phases of the moons, illustrating the five degrees teachings and based on the story about the two moons. See Ishikawa Rikizan, "Transmission of *Kirigami* (Secret Initiation Documents): A Sōtō Practice in Medieval Japan," *The Kōan: Texts and Contexts in Zen Buddhism*, ed. Steven Heine and Dale Wright (New York: Oxford University Press, 2000), 240–41.

26. Heinrich Dumoulin, *Zen Buddhism: A History*, vol. 2, *Japan* (New York: Macmillan, 1990), 207–9. For Gasan see also Bodiford, *Sōtō Zen*, 108–12.

27. Dumoulin, *Zen Buddhism*, vol. 2, 339–40.

28. Cleary and Cleary, *Blue Cliff Record*, 638–39; ibid., 3-volume edition, vol. 2, 467–68.

29. Thomas Yūhō Kirchner, trans., *Entangling Vines: A Classic Collection of Zen Koans* (Boston: Wisdom, 2013), 219.

30. Miura and Sasaki, *Zen Koan*, 63–72. See also Hori, *Zen Sand*, 24–25.

31. Miura and Sasaki, *Zen Koan*, 64.

32. Ibid., 67.

33. See Tanahashi, *Treasury of the True Dharma Eye*, 29. Previously cited in chapter 2 as commentary on Dongshan's "It now is me; I now am not it."

34. Hori, *Zen Sand*, 24.

35. I am indebted for information about echinoderms and their past to personal communications with paleontologists Dr. Kenshu Shimada of the Department of Biological Sciences and Environmental Science and Studies at DePaul University, Chicago, as well as Paul Mayer of the Department of Geology of the Field Museum, Chicago. However, any misunderstandings or misstatements are solely my own responsibility.

36. Stephen Jay Gould, *Wonderful Life: The Burgess Shale and the Nature of History* (New York: Norton, 1989), 302.

37. Pollan, "The Intelligent Plant," 102, 96.

38. Ibid., 99–100.

39. Ibid., 102.

40. Tanahashi, *Treasury of the True Dharma Eye*, 634–35.
41. Cleary, *Shōbōgenzō*, 29.
42. Tanahashi, *Treasury of the True Dharma Eye*, 29. Other useful translations of "Genjōkōan" include Cleary, *Shōbōgenzō*, 32–35; Waddell and Abe, *Heart of Dōgen's Shōbōgenzō*, 39–45; and Okumura, *Realizing Genjōkōan*, 1–5, translation, and with excellent commentary throughout the book.
43. Bokusan et al., *Dōgen's Genjo Koan*, 29–39, 97–99, 154–67. The lack of reference to the five degrees for the first paragraph also applies to the excellent recent "Genjōkōan" commentary in Okumura, *Realizing Genjōkōan*, 24–46.
44. Leighton and Okumura, *Dōgen's Extensive Record*, 257–58.
45. See Taigen Dan Leighton, *Zen Questions: Zazen, Dōgen, and the Spirit of Creative Inquiry* (Boston: Wisdom, 2011), 125–34.

Selected Bibliography

IN CHINESE

Daoyuan, ed., *Jingde Chuandenglu* (*Jingde Transmission of the Lamp*). In Takakusu Junjirō, ed., *Taishō Shinshü Daizōkyō*, T2076: 51.321b–323b. Tokyo: Taishō Issaikyō Kankokai, 1924–33.

Ruizhou Dongshan Liangjie Chanshi Yulu (*Dongshan Yulu*, for short; *Recorded Sayings of Dongshan*). In Takakusu Junjirō, ed., *Taishō Shinshü Daizōkyō*, T1986: 47.519b–526c. Tokyo: Taishō Issaikyō Kankokai, 1924–33.

IN ENGLISH

Abe, Ryūichi, and Peter Haskel, trans. with essays. *Great Fool: Zen Master Ryōkan —Poems, Letters, and Other Writings*. Honolulu: University of Hawai'i Press, 1996.

Aitken, Robert. *The Gateless Barrier: The Wu-men Kuan (Mumonkan)*. San Francisco: North Point Press, 1990.

Anderson, Reb. *Being Upright: Zen Meditation and the Bodhisattva Precepts.* Berkeley: Rodmell Press, 2001.

———. *The Third Turning of the Wheel: Wisdom of the Samdhinirmocana Sutra.* Berkeley, Rodmell Press, 2012.

———. *Warm Smiles from Cold Mountains.* San Francisco: San Francisco Zen Center, 1995.

App, Urs, trans. *Master Yunmen: From the Record of the Chan Master "Gate of the Clouds."* New York: Kodansha International, 1994.

Benn, James. *Burning for the Buddha: Self-Immolation in Chinese Buddhism.* Honolulu: University of Hawai'i Press, 2007.

———. "The Lotus Sutra and Self-Immolation." In *Readings of the Lotus Sutra*, edited by Stephen Teiser and Jacqueline Stone. New York: Columbia University Press, 2009.

Blofeld, John, trans. *The Zen Teaching of Huang Po: On the Transmission of Mind.* New York: Grove Press, 1958.

Blum, Mark. *The Nirvana Sutra*. Berkeley: Numata Center for Buddhist Translation and Research, 2013.

Bodiford, William. *Sōtō Zen in Medieval Japan*. Honolulu: University of Hawai'i Press, 1993.

Bokusan, Nishiari, Shohaku Okumura, Shunryu Suzuki, Kosho Uchiyama, Sojun Mel Weitsman, Kazuaki Tanahashi, and Michael Wenger, trans. and commentaries. *Dogen's Genjo Koan: Three Commentaries*. Berkeley: Counterpoint, 2011.

Bolleter, Ross. *Dongshan's Five Ranks: Keys to Enlightenment*. Somerville, MA: Wisdom Publications, 2014.

Buswell, Robert, Jr. *Tracing Back the Radiance: Chinul's Way of Zen*. Honolulu: University of Hawai'i Press, 1991.

Buswell, Robert, Jr., and Robert Gimello, ed. *Paths to Liberation: The Mārga and Its Transformations in Buddhist Thought*. Honolulu: University of Hawai'i Press, 1992.

Carroll, Lewis. *Alice's Adventures in Wonderland & Through the Looking-Glass, with Alice's Adventures*. 1865. Reprint, New York: New American Library, 1960.

Carter, John Ross, and Mahinda Palihawadana, trans. with annotation. *The Dhammapada*. New York: Oxford University Press, 1987.

Chan Khong. *Learning True Love: How I Learned & Practiced Social Change in Vietnam*. Berkeley: Parallax Press, 1993.

Chang, Garma C. C. *The Buddhist Teaching of Totality: The Philosophy of Hwa Yen Buddhism*. University Park: Pennsylvania State University Press, 1971.

———, ed. *A Treasury of Mahāyāna Sūtras: Selections from the Mahāratnakūta Sūtra*. University Park: Pennsylvania State University Press, 1983.

Chang Chung-yuan, trans. *Original Teachings of Ch'an Buddhism*. New York: Vintage Books, 1969.

Chang Po-Tuan. *The Inner Teachings of Taoism*. Commentary by Liu I-ming. Translated by Thomas Cleary. Boston: Shambhala, 1986.

Cheng, Man-jan. *Lao-tzu: "My Words Are Very Easy to Understand."* Translated by Tam Gibbs. Richmond, CA: North Atlantic Books, 1981.

Cheng Chien Bhikshu (Mario Poceski). *Sun-Face Buddha: The Teaching of Ma-Tsu and the Hung-chou School of Ch'an*. Berkeley: Asian Humanities Press, 1992.

Chih-hsu Ou-i. *The Buddhist I Ching*. Translated by Thomas Cleary. Boston: Shambhala, 1987.

Cleary, Thomas, trans. *The Book of Serenity*. Boston: Shambhala, 2005.

———. *Entry into the Inconceivable: An Introduction to Hua-yen Buddhism*. Honolulu: University of Hawai'i Press, 1983.

———. *The Essential Tao*. San Francisco: HarperSanFrancisco, 1991.

———. *The Five Houses of Zen*. Boston: Shambhala, 1997.

———. *The Flower Ornament Scripture.* Boston: Shambhala, 1984–93.

———. *No Barrier: Unlocking the Zen Koan.* New York: Bantam Books, 1993.

———. *Sayings and Doings of Pai-chang: Ch'an Master of Great Wisdom.* Los Angeles: Center Publications, 1978.

———. *Shōbōgenzō: Zen Essays by Dōgen.* Honolulu: University of Hawai'i Press, 1986.

———. *The Sutra of Hui-neng, Grand Master of Zen.* With Hui-neng's Commentary on the *Diamond Sutra.* Boston: Shambhala, 1998.

———. *The Taoist I Ching.* Boston: Shambhala, 1986.

———. *Timeless Spring: A Soto Zen Anthology.* Tokyo: Weatherhill, 1980.

———. *Transmission of Light: Zen in the Art of Enlightenment.* San Francisco: North Point Press, 1990.

Cleary, Thomas, and J. C. Cleary, trans. *The Blue Cliff Record.* Boston: Shambhala, 3-volume edition, 1977; 1-volume edition, 2005.

Connelly, Ben. *Inside the Grass Hut: Living Shitou's Classic Zen Poem.* Somerville, MA.: Wisdom Publications, 2014.

Conze, Edward, trans. *The Large Sutra on Perfect Wisdom.* Berkeley: University of California Press, 1975.

———. *The Perfect Wisdom in Eight Thousand Lines & Its Verse Summary.* Bolinas, CA: Four Seasons Foundation, 1973.

Cook, Francis, trans. *The Record of Transmitting the Light: Zen Master Keizan's Denkoroku.* Somerville, MA: Wisdom Publications, 2003.

Copp, Paul. "Anointing Phrases and Narrative Power: A Tang Buddhist Poetics of Incantation." *History of Religions* 52, no. 2 (2012): 142–72.

———. *The Body Incantatory: Spells and the Ritual Imagination in Medieval Chinese Buddhism.* New York: Columbia University Press, 2013.

Dumoulin, Heinrich. *Zen Buddhism: A History.* Vol. 1, *India and China.* New York: Macmillan, 1988.

———. *Zen Buddhism: A History.* Vol. 2, *Japan.* New York: Macmillan, 1990.

Dylan, Bob. *Lyrics 1962–2001.* New York: Simon & Schuster, 2004.

Epstein, Mark. *Thoughts without a Thinker.* New York: HarperCollins, 1995.

Faure, Bernard. *Visions of Power: Imagining Medieval Japanese Buddhism.* Princeton, NJ: Princeton University Press, 1996.

Ferguson, Andrew. *Zen's Chinese Heritage.* Somerville, MA: Wisdom Publications, 2000.

Foulk, Griffith. "Controversies Concerning the 'Separate Transmission.'" In *Buddhism in the Sung,* edited by Peter Gregory and Daniel Getz, Jr., 220–94. Honolulu: University of Hawai'i Press, 1999.

Fowlie, Wallace, trans. *Rimbaud: Complete Works, Selected Letters.* Chicago: University of Chicago Press, 1966.

Fronsdal, Gil, trans. with annotation. *The Dhammapada.* Boston: Shambhala, 2005.

Furth, Charlotte, Judith Zeitlin, and Ping-chen Hsiung, eds. *Thinking with Cases: Specialist Knowledge in Chinese Cultural History*. Honolulu: University of Hawai'i Press, 2007.

Gould, Stephen Jay. *Wonderful Life: The Burgess Shale and the Nature of History*. New York: Norton, 1989.

Greene, Brian. *The Elegant Universe: Superstrings, Hidden Dimensions, and the Quest for the Ultimate Theory*. New York: Vintage, 2003.

———. *The Hidden Reality: Parallel Universes and the Deep Laws of the Cosmos*. New York: Vintage, 2011.

Gregory, Peter. *Tsung-mi and the Sinification of Buddhism*. Honolulu: University of Hawai'i Press, 2002.

Gregory, Peter, and Daniel Getz, Jr. *Buddhism in the Sung*. Honolulu: University of Hawaii Press, 1999.

Hakeda, Yoshito. *Kūkai: Major Works*. New York: Columbia University Press, 1972.

Heine, Steven. *Bargainin' for Salvation: Bob Dylan, a Zen Master?* New York: Continuum, 2009.

———. *Dōgen and the Kōan Tradition: A Tale of Two Shōbōgenzō Texts*. Albany: State University of New York Press, 1994.

———, ed. *Dōgen Textual and Historical Studies*. New York: Oxford University Press, 2012.

———. *Shifting Shape, Shaping Text: Philosophy and Folklore in the Fox Kōan*. Honolulu: University of Hawai'i Press, 1999.

Heine, Steven, and Dale Wright, eds. *The Kōan: Texts and Contexts in Zen Buddhism*. New York: Oxford University Press, 2000.

Hirakawa Akira. *A History of Indian Buddhism: From Śākyamuni to Early Mahāyāna*. Honolulu: University of Hawai'i Press, 1990.

Hori, Victor Sōgen. *Zen Sand: The Book of Capping Phrases for Kōan Practice*. Honolulu: University of Hawai'i Press, 2003.

Hurvitz, Leon. *Scripture of the Lotus Blossom of the Fine Dharma* (rev. ed.). New York: Columbia University Press, 2009.

Ishikawa Rikizan. "Transmission of *Kirigami* (Secret Initiation Documents): A Sōtō Practice in Medieval Japan." In *The Kōan: Texts and Contexts in Zen Buddhism*, edited by Steven Heine and Dale Wright. New York: Oxford University Press, 2000.

Kasulis, Thomas. *Zen Action/Zen Person*. Honolulu: University of Hawai'i Press, 1981.

Kieschnick, John, and Meir Shahas, eds. *India in the Chinese Imagination: Buddhism and the Formation of Medieval Chinese Culture*. Philadelphia: University of Pennsylvania Press, 2013.

Kim, Hee-Jin. *Flowers of Emptiness: Selections from Dōgen's Shōbōgenzō*. Lewiston, NY: Edwin Mellen Press, 1985.

Kim, Young-ho. *Tao-Sheng's Commentary on the Lotus Sutra*. Albany: State University of New York Press, 1990.

King, Sallie. *Buddha Nature*. Albany: State University of New York Press, 1991.

Kirchner, Thomas Yūhō, trans. *Entangling Vines: A Classic Collection of Zen Koans*. Somerville, MA: Wisdom Publications, 2013.

Kodera, Takashi James. *Dogen's Formative Years in China: An Historical Study and Annotated Translation of the Hōkyō-ki*. Boulder, CO: Prajña Press, 1980.

Leekley, Guy. *Tao Te Ching: A New Version for All Seekers*. Woodlands, Texas: Anusara, 2004.

Leighton, Taigen Dan. *Faces of Compassion: Classic Bodhisattva Archetypes and Their Modern Expression* (rev. ed.). Somerville, MA: Wisdom Publications, 2012.

———. *Visions of Awakening Space and Time: Dōgen and the Lotus Sutra*. New York: Oxford University Press, 2007.

———. *Zen Questions: Zazen, Dōgen, and the Spirit of Creative Inquiry*. Somerville, MA: Wisdom Publications, 2011.

Leighton, Taigen Dan, and Shohaku Okumura, trans. *Dōgen's Extensive Record: A Translation of Eihei Kōroku*. Somerville, MA: Wisdom Publications, 2004.

———. *Dōgen's Pure Standards for the Zen Community: A Translation of Eihei Shingi*. Albany: State University of New York Press, 1996.

Leighton, Taigen Dan, with Yi Wu, trans. *Cultivating the Empty Field: The Silent Illumination of Zen Master Hongzhi*. Boston: Tuttle, 2000.

Leitch, Donovan. *The Autobiography of Donovan: The Hurdy Gurdy Man*. New York: St. Martin's Press, 2005.

London, Jack. *To Build a Fire and Other Favorite Stories*. Mineola, NY: Dover, 2008.

Lu K'uan Yü [Charles Luk]. *Ch'an and Zen Teaching*, series 2. London: Rider, 1961.

Lusthaus, Dan. *Buddhist Phenomenology: A Philosophical Investigation of Yogācāra Buddhism and the Ch'eng Wei-shih lun*. London: RoutledgeCurzon, 2002.

Marcus, Greil. *Invisible Republic: Bob Dylan's Basement Tapes*. New York: Henry Holt, 1997.

McKibben, Bill. *Eaarth: Making a Life on a Tough New Planet*. New York: St. Martin's Griffin, 2010, 2011.

McRae, John. *Seeing Through Zen*. Berkeley: University of California Press, 2003.

Mitchell, Donald. *Buddhism: Introducing the Buddhist Experience* (2nd ed.). New York: Oxford University Press, 2002, 2008.

Miura, Isshū, and Ruth Fuller Sasaki. *The Zen Koan: Its History and Use in Rinzai Zen*. New York: Harcourt, Brace & World, 1965.

———. *Zen Dust: The History of the Koan and Koan Study in Rinzai (Lin-Chi) Zen*. New York: Harcourt, Brace & World, 1966.

Morrell, Robert. *Early Kamakura Buddhism: A Minority Report.* Berkeley: Asian Humanities Press, 1987.

Ñāṇamoli, Bhikku, and Bhikku Bodhi, trans. *The Middle Length Discourses of the Buddha: A Translation of the Majjhima Nikāya.* Somerville, MA: Wisdom Publications, 1995.

Nattier, Jan. "The *Heart Sūtra:* A Chinese Apocryphal Text?" *Journal of the International Association of Buddhist Studies* 15, no. 2 (1992): 153–224.

Nishijima, Gudo Wafu. *Master Dogen's Shinji Shobogenzo.* Essex, UK: Windbell Publications, 2003.

Ogata, Sohaku, trans. *The Transmission of the Lamp: Early Masters.* Durango, CO: Longwood Academic, 1986.

Okumura, Shohaku. *Realizing Genjōkōan: The Key to Dōgen's Shōbōgenzō.* Somerville, MA: Wisdom Publications, 2010.

Okumura, Shohaku, and Taigen Dan Leighton, trans. *The Wholehearted Way: A Translation of Eihei Dōgen's Bendōwa.* With Commentary by Kōshō Uchiyama Roshi. Boston: Tuttle, 1997.

Penkower, Linda. "T'ien-t'ai during the T'ang Dynasty: Chan-jan and the Sinification of Buddhism." PhD diss., Columbia University, 1993.

Pollan, Michael. "The Intelligent Plant." *The New Yorker* (December 23 & 30, 2013): 92–105.

Powell, William. *The Record of Tung-shan.* Honolulu: University of Hawai'i Press, 1986.

Rahula, Walpola. *What the Buddha Taught.* New York: Grove Press, 2d edition, 1974.

Red Pine, trans. and commentary. *The Lankavatara Sutra.* Berkeley: Counterpoint, 2012.

Reeves, Gene. *The Lotus Sutra.* Somerville, MA: Wisdom Publications, 2008.

Sangharakshita. *The Eternal Legacy: An Introduction to the Canonical Literature of Buddhism.* London: Tharpa Publications, 1985.

Śāntideva. *The Bodhicaryāvatāra.* Translated by Kate Crosby and Andrew Skilton. New York: Oxford University Press, 1995.

———. *A Guide to the Bodhisattva Way of Life.* Translated by Vesna A. Wallace and B. Alan Wallace. Ithaca, NY: Snow Lion Publications, 1997.

Sasaki, Ruth Fuller, Yoshitaka Iriya, and Dana Fraser, trans. *The Recorded Sayings of Layman P'ang: A Ninth-Century Zen Classic.* New York: Weatherhill, 1971.

Saunders, Dale. *Mudrā: A Study of Symbolic Gestures in Japanese Buddhist Sculpture.* Princeton, NJ: Princeton University Press, 1960.

Schlütter, Morten. *How Zen Became Zen: The Dispute over Enlightenment and the Formation of Chan Buddhism in Song-Dynasty China.* Honolulu: University of Hawai'i Press, 2008.

Schmithausen, Lambert. *Plants in Early Buddhism and the Far Eastern Idea of the Buddha-Nature of Grasses and Trees.* Lumbini, Nepal: Lumbini International Research Institute, 2009.

Seaton, J. P., and James Cryer, trans. *Bright Moon, Perching Bird: Poems by Li Po and Tu Fu.* Middletown, CT: Wesleyan University Press, 1987.

Shantideva. *A Guide to the Bodhisattva's Way of Life.* Translated by Stephen Batchelor. Dharamsala, India: Library of Tibetan Works and Archives, 1979.

Sharf, Robert. *Coming to Terms with Chinese Buddhism: A Reading of the Treasure Store Treatise.* Honolulu: University of Hawai'i Press, 2002.

———. "How to Think with Chan Gong'an." In *Thinking with Cases: Specialist Knowledge in Chinese Cultural History,* edited by Charlotte Furth, Judith Zeitlin, and Ping-chen Hsiung, 213–14. Honolulu: University of Hawai'i Press, 2007.

———. "Is Nirvāna the Same as Insentience? Chinese Struggles with an Indian Buddhist Ideal." In *India in the Chinese Imagination: Buddhism and the Formation of Medieval Chinese Culture,* edited by John Kieschnick and Meir Shahas. Philadelphia: University of Pennsylvania Press, 2013.

———. "On the Buddha-nature of Insentient Things: How to Think about a Ch'an Kung-an." http://kr.buddhism.org/zen/koan/Robert_Sharf-e.htm.

Sheng-yen. *The Infinite Mirror: Commentaries on Two Chan Classics.* Boston: Shambhala, 2006.

———. *The Poetry of Enlightenment: Poems by Ancient Ch'an Masters.* Elmhurst, NY: Dharma Drum Publications, 1987.

Shibayama, Zenkei. *The Gateless Barrier: Zen Comments on the Mumonkan.* Boston: Shambhala, 2000.

Snyder, Gary. *The Practice of the Wild.* Berkeley: Counterpoint, 1990.

Soothill, William Edward, and Lewis Hodous. *A Dictionary of Chinese Buddhist Terms.* Delhi, India: Motilal Banarsidass, 1937, reprinted 1987.

Sōtō Zen Text Project. *Soto School Scriptures for Daily Services and Practice.* Tokyo: Sōtōshū Shūmucho, 2001.

Stone, Jacqueline. *Original Enlightenment and the Transformation of Medieval Japanese Buddhism.* Honolulu: University of Hawai'i Press, 1999.

Susskind, Leonard. *Cosmic Landscape: String Theory and the Illusion of Intelligent Design.* New York: Little, Brown, 2006.

Suzuki, D. T. *Manual of Zen Buddhism.* New York: Grove Weidenfeld, 1960.

Suzuki, Shunryu. *Branching Streams Flow in the Darkness: Zen Talks on the Sandokai,* edited by Mel Weitsman and Michael Wenger. Berkeley: University of California Press, 1999.

———. *Not Always So: Practicing the True Spirit of Zen,* edited by Edward Espe Brown. New York: HarperCollins Publishers, 2002.

Tagawa Shun'ei. *Living Yogācāra.* Somerville, Mass.: Wisdom Publications, 2009.

Tanahashi, Kazuaki. *Sky Above, Great Wind: The Life and Poetry of Zen Master Ryokan.* Boston: Shambhala, 2012.

———, trans. and ed. *Treasury of the True Dharma Eye: Zen Master Dōgen's Shōbō-genzō*. Boston: Shambhala, 2010.

Tanahashi, Kazuaki, and John Daido Loori, trans., with commentary and verse by John Daido Loori. *The True Dharma Eye: Zen Master Dōgen's Three Hundred Koans*. Boston: Shambhala, 2005.

Tanahashi, Kazuaki, and Tensho David Schneider, eds. *Essential Zen*. San Francisco: HarperSanFrancisco, 1994.

Teiser, Stephen, and Jacqueline Stone. "Interpreting the *Lotus Sūtra*." In *Readings of the* Lotus Sūtra, edited by Stephen Teiser and Jacqueline Stone. New York: Columbia University Press, 2009.

———, eds. *Readings of the* Lotus Sutra. New York: Columbia University Press, 2009.

Thurman, Robert, trans. *The Holy Teaching of Vimalakīrti: A Mahāyāna Scripture*. University Park: Pennsylvania State University Press, 1976.

Verdu, Alfonso. *Dialectical Aspects in Buddhist Thought: Studies in Sino-Japanese Mahāyāna Idealism*. Lawrence: University of Kansas, Center for East Asian Studies, 1974.

Waddell, Norman, and Masao Abe, trans. *The Heart of Dōgen's Shōbōgenzō*. Albany: State University of New York Press, 2002.

Waley, Arthur. *The Way and Its Power: A Study of the Tao Te Ching and Its Place in Chinese Thought*. New York: Grove Press, 1958.

Welter, Albert. *The Linji Lu and the Creation of Chan Orthodoxy: The Development of Chan's Records of Sayings Literature*. New York: Oxford University Press, 2008.

———. *Monks, Rulers, and Literati: The Political Ascendancy of Chan Buddhism*. New York: Oxford University Press, 2006.

———. "Zen Syncretism: An Examination of Dōgen's Zen Thought in Light of Yongming Yanshou's Chan Teachings in the *Zongjing Lu*." In *Dōgen Textual and Historical Studies*, edited by Steven Heine, 188–91. New York: Oxford University Press, 2012.

Wilhelm, Richard, and Cary Baynes, trans. *The I Ching or Book of Changes*. Princeton, NJ: Princeton University Press, 1950, 3d edition 1967.

Williams, Paul. *Mahāyāna Buddhism: The Doctrinal Foundations*. London: Routledge, 1989.

Wong, Eva, trans. *Lieh-Tzu: A Taoist Guide to Practical Living*. Boston: Shambhala, 2001.

Wu, John. *The Golden Age of Zen*. Taipei, Taiwan: United Publishing Center, 1975.

Wu, Yi. *The Book of Lao Tzu (The Tao Te Ching)*. San Francisco: Great Learning, 1989.

———. *The Mind of Chinese Ch'an (Zen): The Ch'an School Masters and Their Kung-ans*. San Francisco: Great Learning, 1989.

Yampolsky, Philip. *The Platform Sutra of the Sixth Patriarch*. New York: Columbia University Press, 1967.

Yifa. *The Origins of Buddhist Monastic Codes in China: An Annotated Translation and Study of the Chanyuan Qinggui*. Honolulu: University of Hawai'i Press, 2009.

Ziporyn, Brook. "The Use of the Li Hexagram in Chan Buddhism and Its This-Worldly Implications." In *Shengyanyanjiu*, vol. 3 (May 2012): 83–124.

Index

childhood eyes and ears, 19–20
and Chinese Buddha nature
   background, 22–23
commentaries on, 11–12
Dharma inquiry, 20–21
five ranks teaching, 6
grass shack in his background, 79–80
"It now is me; I now am not it," 34–46
lineage, 7–8
on nonsentient beings, 32 (see also
   nonsentient beings)
passing, 157–58
provenance of stories about, 3–6
on the senses, 29–30
speaking with silence, 31
stupa, 14f
suchness and, 8–9 (see also suchness)
teaching style, 10–11, 31
temple, 15f
three roads, 116–17
See also specific topics
Donovan, 131–32
duality. See nonduality
Dylan, Bob, 38–39, 119, 151, 245n10

Earth, changes in, 89–91. See also
   climate change
echinoderms, 231–33
ego, 37, 40, 180
Eihei Kōroku (Dōgen), 141, 143, 153–54,
   235
embraced within the real, 188, 189
emperor's personal name, taboo
   against saying, 147–49
emptiness, 9, 10, 123
   attachment and, 10, 55, 81, 114, 115, 130
   Daowu Yuanzhi on, 64
   death and, 51, 160, 230
   diligent practice and the empty
      realm, 160
   Hongzhi Zhengjue and, 153
   overcoming, 130–32
   realization and, 130
   realization of, 130
"emptiness of the pot of ages," 152–54
Engo Kokugon. See Yuanwu Keqin
enlightenment. See awakening/
   enlightenment/realization

environmentalism, 89–91
"everywhere I meet him," 41–42, 47.
   See also Yunyan Tansheng: meeting
   him everywhere
"everywhere I meet it," 34, 35

face, original, 113–14
Fazang, 22, 139–40
Fengxue, 220
fire, 85–88, 176. See also Illumination
   hexagram
five degrees
   of accomplishment, verses on, 217–21
   after Dongshan, 221–24
   Caodong/Sōtō tradition and, 7, 22,
      36, 172, 184, 212, 222, 227–28
   context and background of, 211–13
   Dōgen and, 6, 97, 228–30, 233–37
   Dōgen's implicit commentaries on,
      233–37
   Dongshan's verses on the, 214–17
   Hongzhi Zhengjue and, 205, 225–27
   later Caodong five degrees study,
      224–28
   Linji and Hakuin use of, 229–31
   and the practice of suchness, 237–38
   realization and, 234
   See also five ranks; specific topics
five degrees dialectics, 221, 222, 228
five degrees system
   Linji school and, 94, 212, 229
   Linji Yixuan and, 209
five positions/modes, 6, 212, 223, 223f,
   238
five ranks, 6, 7, 97, 212–13, 229, 230,
   233–34. See also five degrees
five relationships. See five degrees
fivefold, pentamerous reality, 231
fivefold classifications, 230
fivefold interaction, 170–71, 188–90,
   214–15, 221
fivefold radial symmetry, 232
fivefold structure, 222, 233. See also
   "Song of the Jewel Mirror Samādhi"
"Flowers in the Sky" ("Kūge"), 176–77
"forest of thorns," 76
form, 19
Four Noble Truths, 112

temperature. *See* heat and cold
Ten Stages Sutra, 115
Tendai, 139, 140
"three roads," Dongshan's, 116–17
Tiantai school, 22
Tibetan Buddhism, 88
"To Build a Fire" (London), 85–86
Touzi Yiqing, 13, 224
Tōzan Ryōkai. *See* Dongshan Liangjie
transcendence, 50–51
true, 188
   coming from within the, 225
   partial within the, 225, 226
   See also real
"True within the Partial," 225
truth, 188
"Truth Is a Pathless Land"
   (Krishnamurti), 126
"Turning away and touching are both
   wrong" (Dongshan), 143, 150, 169,
   175–77, 185
Twain, Mark, 90–91

Ungan Donjō. *See* Yunyan Tansheng
Ungō Dōyō. *See* Yunju Daoying
Unity Attained, 230
universal and particular, 8, 22, 35–36,
   40, 93–95, 144, 170, 173, 174, 177, 181,
   185, 188, 208, 212–14, 220–22, 230–31,
   236, 237. *See also* phenomenal
   and ultimate/universal; real and
   apparent
universal liberation, 102, 112
universal/ultimate and phenomenal,
   79, 93, 144, 184, 189, 209, 214, 228
universal/ultimate reality, 20, 22, 140,
   173, 177, 181, 189, 192, 213, 215
Unmon Bun'en. *See* Yunmen Wenyan

vajra, 182–83
Verdu, Alfonso, 212, 214, 220, 228
Vietnam War, 87–88
Vipaśyin (Vipassī) Buddha, 142, 143

Wanshi Shōgaku. *See* Hongzhi
   Zhengjue
Wansong Xingxiu
   on awakening, 102

bodhisattvas and, 63, 106
Book of Serenity and, 5, 13, 28–29, 43,
   52, 53, 63, 74, 102, 107–8, 147, 148, 159
buddhas and, 53, 147, 202
Daowu Yuanzhi and, 60, 61, 63
   on death, 159, 160, 162
Dongshan and, 60, 107, 147–49, 159,
   163
   on enlightenment, 102
Hongzhi Zhengjue and, 63, 162
Lotus Sutra and, 105, 106
moon(s) and, 61, 63–64
nature, plants, and, 63, 74
Shitou and, 162
suchness and, 60
Yunyan Tansheng and, 53, 60, 61, 63
Way, the, 121
"What is it?," 51, 217
white rabbit
   down the hole of the, 108–9
   how high a rabbit jumps, 101–3
   in the moon, 108
"White Rabbit" (song), 109–10
white rabbit practice, 109–10
wholeness, 61–62, 65, 237
Williams, Hank, 205
Williams, Paul, 128
wisdom, 75
   perfection of (*see* Perfection of
   Wisdom)
   See also under speaking
Wisdom Awakening, 158
Wumen Huikai, 5

Xiangyan Zhixian, 204
Xiujing, Huayan, 75, 115
Xuanjiang, Deshan, 67
Xuedou Chongjian, 5, 93, 95–97
Xuefeng Yicun, 147–48, 176

Yakusan Igen. *See* Yaoshan Weiyan
Yangshan Huiji, 64, 124, 223
Yao, Emperor, 202–3, 218
Yaoshan Weiyan, 148
   Baizhang Huaihai and, 50, 51, 57
   on birth and death, 50
   Daowu Yuanzhi and, 50, 55–58
   lineage, 7, 50

About the Author

Taigen Dan Leighton is a Sōtō Zen priest and Dharma successor in the lineage of Shunryū Suzuki of the San Francisco Zen Center, where he was ordained in 1986 and received Dharma transmission in 2000 from Tenshin Reb Anderson. He is also an authorized teacher in the Japanese Sōtō school and now is resident Dharma teacher of the Ancient Dragon Zen Gate temple in Chicago.

Leighton is author of *Faces of Compassion: Classic Bodhisattva Archetypes and Their Modern Expression*; *Visions of Awakening Space and Time: Dōgen and the Lotus Sutra*; and *Zen Questions: Zazen, Dōgen, and the Spirit of Creative Inquiry*. He is cotranslator and editor of several Zen texts, including *Dōgen's Extensive Record*; *Cultivating the Empty Field: The Silent Illumination of Zen Master Hongzhi*; *The Wholehearted Way: A Translation of Dōgen's "Bendōwa" with Commentary by Kōshō Uchiyama Roshi*; and *Dōgen's Pure Standards for the Zen Community: A Translation of "Eihei Shingi."* He has contributed to other translations and also published articles in many books and journals.

Leighton has taught at many universities and currently teaches online at the Institute of Buddhist Studies of the Graduate Theological Union in Berkeley, from where he has a PhD.

01 14